THE LOOK

TRANSFORM YOUR HOME WITH FABRIC

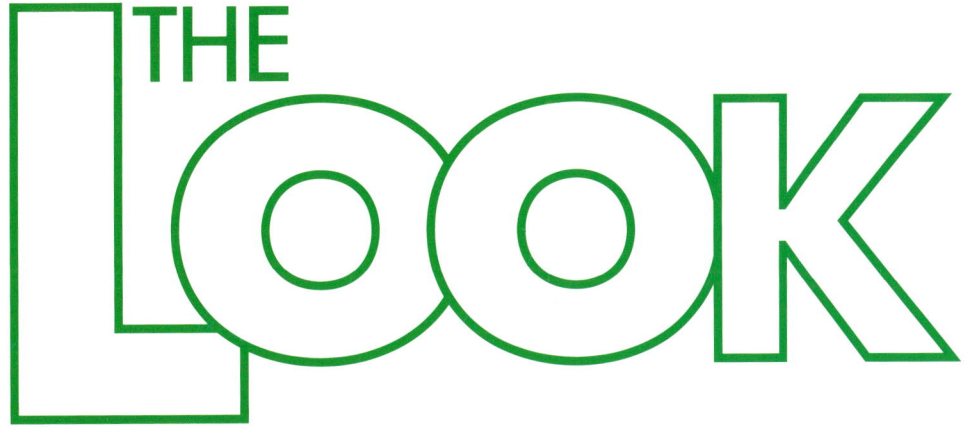

CONTENTS

Transform your home - room by room & step by step

Clearly divided into eight sections, **The Look** couldn't be easier to use. Projects are housed in their relevant 'rooms', making them quick to locate, and each one is explained in easy stages with detailed Illustrations. All the skills you'll need to achieve the projects are explained clearly in the 'Workshop', and there's also a guide to how long it will take you to complete each make. Instant looks, room scheme ideas and fabric suggestions are all dealt with separately for easy reference.

▼ **How to make each project is described clearly in numbered stages. Simply follow the steps, and you can't go wrong**

windows and walls

Window dressings can make or break a room, and here we provide you with all the inspiration you need to make a real style statement. Learn how to stick, sew, staple and scrunch fabric to make all variety of curtains and blinds; to add drama to a setting with fabric-covered pelmets, and to make quick tie-backs. There are also occasional projects for hanging on walls.

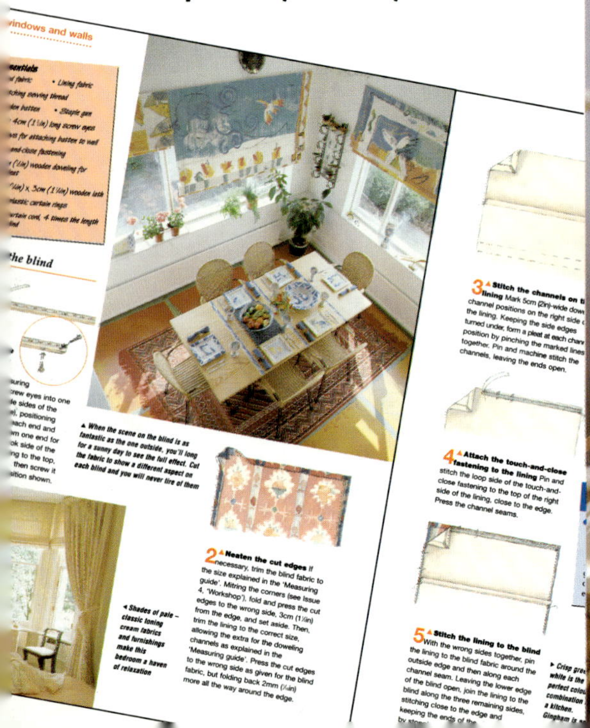

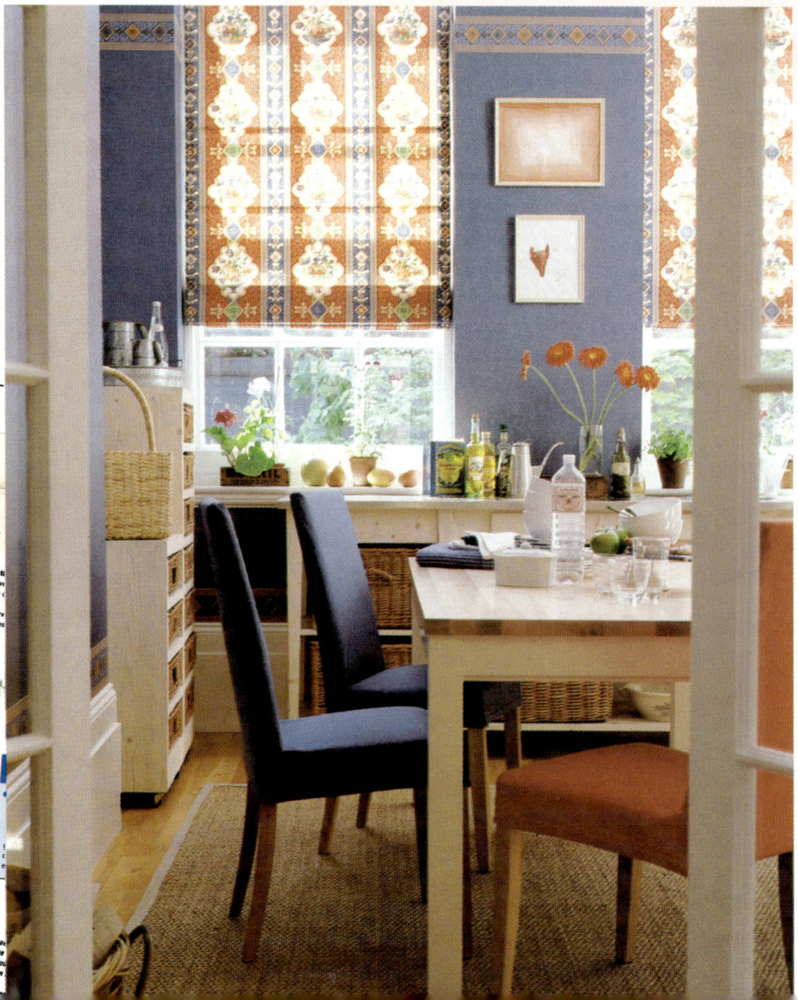

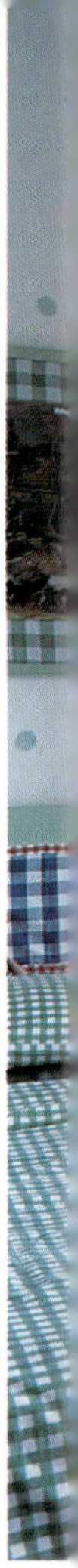

Create inspirational bedroom settings to make your dreams come true, plus a wide range of items guaranteed to give your bathroom a boost. From matching bed linen to nursery projects, and from easy shower curtains to bath mats with a difference, there's ample ammunition here for you to achieve just the kind of look you want.

instant style

The emphasis is firmly on instant makes and quick ideas in this no-nonsense section, where projects take only a matter of minutes to complete but give big rewards. Stick, staple, drape and tie fabric for rapid and exciting results.

living spaces

Here the spotlight falls on living rooms and you'll discover just how easy it can be to create an impact with your own lampshades, cushions, fabric-covered screens and other accessories. Even stylish slip-over chair covers and re-upholstering are made simple by following the clear, step by step instructions.

From sticking ▲ and stapling, to scrunching and sewing fabric, The Look is overflowing with all sorts of creative ideas

◀ Detailed illustrations provide essential information and show you exactly what you should be doing in the project steps

◄ *All the help and information you need, delivered clearly and step by step, means guaranteed results*

workshop

To get the best results from the projects in *The Look*, you'll need the right approach. And while some of you may already have the know-how to get started straight away, all the essential techniques are explained here in easy terms with illustrations – from creative know-how to fabric painting, basic sewing skills and DIY.

kitchens, diners and patios

Contemporary dining is an art in itself and here we give you a helping hand to creating all sorts of delectable settings for your kitchen and dining room. Plus, with the sun-filled days of summer never far away, there are also projects for stylish al fresco living in the garden and on the patio.

 # creating your look

Putting a room scheme together and developing a look takes judgement, and confidence. This section delivers all the information you'll need to plan interiors with conviction and guides you through various techniques for combining colour, shape and texture to achieve a range of effects. From Shaker style to creating a welcoming hallway, all the inspiration you'll need is provided here.

◀ *Any skills needed to complete the sewing based projects featured in The Look are basic ones and are clearly explained in the 'Workshop'*

 # fabric file

Which fabrics you select to make the projects featured in *The Look* is up to you. But to provide you with some idea of what might make a good choice, in this section we give you the low-down on the different types of fabric available, plus show you a gallery of the latest designs.

take a break

Give your sofa a spring make-over with a striped floral throw with a brilliantly coloured fringed edging. Make it in minutes!

The beauty of working with fabric throws is that you can use a texture to transform a piece of furniture which you could not use to cover it conventionally. A lightweight cotton would be unsuitable as an upholstery fabric, but as a throw or coverlet, you can get away with it. You will then have huge amounts of choice for colour and pattern.

Just make sure you turn neat and secure hems on all the edges and add a fringed braid to trim and to give the throw weight. It's so quick you can make another when your mood changes. Now sit back and take a break!

▲ *Floral feast*
A splash of light lifts a tired sofa into springtime freshness

sheer delight

Choose from the latest designs in sheer fabrics for this no-nonsense curtain project, where privacy and style go hand-in-hand

Gone are the days when sheer curtains meant nothing but white nylon lace embossed with flowers. Sheer fabrics have undergone a transformation so radical that while traditional white nylon is still an option, so too are a new range of fabrics including soft, billowycotton voiles, translucent sheer weaves and jewel-bright coloured panels.

Sheer curtains are actually very easy to make as long as you observe two basic rules. The first is to avoid joining fabric widths, as any seams will show unless the curtain is very full; so if you have a very wide window, the best solution is to hang several widths of fabric side by side. The second rule is always to turn under double width hems at the sides and at the top and bottom edges to give the curtains extra weight. Meanwhile, remember that the more fabric you gather across the window, the more light you will restrict; so to gain maximum daylight while retaining privacy, use fabric up to one-and-a-half times the width of the window.

If economy is the basis for sheer curtains, then one of the cheapest solutions fabric-wise is butter muslin. You'll often find this in a dress-fabric shop where it's used as pressing cloth. It's pure cotton, so you can easily dye it a glorious colour.

Affordable style

The easiest and least expensive way to hang sheer curtains is by stitching a simple casing – a narrow channel formed by two rows of stitching – across the top hem and slotting through a length of plastic-covered, sprung wire.

Other options for hanging sheers include: fine brass or metal poles that can be slotted through a narrow casing at the top of the curtain; tension rods, which contain a concealed central spring; and fine white plastic rods. In our own example we show you how to make the ever-popular covered wire variety.

Making the curtain

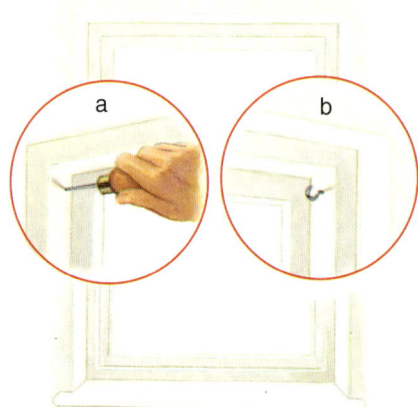

1 ▲ Fix the hooks Once you have decided on the best position for the wire, measure an equal distance down from the top of the frame at each side of the window and mark with a pencil. Use the bradawl or any other sharp, pointed tool to make a single starter hole at each pencil mark (**a**), then screw the hooks into the wood so that they face upwards (**b**).

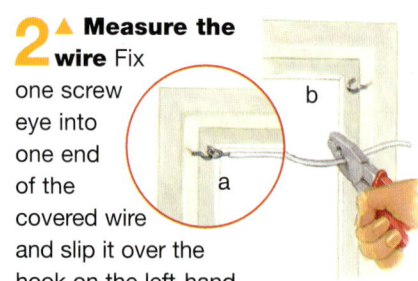

2 ▲ Measure the wire Fix one screw eye into one end of the covered wire and slip it over the hook on the left-hand side of the window (**a**). Stretch the wire very tightly across to the opposite hook and, with the pencil, mark the required length on the wire. Use the pliers to cut the wire (**b**), then fix the second screw eye into the cut end. Slip it over the hook on the right-hand side of the window and check that the wire is taut across the width.

Measuring and cutting guide

- **To calculate the width**
  1 First decide on the best position for the covered wire. Generally this is fitted across the window inside the frame, but it can also be fixed with the ends outside the window boundary.
  2 Then measure across the window from hook to hook (see Step 1) and allow for up to one-and-a-half times this measurement for fullness, plus 2.5–5cm (1-2in) for each side hem, depending on the size of the window and the type of fabric you are using.
  3 If the curtain is to be flat without fullness, simply add the side hem allowance to the window measurement.

- **To calculate the length**
  On set-in windows, sheer curtains can hang from the top and fall to the sill. You can also make café curtains in this way that fall from half-way down to the sill.

  Fixing outside the window frame however, provides more scope for different lengths. You can allow your curtains to fall to the sill, to the floor, or to just above a radiator or below the sill, depending on the proportions of the room. Measure from the hook down to your chosen length, then add 3cm (1¼in) for the top hem and 4cm (1½in) for the bottom hem.

◀ **Overlap expansive sheers in lighter and darker colours for a dramatic effect that still lets through the light**

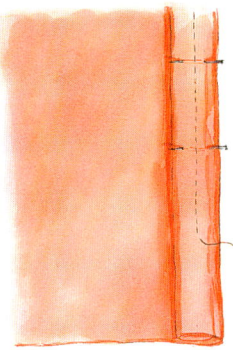

3 ◄ **Stitch the side hems** Turn under double 12mm (½in) hems down each side of the fabric (turn under 12mm and 12mm again), then pin and machine stitch. If the sheer fabric has decorative selvedges, however, these are meant to be seen and turnings are not necessary.

MAKE IT SIMPLE

no-sew sheers

For a no-sew option, if you've a particular sheer fabric that you'd like to use, turn it into curtains the quick and easy seamless way.

1 Simply neaten any edges (top, bottom and sides) with narrow hems held in place with easy to use iron-on bonding tape.

2 Then to hang the curtains, rather than creating a casing for a wire, instead attach small metal curtain clips (like the ones shown here) at regular intervals along the top edge. These grip the fabric firmly and can then be slotted directly over your rod or pole.

4 ▶ **Stitch the casing** Turn under a double 2cm (¾in) hem along the top edge of the fabric (turn under 2cm and 2cm again), then pin and machine stitch close to the hem edge. Stitch across the curtain again, inside the folded top edge, to make a narrow casing (channel) for the wire.

5 **Stitch the bottom hem** Turn under a double 4cm (1½in) hem along the bottom edge (turn under 4cm and 4cm again), then pin and stitch.

6 ▲ **Hang the curtain** Slot the covered wire through the casing, gathering the fabric evenly as you feed it through, then hang the curtain tautly across the window on the hooks. If your window is very wide, you may need to fix another small hook to support the wire in the middle of the frame, to prevent the curtain from sagging.

TAKE ANOTHER LOOK

star-stamped sheers

Stamp a pattern for instant appeal Use a rubber stamp, such as a star or fleur-de-lys to decorate bought sheer curtains. See 'Stamp of approval', p20, for clear instructions on stamping. Arrange the motifs in whatever pattern you like – either at random, or using a symmetrical design as shown.

STAMP IT

light as a breeze

Sensuous sheer fabrics will give any room a light and airy ambiance. And these days there's no need to stick with plain white, as this selection shows

1

2

3

Tantalizing and tasteful, sheer fabrics can be used on their own or to complement existing curtains. Available in a wide array of colours and patterns, they make simple curtains that are easy to hang. And, because most sheer fabrics are synthetics, they're inexpensive as well.

Before choosing your fabric, consider how it will work with your existing scheme. Use sheers to pick out hues in furnishing fabrics, such as checked or floral prints, or to reflect muted solids. Layering sheers produces exotic effects, as curtain folds create ever-changing colour drifts in the breeze.

Alternatively, cover chairs in sheers to add a fresh touch to a bedroom or dining area – fabrics stamped with metallic shapes like gold stars are especially appealing.

▲ **Mix patterned curtains with large, gingham checked sheers for a bright, modern approach to window dressing**

• **See p100 for a dreamy sheer canopy stamped with stars**

checklist
Sheer fabrics

● **Fibre content** Sheer fabrics are synthetics, or blends of man-made and natural fibres, which means that they are shrink- and crease-resistant. Synthetics fray quite easily, so leave plenty of seam allowance in case you have a problem.

● **Sewing sheers** Take care as sheers tend to be quite slippery. You'll need to tack pieces together to hold them in place for stitching. For stitching finished seams, use a polyester thread as it has a certain amount of 'give'.

● **Quick seams** For simple seams use iron-on bonding tape. This is plain white and hardly visible along a hem. Instead of turning side hems, on curtains for example, leave the woven selvedges.

● **Variety of effects** Not all sheers are plain, boring white – there are lots of different colours, printed patterns and woven effects that add interesting texture.

● **Aftercare** Most sheer fabrics will go in the washing machine quite happily. They should need very little ironing if you've followed the care instructions carefully, but always use a cool iron.

1 Add a dash of Renaissance opulence to a sitting or dining room with Italian script voile. Try mixing with deep, rich velvets for a luxurious look

2 A soft green-and-white Victorian floral print is easy on the eye and lends fresh country charm to any room in the house

3 Embossed leaves whisper across this pastel organza, forming a backdrop of natural beauty

4 Wispy blue-and-white large-checked sheers bring to mind lazy days at the seaside and are perfect for French door curtains

5 A continental wheat sheaf print sets off stripes of dusty blue for an elegant curtain. Co-ordinate with tableware for breezy dining

6 Go dotty with a silver-spotted sheer that tones well with the pastel shades of retro interior styles, such as the 1950s look

take

STAMP IT
a leaf

Give bare boards or plain carpets an instant uplift with printed floor cloths. Not only do they look great – they're easy to make and low cost too

Add warmth and vitality to plain, bare areas of flooring throughout the house with modern day floor cloths. Originally a Victorian idea, floor cloths were a cheap way of providing protective covering for areas of considerably more expensive carpeting. Now they are a form of 'painting' on the floor by using decorative techniques to create your own contemporary style statement.

An undaunting mat-size, floor cloths are brimming with impact both visually and artistically. By employing only simple printmaking skills, you can decorate them with graphic images, while a final coat of clear varnish protects both your artwork and the cloth from inevitable wear and tear. And the big bonus is that they need no sewing at all.

Natural success

Apart from the small costs of artists' canvas and paints, your expenditure for a floor cloth is minimal. Don't be deterred by having to use a roller for printing. It's a small, hand-held tool that's easily available from an artists' suppliers for a nominal sum.

We've used leaves as the design basis of this floor cloth. When you're out walking, it's easy to scour the pathways for fallen leaves to use for printing – and they cost nothing at all. But make sure that they're in good condition for the best printing results. Another idea is to use the stamps or stencils, available from craft shops, to decorate smaller cloths.

Practice makes perfect

Don't launch straight into your project, however. It's important to practise first because once you've imprinted your leaf or other design on the cloth, there's no chance to make corrections. When you've cut your canvas to size, you'll most likely have left-over material – so make a number of test runs with printing leaves to determine the amount of paint to apply and how much pressure you'll need on the roller. And, in no time at all, you'll have created your own, unique work of art that'll look great on floors throughout the house.

Measuring and cutting guide

- Measure your canvas and cut it to the required size, adding 6cm (2¼in) to each measurement for the turnings. As a guide to size, the finished measurement of our rug is 52 x 94cm (20½ x 37in). Make sure that all the edges are square by following the straight weave of the canvas.

Essentials

- Heavyweight unprimed artists' canvas
- Selection of fresh leaves
- Ready-mixed acrylic paint in bright green, dark green, orange and yellow
- Iron-on bonding tape
- Paint brushes and mixing tray
- Hard printmakers' roller
- Long ruler
- Wide masking tape
- Clear acrylic varnish
- Clean sheets of paper
- Hard pencil
- Scissors

Making the cloth

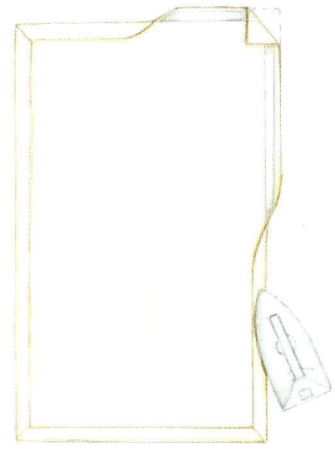

1 ▲ Hem the canvas Turn 3cm (1¼in) to the wrong side around each edge of the canvas and press in place. Open out and make a diagonal fold across each corner from one pressed line to another. Then, fold the

◄ Off-set a plain armchair with a striking, patterned floor cloth. Try an arrangement of simple geometric shapes for an eye-catching design

sides again so that the previously folded corner forms a neat mitre (diagonal line at the corner). Place strips of the iron-on bonding tape between the two layers of canvas and stick the hem in place, following the manufacturer's instructions.

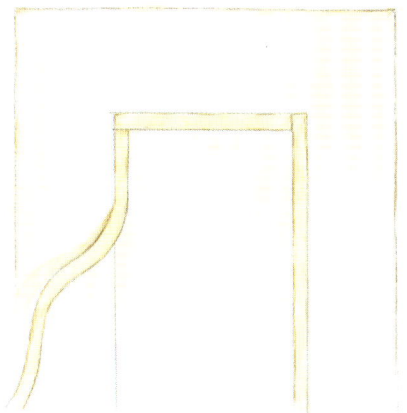

2 ▲ Mark the border Using a long ruler and hard pencil, mark a border on the right side of the canvas 13cm (5in) from the folded hem edges. Make sure that any pencil marks you make are faint enough to be covered by the border paint.

Apply masking tape along the outer edges (ie outside the marked border) of the pencil lines, cutting it neatly at the corners to achieve a smooth line. The masking tape prevents paint from bleeding into the centre panel.

3 ▲ Paint the border Using bright green paint and a large brush, carefully paint the outer border of the cloth, working over the masking tape at the inner edge. Leave until the paint is dry (about an hour), then carefully peel off the masking tape.

TAKE ANOTHER LOOK

autumnal floor cloths

4 ▲ **Mark the centre panel**
Select a leaf (ours is a maple) that's in good condition and large enough to repeat three times in the unpainted centre panel. Try placing a few leaves on the canvas until you achieve the desired effect. When you're happy with the arrangement, mark the position of the leaves with a few pencil marks (these will be covered up later).

Create a different version of the leaf-print floor cloth. It's a larger size, so cut a piece of canvas 124 x 66cm (49 x 26in).

1 Following Step 1 on page 15, hem the canvas, then mark the coloured borders that divide the canvas into squares. First draw a faint line 3cm (1¼in) from the outer edges. Divide the short edges in half and mark in another 3cm (1¼in) border down the length of the canvas. Then mark the long edges into four sections with borders separating them. Lay masking tape along the inner edges of each marked out square.

2 When you are ready, paint in the borders between the taped lines, then print one large leaf, or a group of smaller ones, in each square.

5 ▲ **Decorate the centre panel**
Using dark green paint, apply a thick layer on to the underside (veined side) of the leaf. Carefully place the leaf face down in position on the canvas, cover with a clean sheet of paper and working in the same direction each time, use the hard roller to press the leaf firmly on to the canvas. Repeat with the other leaves to complete the centre section.

6 ▲ **Work the corners** Using a mid-size leaf, such as lime, and orange paint, print a leaf motif in two diagonally opposite corners following Steps 4 and 5. Place them centrally on the green border, pointing inwards and at a 45 degree angle to the corner.

7 ▲ **Complete the border** Using large oak leaves and orange and yellow paint alternately, work outwards from the corner motifs and print three motifs on the long edge and two leaves along the short edge of the canvas. Leave until completely dry.

8 ▲ **Varnish the cloth** Protect the design and prolong the life of the finished cloth by carefully applying one coat of clear acrylic varnish, working right up to the edge and over on to the turned hem on the wrong side. Again, leave overnight to allow the rug to dry.

lashings of style

Bold metal eyelets and audacious rope lashings are the perfect adornments for smart modern settings

L arge metal eyelets lashed with white or beige cords, ropes or twine are just the thing to add visual interest to contemporary interiors. They keep modern rooms from looking too severe by softening hard edges on screens, windows and sofas. Eyelets also harmonize with uncomplicated and minimalist settings, without detracting from the desired effect.

Evoking a maritime theme, rope and eyelet ornaments are suitable for bathrooms, studies, kids' rooms, kitchens and conservatories – in fact, anywhere that a pert and bright unconventional look is required.

Lashing low-down

The trick to decorating with metal eyelets is to use them sparingly on appropriate fabrics. They look best widely spaced on stark white, neutral and boldly coloured plain fabrics, or on simple, vivid stripes and plaids. Canvas, ticking or other strong, densely woven materials are the essential foundation for heavy eyelets. Metal ones simply won't be held secure in loosely woven fabrics.

Eyelets are easy to fix – simply punch into the fabric using the tool provided when you purchase a pack. Then use them with lashings to lace up cushion covers, for Roman blind pull-ups, to secure curtains to curtain poles, or to tie seats and chair-backs to director's chairs. Alternatively, you can apply them as pure decoration around cushion covers, lampshades, and roller blinds. So take your pick – and get lashing!

▲ Chic shower
A combination of a single starfish and frayed-edged twines and ropes adds natural charm to a bathroom

◄ Cheeky cushions
These cushions in sharp contrasting colours are ideal for kids' rooms, which look best decorated with bold soft furnishings

▶ *Cord, laced in crosses through brass eyelets on a lampshade, contributes a fabulous contrast of texture to a room scheme which evokes an ocean landscape. Buy an eyelet kit that includes a two-part insertion tool, then you can adapt an existing lampshade*

Make it!

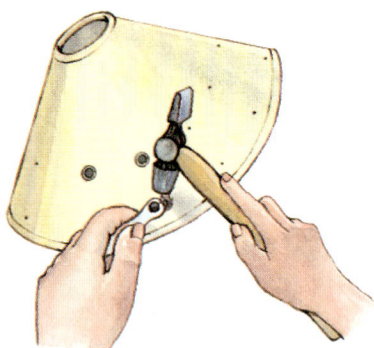

1 ▲ **Insert the eyelets** Using a pencil, lightly mark the position of the eyelet holes around the lower half of the lampshade. Place the shade over a firm surface with the lower section of the eyelet device underneath. Position the eyelet, hold the upper section of the device in place and hammer the eyelet home. Repeat with the remaining eyelets.

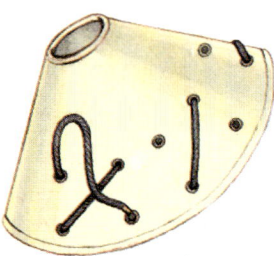

2 ▲ **Thread the laces** Cut a long length of thick cord so that you can thread it through the holes in a continuous line. Neatly secure the ends of the cord on the inside of the shade with small pieces of masking tape. Then work the first diagonal lines of the crosses in the same direction and return in the opposite direction to complete each cross.

▶ ***Nautical but nice***
Yachting accessories, where eyelets, rope lashings and thick cords appear in abundance, are the inspiration for this selection of maritime cushion designs

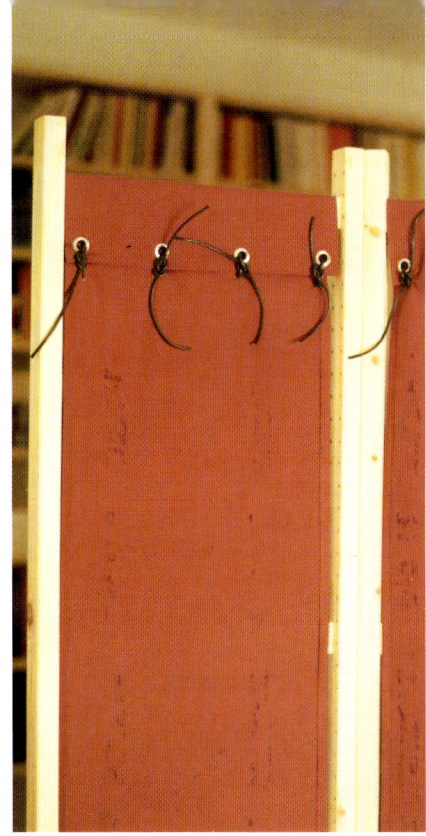

◄ Screen it
A loud red canvas screen divider, with eye-catching eyelets and modern lashings, cleverly draws attention away from the clutter of a busy home study area. Fold the required amount of canvas over the top bar of the screen and punch two corresponding eyelets at regular intervals. Thread with electrical wire to secure

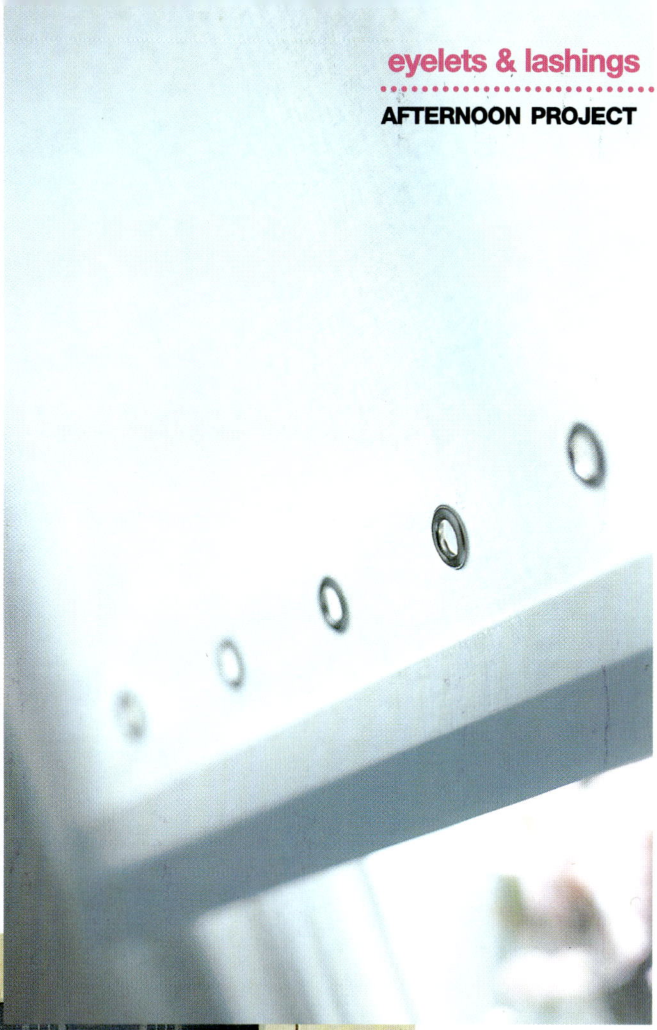

▲ Blinding eyelets
Widely spaced chrome eyelets transform a white blind into a stylish design statement. Simple curves and circles are the perfect foil to a hard-edged interior and soften the overall look of the setting

◄ All tied up
Liven up a guest bedroom, or a breakfast room, with this Roman blind. Punch brazen brass eyelets in vertical lines where you want the blind to pleat up. Thread with a chunky cotton rope for a decorative and functional finish

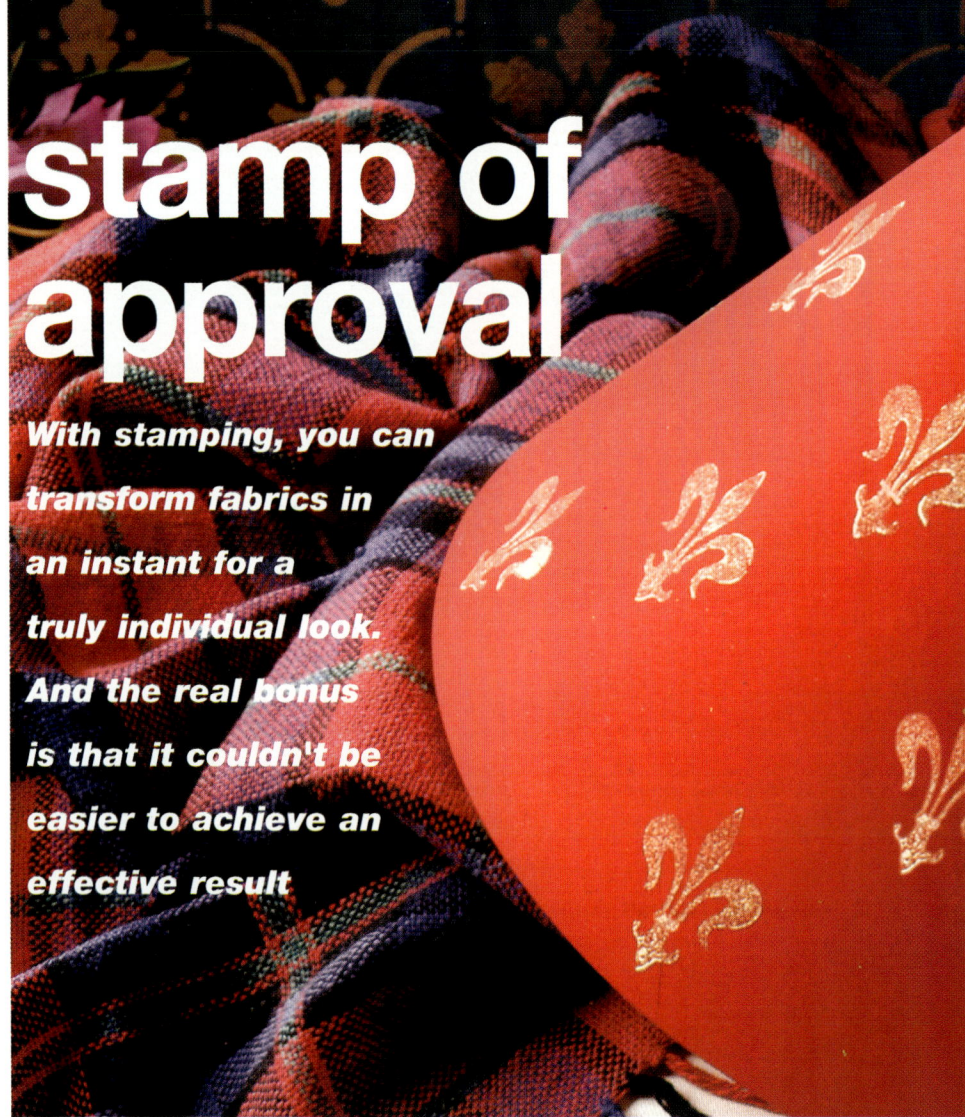

stamp of approval

With stamping, you can transform fabrics in an instant for a truly individual look. And the real bonus is that it couldn't be easier to achieve an effective result

Stamping looks like if it could be a complex technique to master because the results are so dramatic – as the pictures on these pages show. But in fact stamping requires no special skills whatsoever, which makes it one of the easiest ways to decorate fabric in a truly individual way.

There is a wide range of rubber and wooden stamps, and specific stamping pads and paint, available in craft shops and by mail order. Here we've used an elegant fleur-de-lys motif to decorate a fabric lampshade in gold paint, but you can apply as simple or as intricate a design as you want – whether it's to transform a plain fabric, or to brighten up any fabric object that you've bought.

Simply stylish

The process is simple: all you have to do is coat the stamp with a liquid fabric paint (available from department stores or craft shops) using a small artist's paint brush, and then press the stamp firmly on to the surface of the fabric. You can print the motif randomly over the fabric or, alternatively, apply it according to a previously measured and marked out pattern – as we have in the case of this lampshade.

Choose wisely

As a rule, always choose smooth fabrics that will give a clear image when stamped. Natural fabrics, such as cottons, are a good option, as they tend to absorb paint well. Avoid synthetics or fabrics with man-made finishes, however, as these can prevent the paint from fixing properly; also avoid textured fabrics which may break up the motif's outline. And before you start stamping, remember first to press the fabric to remove any creases, and then stretch and tape it to a flat surface so that it will not slide about.

Stamping, then, is a simple technique; but don't rush into it – there are a few things to think about first, so for the best possible results, work through the checklist on the right before you begin.

▶ *Fabric stamps can be used in all sorts of ways, on a variety of different fabrics. This regal crown motif, stamped on the corner of a napkin, has been oversewn for a dramatic finish*

Essentials
- *Fabric lampshade*
- *Fleur de lys stamp*
- *Shallow dish*
- *Liquid fabric paint*
- *Small, soft paintbrush*
- *Soft pencil (B or 2B)*

▶ **Paisley stamps create an opulent border on a curtain**

checklist
Stamping fabrics

- **Plan your design** Always decide on your design before you start stamping, as badly positioned motifs can be difficult to remove.
- **Mark the positions of the motifs** Measure carefully between your motifs for an even design. Instead of a tape measure you can use card. Cut a strip of card to the width of the spaces you wish to create. Line up the left-hand edge of the card with the right-hand edge of the first motif, then print the next motif at the opposite edge.
- **Test the stamp** Do a trial run on a scrap of your chosen fabric first. This will give you some idea of the fabric's absorbency and show you what the finished colour of your motifs will be, as colours can change when applied to different background shades.
- **Do not re-stamp a motif** It is almost impossible to stamp exactly over a first outline, and re-stamping will produce an 'echo' effect.
- **Separate layers of fabric** When stamping on double-layered items such as cushion covers, separate out the fabric to prevent the paint from seeping through the top layer. You can do this by sliding a piece of card, or a sheet of plastic, between the two layers.

How to stamp the lampshade

1 ▶ **Position the motifs** Measure the shade from top to bottom edges and decide how many rows of the motif you want. Using a soft pencil, lightly mark the positions for the rows. Choose how much spacing you would like between the motifs around the shade and mark their positions in the same way.

2 ▶ **Prepare the paint** Pour a small amount of fabric paint into a shallow dish.

3 ▶ **Apply paint to the stamp** Coat the paintbrush with the paint and brush it evenly over the stamp motif, taking care not to overload the motif with paint.

4 ▶ **Stamp the lampshade** Using the flat, open palm of your hand to support the shade from the inside, stamp firmly on the fabric at the first marked position, applying even pressure. Leave for a few seconds, then carefully lift the stamp.

5 **Add the next motif** Re-coat the stamp with paint and apply again at the next marked position, continuing until you have stamped all around the shade.

6 **Fix the paint** Allow the paint to dry. Wash your brush and the dish in cold water.

all tied up

If you want a duvet with a difference, try making this matching bed set with stylish tie-fastenings. There's not a popper in sight

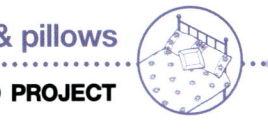

As the modern alternative to blankets and bedspreads, duvets can stamp a definite personality on any bedroom and come with an added bonus: duvet covers are simple to make.

In essence, duvet covers are simply large, rectangular fabric bags with an opening along one edge. However, not all duvets have to look the same, and both the fabric used and the way in which the opening is fastened can make all the difference. In this project we show you how to make a double duvet cover and matching pillowcases with a contemporary feel, featuring ties that can be fashioned into bows as a stylish alternative to poppers.

Freedom of choice

It's the choice of fabric that will make your duvet truly individual and here we've gone for bold citrus colours. What kind of effect you want to achieve is up to you, though, and you can choose anything from soft floral prints to smart stripes.

Another plus point is that modern sheeting fabrics they come in 230cm (90in) and 280cm (110in) widths, and this means that the front and the back sections of the duvet cover can be cut in single pieces. The amount of fabric you need, and the cutting requirements, will differ according to the size of cover you're making. So refer to the chart below.

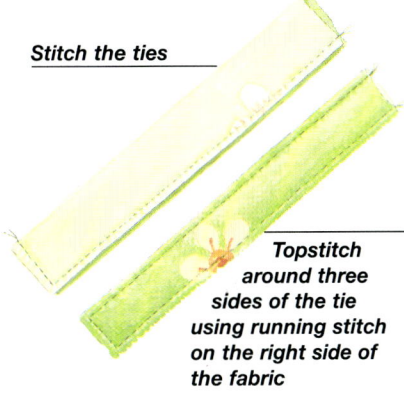

Essentials
- Sheeting fabric
- Matching sewing thread
- Scissors
- Pins
- Tape measure

Making the cover

Stitch the ties

Topstitch around three sides of the tie using running stitch on the right side of the fabric

1 ▲ Make the ties Cut eight ties and fold the strips lengthways in half with right sides and cut edges together. Pin and stitch along one long side and across one short end taking a 6mm (¼in) seam allowance. Trim the fabric across each corner, then turn the tie right side out and press with the seam to the edge. Topstitch all around three sides of the tie using normal running stitch, taking a 6mm (¼in) seam allowance. Make eight front and eight back ties in the same way.

2 ▲ Position the front ties Lay out the duvet front with the right side uppermost. Position the first tie 15cm (6in) along the base edge with cut edges together and the tie facing inward. Position another tie 15cm from the opposite edge and then space the remaining six ties equally in between. Pin and tack each tie in place.

Measuring and cutting guide

	Single duvet	Double duvet	King size duvet	Pillowcase
Size	140 x 200cm	200 x 200cm	230 x 220cm	75 x 50cm
	54 x 78in	78 x 78in	90 x 86in	30 x 20in
Amount required	410 x 230cm	450 x 230cm	480 x 230cm	210 x 50cm
	4½yd x 90in	5yd x 90in	5⅓yd x 90in	2½yd x 20in
Front	143 x 203cm	203 x 203cm	233 x 223cm	80 x 50cm
	56 x 80in	80 x 80in	92 x 88in	31½ x 20in
Back	143 x 206.5cm	203 x 206.5cm	233 x 226.5cm	80 x 50cm
	56 x 81in	80 x 81in	92 x 89in	31½ x 20in
Flap	143 x 40cm	203 x 40cm	233 x 40cm	24 x 50cm
	56 x 16in	80 x 16in	92 x 16in	9½ x 20in
Front ties	40 x 6cm	40 x 6cm	40 x 6cm	40 x 6cm
	16 x 2¼in	16 x 21/4in	16 x 2¼in	16 x 2¼in
Back ties	43 x 6cm	43 x 6cm	43 x 6cm	43 x 6cm
	17 x 2¼in	17 x 2¼in	17 x 2¼in	17 x 2¼in

3 ▲ **Hem the flap** Neaten one long edge of the flap by turning under a double 2cm (¾in) hem (turn under the cut edge 2cm and 2cm again). Pin and stitch along the hem.

4 ▲ **Join the flap to the duvet front** With right sides together, place the flap over the base edge of the duvet front, matching the cut edges and enclosing the tie ends. Pin and tack, taking a 1.5cm (⅝in) seam allowance. Then, stitch the flap and duvet front together, sandwiching the ties in between. Trim the seam allowance and leave the flap in place on the right side of the duvet front.

5 ▲ **Position the back ties** Lay out the duvet back with the right side uppermost. Position the eight

back ties along the base edge so they will match up with the ties along the duvet front, with the cut edges matching and the ties facing inward. Pin and stitch each tie in place.

Then, turn under the base edge to the wrong side to form a double 2.5cm (1in) hem, turning under the ties with the hem at the same time. Fold back the ties so that they protrude from under it and pin and stitch across the hem, stitching across the ties in the process as shown. Topstitch also across the top of the hem edge.

6 ▲ **Stitch the cover together** Place the duvet back and front sections together with the right sides

facing and the cut edges matching. Overlap the flap, so that it covers the top edge of the back. Pin and stitch around three sides, taking a 12mm (½in) seam allowance and catching down the sides of the flap in the seam.

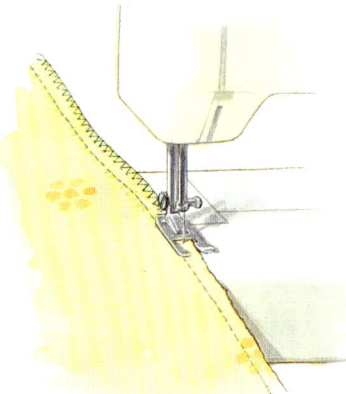

7 ▲ **Neaten the seams** Although the finished seams are hidden on the inside of the duvet cover, make sure that they don't fray by neatening them using the zigzag attachment on your sewing machine. Press the seam allowances together, set the dial to a medium stitch and length and, using a matching sewing thread, stitch over the edge of the fabric. Finally, turn the cover through to the right side.

◄ *Ties look stylish and, as an added bonus, are less likely to come undone than the traditional popper fastenings*

Making the pillowcases

1 **Make the ties** Make up two pairs of front and two pairs of back ties as given for the duvet cover.

2 ▲ **Position the front ties** Lay out the pillowcase front with the right side uppermost. Position the front ties equally spaced along the front edge, then pin and tack in place. Hem one long side of the flap and stitch it in place as for the duvet cover. Turn the flap to the wrong side and pin the side edges.

3 **Position the back ties** Hem the top edge of the back section, incorporating the ties in the same way as for the duvet cover.

4 **Stitch the pillowcase** Place the front and back sections together with right sides facing (see Step 6 of the duvet cover). Pin and stitch around three sides taking a 12mm (½in) seam allowance. Neaten the seams by zigzagging and turn the pillowcase through to the right side.

MAKE IT SIMPLE

adding ribbon ties

For a speedier version of this project, you can bypass making the ties for the fastenings by using ribbons instead. Simply make a plain duvet or pillowcase following the steps on these pages, but replace the matching ties with bought ribbons or braids (like the wonderful selection shown here). Another even quicker option is to buy a duvet cover and then simply jazz it up by attaching ribbon fastenings. All you have to do is neaten the ends of the ribbons as shown below and refer to the instructions on the previous pages for where you should position the ties.

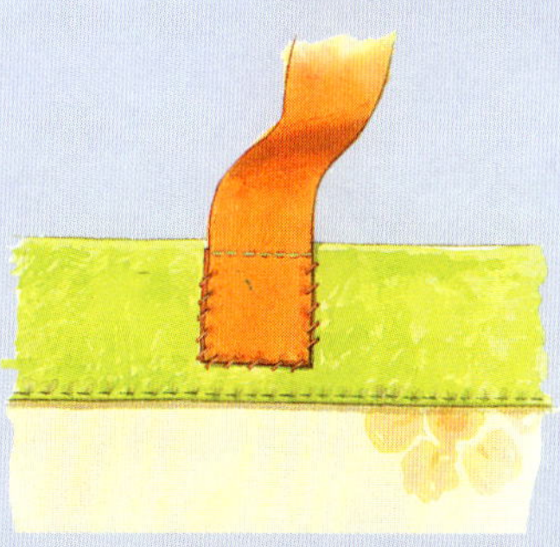

1 ◄ **Attach the ribbons** Turn under 12mm (½in) at one end of the ribbon. Position the folded end just inside the inner edge of the duvet or pillowcase, with the ties extended. Using matching sewing thread, slip-stitch around three sides of the folded ribbon as shown, then secure the fourth side with a line of neat running stitches.

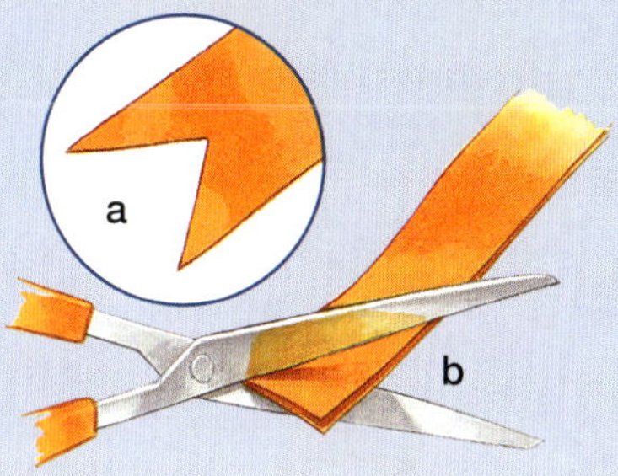

2 ◄ **Neaten the ends** Prevent the free ends of the ribbon fraying by cutting them straight across in a diagonal line. Alternatively, form a V shape (a) by folding the ends together widthways and then cutting diagonally, angling the scissor blades down from the outer edge (b).

drop in anytime

Add a burst of new life to your dining area by re-covering drop-in seats. No specialist techniques are required, so you can get started straight away

Re-covering a single or group of dining chairs need not be a daunting prospect – especially if the chairs have seats that drop into their frames and are easy to lift out. In fact the re-covering process requires very little preparation and no specialist equipment if you retain the existing seat stuffing; so there's nothing to stop you from starting the transformation straight away.

A change of scene

If you want to stay close to your existing look, you can replace worn or faded fabric with a similar variety. But you may get the urge to try a new approach. For a dramatic change, swap pale pastels for bold primary colours; alternatively, replace formal stripes with abstract checks or large motifs.

Wear and tear

But whatever your choice of fabric, you should check that it is the correct weight for the job in hand. Mediumweight fabric is best, particularly for chairs that are used every day. Also, make sure that the fabric is closely woven so that it holds its shape and wears well. And if you are re-covering a set of chairs, take care to select a fabric that does not fade easily, or any chairs exposed individually to bright light will soon appear less vibrant than the others – moving your chairs around every few months should help prevent this.

◀ *Create a pretty dining room chair with a seat covered in a fancy check pattern to complement the floral curtains*

Measuring and cutting guide

- **To calculate the fabric** To work out how much fabric you will need, measure the widest part of the seat lengthways and widthways, then add about 20cm (8in) to both measurements. You will need extra if you are using a patterned fabric to allow for centring motifs and matching the pattern on each chair; also if your chair seat is especially thick.
- **To calculate the hessian** The hessian for the underside should measure about 2cm (¾in) wider than the seat all the way around.

Essentials

- Seat fabric
- Hessian
- Tack lifter
- 12mm (½in) tacks
- 15mm (⅝in) tacks
- Hammer
- Staple gun (optional)

Re-covering the seats

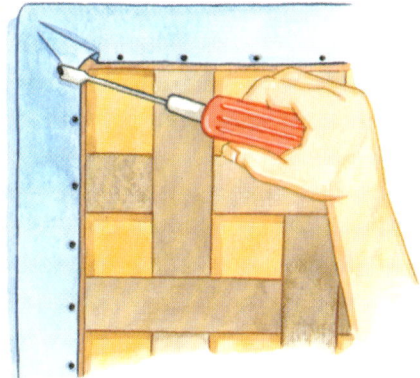

1 ▲ Remove the old fabric
Remove the drop-in seat from the chair and secure it, upside-down, on a work bench or flat surface. Use a tack lifter (which you can buy from any DIY store) to prise out the old tacks, taking care to work through only the hessian covering if there is one, and the top layer of seat fabric. Remove the old fabric and dispose of the old tacks.

2 ▲ **Cut out the new fabric** Using the seat as a template, cut a piece of fabric using the measuring guide provided, taking care to centre any motifs. Leave enough fabric to wrap around the sides and under the frame. If your seat padding is very thick, or your frame is very deep, you may need to allow for slightly more fabric.

3 ▲ **Tack the new fabric in place temporarily** Lay out the fabric, wrong side up, with the seat turned upside-down and centred on top. Wrap the fabric over the seat frame and secure it temporarily over the front and back rails, close to the inner edge of the frame, using a few 15mm (⅝in) tacks. Do this by knocking the tacks only half-way into the wood. Secure the fabric along each of the remaining sides in the same fashion.

4 **Tack the new fabric in place permanently** When you are satisfied that the fabric is in the correct position and is evenly taut, tack it into place permanently, using 12mm (½in) tacks spaced every 4cm (1½in). Leave 5cm (2in) of fabric free from each inner corner, then hammer home the temporary tacks.

MAKE IT SIMPLE

using a staple gun

Staple guns are a quick and efficient alternative to re-covering chair seats using the traditional tacks method. Simply position the staple gun flush against the frame on the underside of the seat and squeeze the handle firmly and steadily to staple the fabric in place.

CHOOSING A STAPLE GUN
When buying a staple gun, choose a mediumweight one that's recommended for upholstery work – a heavy gun is difficult to handle and may result in you splitting the frame, or firing metal staples into the wood at awkward angles.

5 ▲ **Cover the corners** Pull the corners of fabric across each corner of the chair frame and tack in place. Then fold the two side pleats towards the tack to form a neat corner. Crease the fabric firmly and trim away the excess fabric, taking care not to cut too close to the outer edge of the frame. Fold in one of the side flaps and secure it with a 12mm (½in) tack. Repeat with the other side flap and trim away any excess fabric protruding underneath.

6 ▲ **Cover the underside with hessian** Make turnings along each edge of the piece of hessian by folding under 2cm (¾in) to the wrong side and creasing firmly. Place the neatened piece of hessian over the underside of the frame to cover the raw edge of the seat fabric. Secure first with temporary, then permanent, tacks close to the outer edge of the frame, following Steps 3 and 4.

Make sure you have the following basic items in your workbasket or at hand for creating the projects in this book. Any extra equipment is listed in the 'Essentials' box at the start of every new make.

Measuring

Tape measure Buy a non-stretch tape with metal ends. They are usually about 150cm (60in) long.
Metal tape An expandable metal tape measure is essential for accurately measuring large items such as windows and beds.
Wooden or metal ruler Essential for marking and cutting fabric.

Cutting

Dressmaker's shears These scissors have 20–25cm (8–10in) blades and are used for cutting out fabric. Shears with angled handles allow the fabric to be kept flat during cutting, giving a more reliable and accurate result.
General sewing scissors Smaller, straight-handled scissors are useful for trimming seams and clipping thread ends.
Pinking shears Used to neaten seam allowances, these scissors have zigzag-edged blades. Remember, though, that fabric should never be cut out using pinking shears, since it is difficult to measure accurately from a zigzag edge.
Household scissors Keep a pair of everyday scissors handy in your workbasket to cut paper, string and so on, since fabric scissors can quickly become blunt if they are used to cut other materials.

Marking

Tailor's chalk This is available in different colours, in chalk or pencil form. Choose a shade that shows up on your fabric, but avoid marking a very pale fabric with dark chalk.
Marking pens Marks made with these pens either disappear after several hours, or can be washed out of fabrics that can be laundered.

stitching for starters

To get the best results from the projects in The Look, the right equipment and some basic sewing know-how, are a must.

Sewing

Pins There is a huge range of pins available in various lengths. Check the box label and pick the appropriate type for your fabric.
Hand sewing needles Match the needle type and size to the project and fabric. Use 'sharps' in various sizes for general sewing; shorter 'betweens' for hemming; and blunt 'bodkins' for threading ribbon and tape through casings.

Thimble This allows you to push, rather than pull, the needle through heavy furnishing fabrics or through several layers. Buy the metal variety and make sure it fits your middle finger properly.
Threader Even if you've keen eyesight, this small gadget makes threading fine needles quick and easy.
Unpicker A handy device with razor-sharp points that's ideal for removing unwanted machine stitching and tacking stitches.

Plain or flat seam

This is the seam that you'll need most often for sewing projects. The reverse stitching at either end of the seam gives an important bit of added strength.

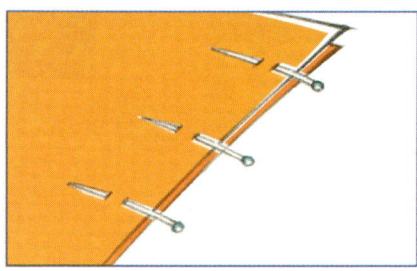

1 ▲ Place the fabric pieces with right sides and raw or cut edges together. Secure with pins inserted at right angles to the fabric edges and the pin heads outside the fabric so that they can be removed as you stitch the seam. If necessary, tack the pieces together alongside the seamline before stitching.

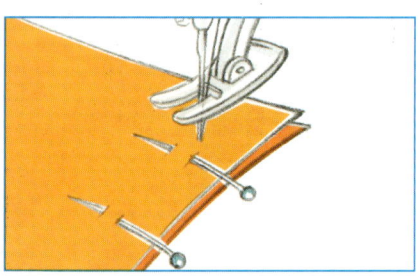

2 ▲ Position the needle in the fabric, the given distance from the raw or cut edges and 1.5cm (⅝in) down from

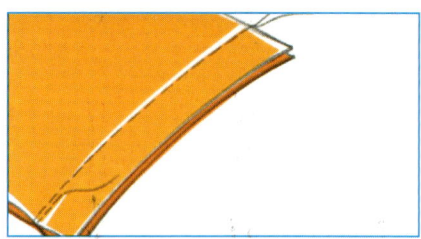

the top edge. Lower the presser foot, set the sewing machine in reverse and stitch back to the top edge.

3 ▲ Change the setting to forwards and stitch the seam, keeping an even distance from the cut edges. Remove the pins as you stitch to avoid breaking the needle. At the end, change the setting to reverse and work a few backstitches. Raise the foot and needle. Pull the fabric and threads to the back of the machine and cut and trim the ends.

4 ▶ Press over the stitched seam to set the stitches (**a**), then press the seam open (**b**) if required (see individual projects).

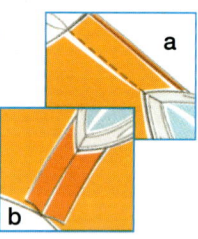

Zigzag stitching

One of the most useful functions of the zigzag attachment on your sewing machine is for neatening the cut edges of seams. You can alter the stitch in both length and width depending on the purpose. Alter the length in the same way as straight stitching (see right), and the width (the distance the needle moves from side to side) by altering the width regulator.

A short stitch length produces a tightly worked satin stitch, while the higher the number on the width regulator dial, the wider the stitch. Test different mixtures of stitch lengths and widths on the fabric you're using.

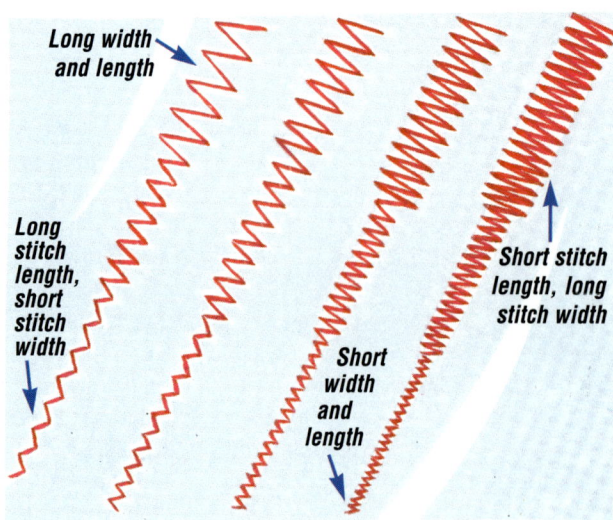

Long width and length

Long stitch length, short stitch width

Short width and length

Short stitch length, long stitch width

Creating the perfect stitch

1 Set up your sewing machine following your instruction manual. Check that the tension between the upper (spool) and lower (bobbin) threads is correct and that the pressure from the presser foot is neither too heavy, nor too light. If necessary, adjust the settings according to your manual and set the stitch length (between 2 and 3 for most fabrics) and the stitch width (0 for running stitch, various for zigzag stitch).

2 ▶ Place the fabric under the raised presser foot with the bulk of the fabric on the left. Lower the needle into the fabric, then lower the foot and stitch evenly and carefully, supporting and guiding the fabric through the machine as you sew. Most machines have guidelines etched into the needle plate at measured distances from the needle. These will help you to stitch in a straight line if you keep the edge of your fabric butted up against the same mark all the way along.

3 When you have finished stitching, stop the machine with the needle in the highest position. Raise the presser foot and remove the fabric from the machine. Cut both threads together.

Tone on tone ▶
There's nothing dull about a neutral scheme that contains a lively mix of patterns in several tones of the same shade

Sweet ▶ lavender
A combination of cream, cool whites and soothing lavender creates the perfect atmosphere for relaxing

▲ Orange crush
Bring the bright oranges and pinks of garden flowers into the house for a sunny dining room to make mealtimes cheery all year round

making the right choice

When styling your home, be bold with colour and change the rooms to really reflect your style. However, when choosing fabrics and paints, consider the design of your furniture and how the different rooms will complement each other

Homes are definitely looking more colourful these days, but not all of us have the confidence to depart from the safe haven of the neutral schemes we've come to know and love. Hot orange, lime and citrus yellow might look sensational as the basis of an in-store display, but can you live with them in your own home? And, if you decide to take the plunge, is it possible to work in the 'new' colours with what you already have?

Choosing the look
Before you embark on any radical changes, it's important to establish some idea of the overall look you

are trying to achieve. Pay more attention to shop displays, cast a critical eye over friends' houses, study restaurant interiors even, and you'll start to build up a clear picture of what you like. Make up your own personal 'home file' of cuttings, photographs, fabric swatches and paint samples as you go; then add room plans and dimensions and you'll have an up-to-date record that you can refer to each time you redecorate.

Making it work

By the time your research is complete, the chances are you'll have already identified the look you want, but still may not know quite how to achieve it. You certainly won't want to make

expensive mistakes, so how can you be sure that Mediterranean, Shaker, or Scandinavian style – all favourites with interior designers – will work for you?

The room itself must be your most important consideration. When choosing a colour scheme, consider factors such as how the room is used and by whom, what direction it faces and how much natural light it gets. It's a well-known fact that cool, north-facing rooms seem instantly cosier when bathed in a warm colour, like terracotta, while those filled with sunshine need the calming influence of shades such as aqua and lime. Light and airy rooms generally look good in shades of blue, while gloomy

▲ Forge your own style

Modern mix-and-match ranges help you to achieve a totally individual look that was missing in the days when co-ordination was all the rage and everyone's home looked the same

▶ China blue

Reluctant colour-schemers can always rely on tried and tested combinations such as blue and white. Varying the tones from aquamarine to navy gives this bathroom added dimension

◄ Set and match
You'll have no problem mixing patterns if you stick to the same basic shades for fabrics and wallpapers

areas benefit from light-reflecting yellow hues.

But while such guidelines exist, they are no substitute for personal taste. And remember to bear in mind the views of your family as well. There's no reason why a lively youngster can't have a bedroom that's garish and bright, even if your ideal is something more soothing on the eye.

Getting started

Some rooms cry out to be decorated in a certain style. Others can be more difficult, and the huge variety of fabrics and furniture, colours and textures on offer can make it even harder to reach a decision. If you already have a favourite chair, bedspread, or rug that you want to incorporate into the scheme, use it as your starting point and you'll find it easier to build your theme around it. However, if you're starting from scratch, one safe bet is to choose the pattern of your fabric first and let it determine the other colours in the room for you.

Putting it all together

You should also take time to closely examine your chosen fabric. Squinting through half-closed eyes will reveal the predominant colours on which to base your overall scheme – paint, cushions, upholstery and so on. But you don't have to match these exactly, since paler or deeper shades will also work. And if you feel brave enough to introduce additional patterns, such as checks with florals, stick to the same basic colours and you won't go wrong.

Professional designers rely on colour boards to present a scheme and these are useful tools for anyone. All you need is a large piece of card on which to paste all your samples, cuttings, paint splodges, carpet swatches and other bits and pieces; then take it into the room and study it for a while. See how it looks in different lights and at different times of the day, and, if you're happy with what you see, you'll soon feel confident enough to get started.

▲ Mint condition
Green can be an easier colour to live with than you think. Combine it with a gentle floral design and plain upholstery fabric in warm pink and cream for a tranquil sitting room

sheer simplicity

For the ultimate in quick and easy curtains and blinds, dress your windows with fine voiles and muslins in pure white cotton

Long, narrow windows and doors require careful treatment. Curtains hanging at each side can drastically reduce the amount of light coming into the room, and heavy drapes will make the opening appear narrower.

To maximise the light from the window, use sheer fabrics such as voile and muslin in white or soft pastels and let the light flood in.

For the speediest of window dressing, wrap long lengths of the fabric around a wooden pole and let it pool on the floor. For a more structured look, such as the blind on the right, catch the centre of the lower hem up onto the top of the curtain and either bind the two ends or add two luxurious tassles.

▲ Go to great lengths
Long curtains accentuate the height of these French doors, while the simple drape hides the pole or track

▶ Swept away
Narrow windows can be spoilt by over-fussy dressing, but nothing could be more elegant than this sheer blind with its sweeping curves

Lighting has a dramatic effect on the mood and atmosphere of a room. Throw a soft, clear light on living spaces with subtle fabric lampshades, made by simple snipping and glueing

natural shades

Instead of trawling the shops for just the right lampshade, why not make one yourself? It's so easy to re-cover an old shade in a fabric that complements your room style, curtains or wallpaper.

Choosing a frame

Lampshade frames are available from craft shops and haberdashery departments in a variety of exciting shapes and sizes, from classic tapered styles to modern elongated drum designs. And, if you can't find the frame you want, buy a cheap lampshade in the required shape instead. Then take off the fabric cover and replace it with your own – first making sure to strip off all the tape and glue from the old frame, or you won't achieve a smooth shape. Also, if the wire isn't plastic-coated, it may need sanding down first to remove any bumps (Step 1 on the next page explains how to do this).

Suitable fabrics

The lampshades featured here are made in natural scrim (a heavy-weight undyed linen) for one, and a smooth cream linen for the other. But in actual fact you can use virtually any fabric, although very

transparent or open-weave fabrics may not be suitable for this project. To stiffen the fabric, use a self-adhesive plastic card designed specifically for lampshades, which is again available from craft shops and haberdashery departments. It looks solid white on the roll, but magically becomes translucent when held up to the light.

◄ *Create a very modern look by using a soft-printed natural fabric for an elongated cone lampshade. Place it on a tall wooden lampstand, against a neutral background, to accentuate its height*

Measuring and cutting guide

- **Make a pattern** *To find out how much fabric you will need to cover your lampshade, first make a pattern.*

  1 *Roll the wire frame on to a large sheet of paper – brown wrapping paper is ideal. Make a mark on one strut with a pencil or tailor's chalk, then starting with the marked strut, roll the frame on its side, marking the top and bottom of the struts on the paper as you go.*

  2 *Join up the marks with a pencil, following the curve of the shade.*

  3 *Cut out the paper pattern, allowing 1cm (⅜in) for the overlap on all edges. Check that the pattern is the correct shape by holding it around the frame.*

- **Estimate the fabric**

  1 *Place the paper pattern with its centre on the bias (cross grain) of a piece of 115cm (45in) wide fabric.*

  2 *Measure along the selvedge from the top to the bottom edge of the pattern to work out how much fabric you need, allowing a little extra for cutting out.*

Essentials
- Wire lampshade frame
- Binding tape
- Self-adhesive card
- Clear multi-purpose glue
- Paper for pattern • Pencil
- Clothes pegs or bulldog clips

For the string shade:
- Natural scrim fabric
- String or twine

For the muslin shade:
- Cream linen fabric
- Patches of dyed muslin

Making a covered lampshade

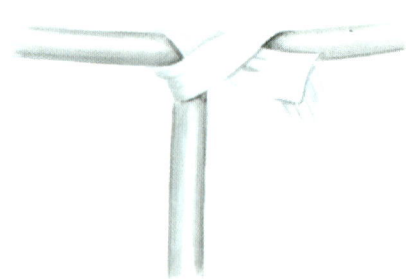

1 ▲ Wrap the frame Using binding tape, wrap the top and bottom rings of the frame to form a firm foundation on which to stick your shade. Use tape in a toning colour so that it doesn't show through the fabric. Wrap the tape tightly, smoothing it to avoid bumps and overlapping as you go. Secure the end with a figure of eight as shown, tucking it under and fixing securely with glue.

◀ *A simple lampshade can transform a dark corner into a bright oasis. Use natural objects, such as these stones, to enhance the theme*

▼ *What could be easier than decorating a lampshade with cut-out shapes. These shells look so effective*

to the backing, wrong side to the sticky surface, smoothing it down as you work to avoid any creases.

grain
of
fabric

2 ▲ Back the fabric From the self-adhesive card and fabric, cut out a square large enough to place the pattern on. Roll the fabric on to a cardboard tube first (this makes it easier to handle as you roll it on to the backing). Remove the backing from the card and lay it, sticky side up, on a flat surface. Slowly roll the material on

3 ▲ Cut out the fabric Lay the pattern on the card-backed fabric, with the grain along one of the straight edges as shown, and mark out the shape with a soft pencil. Cut out the shape carefully using a pair of sharp scissors as it can be quite stiff.

37

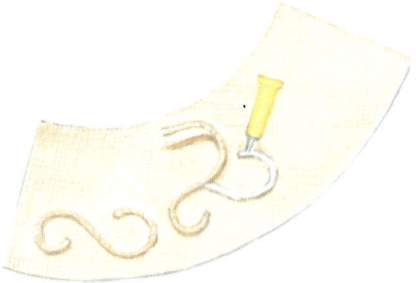

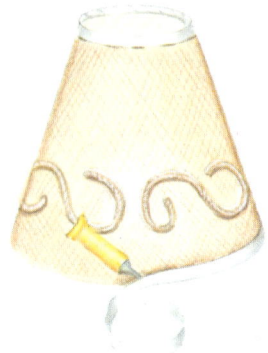

4 ▲ Decorate the shade with string Add the decoration at this stage. Plan your design (mark it out on the paper pattern) and cut some string to the correct length. Transfer the pattern on to the lampshade fabric with clear glue, and then lay the string in place. If the string bounces back when you shape it, try straightening it first by dampening and allowing it to dry. Wait for the glue to dry before proceeding to the next stage.

6 ▲ Glue the shade Using a clear multi-purpose glue, preferably in a tube for ease of use, stick the shade to the frame. Run a line of glue around the top and bottom rings over the tape, and, starting at one end, press down firmly all the way around. You will need to hold the fabric in place with pegs or bulldog clips until it is dry, making sure that they don't stick to the shade.

7 ▲ Trim the frame When the glue has dried, you can straighten any edges and trim them to an exact shape using very sharp scissors. Disguise any rough outer edges with the natural tape used for binding the frame. Glue the tape on one bit at a time, stretching it as you work. Finally, use a steam iron to press out carefully any wrinkles in the scrim.

TAKE ANOTHER LOOK

decorations with a difference

5 ▲ Decorate the shade with muslin Cut several small squares of dyed muslin. Strong pastel shades of green, yellow and burnt sienna will give definition when the light shines through. Fringe the muslin by pulling out an equal number of threads at each edge. Mark the position for the squares on the shade using a pencil and glue them into position.

Be inventive!
The choice of decorations and the possibilities are endless. Cut stars, circles, animals and flowers, or other shapes from patterned fabric and stick them on to an existing shade to match your room scheme.

These shades here are a good example of how resourceful you can be. Following our natural theme, use rope, instead of string, to make swirls and coils. For more dramatic styling that looks great with a wrought iron stand, try black fabric threaded through eyelets to make a looped braid. Or, for a prettier look, punch holes in the fabric and insert a scattering of dried rosebuds.

getting the right mix

A basic understanding of colour and how colours work together will help you to get the best results when decorating fabrics with paint

Colour is a major element in the home. As well as using paints in their pure form, colours can be successfully mixed with each other to create new and original shades.

The colour wheel

The colours of the spectrum (the rainbow) can be simplified into a circle – the colour wheel – in which each colour is shown progressing into the next colour round a circle. Use the colour wheel pictured for a visual explanation of the colour principles.

Colours are divided into three types. First, the **primary colours**: red, blue and yellow. These colours can't be mixed from any other colours; but you can mix every other colour from these three primaries and these are called **secondary colours**. Combine red with yellow to create orange, mix yellow and blue to make green, or produce purple by mixing red and blue together.

As you can see here, primary and secondary colours make up the main colours of the wheel. Finally, **tertiary colours** are created by mixing primary and secondary colours together. For example, add red to green to make brown.

Complementary colours

The colours that lie directly opposite each other on the colour wheel work well together. They produce the strongest contrast of hues, but by placing the opposite sides of the wheel together you balance both warm and cool colours.

In fabric painting, complementary colours prove to be an exciting combination, but only when used in varying amounts. For a more eclectic mix, use one colour to accent or highlight the other, for example adding touches of yellow to accent a blue-based design, creates an eye-catching colour scheme.

Peaceful harmony

Harmonious colours lie between the primary colours on the colour wheel. Take just two colours, for example red and yellow, mix them and see the extensive range of orange and terracotta shades in between with which you can experiment.

A vibrant clash

In harmonious schemes, reds naturally blend into orange. But if you substitute pink, the result is an unexpected clash of colours. Complementary colours also seem to clash when you reverse their strengths. Violet is usually darker than yellow, but put it with a pale mauve and it looks alive.

Tints and shades

Tints are colours mixed with white to lighten them, such as adding white to red to produce pink. Shades are produced when black is added to darken a colour, for example adding a small amount of black to yellow to make mustard.

start stencilling

Follow our steps to successful stencilling and add an individual touch to fabric items all around the home

Stencilling is quick and easy to do: a cut-out shape – the stencil – is lightly sprayed with adhesive and fixed to the fabric, then fabric paint is simply sponged or brushed over the cut-away areas.

And the real plus point is that the options for stencilling are limitless: you can use a single motif repeated as a border, or scatter the shape over your fabric to create a pattern. We used a small synthetic sponge (available from craft shops) as it's quick and easy for beginners. However, a special stencil brush produces just the same effect.

A continuous, undulating ivy stencil will soften and decorate the lower edge of a plain roller blind

Easy steps to stencilling

1 Prepare the surface Iron the fabric to remove any creases. Use the masking tape to hold it firmly in place over a flat surface, such as a table top. In the case of a double-sided fabric, such as our pillowcase, insert a piece of stiff card in between the double layers so that the paint will not sink through.

2▲ Position the stencil Using tailor's chalk, lightly mark the centre of the area you're stencilling (in this example, the corner of the pillowcase). Working from this central point, mark the position of the stencil on the fabric. The chalk marks can be removed by lightly brushing them.

3▲ Fix the stencil in place Place the stencil right side down on a sheet of newspaper and spray it with a light coat of adhesive (spray adhesive is available from a stationer's). Place the sprayed side of the stencil over the positional marks and smooth down firmly. You will find that it sticks in place, yet lifts up quite easily for repositioning.

4▲ Apply the paint Pour a little paint into a clean dish or saucer, then press your sponge lightly into the paint. Pat the sponge on a piece of kitchen paper to remove any excess paint and lightly dab it all over the cut-away parts of the stencil, making sure that you apply an even coat.

5▲ Complete the design Leave the stencil in place for about 10 minutes until the paint is almost dry and then carefully peel it off the fabric.

6▲ Fix the paint Allow the stencilled fabric to dry overnight, then fix the paint by running a hot iron over it. Use a clean, dry cloth to protect the surface of your stencilling. When you have finished with the stencil, clean it by sponging it with warm, soapy water. Rinse the stencil and hang it up to dry so that it's ready to re-use on another occasion.

spot the dog

Children everywhere will fall for the magic appeal of this Dalmatian wall hanging to store their bits and pieces

He's such a cute character – with his cartoon-style expression and realistic fake fur coat – that our spotty dog is hard to resist. A cross between a decorative picture and practical storage, this wall hanging is perfect for a child's room – and you don't even need any sewing skills to make it.

Shape up

You'll need to follow the diagrams in the 'Measuring and cutting guide' (see right) to make paper templates to cut out the shapes for the dog. All you have to do is measure and adapt square or rectangular shapes, or draw circles – so don't worry if your drawing skills aren't perfect.

Once you've cut out the sections of the dog, it's easy to stick them on to the background fabric. Bold metal rivets add a decorative touch as well as a functional one – they hold the tabs at the top of the hanging in position. To hang up your 'picture', just slip a length of wooden dowelling through the felt loops, insert a screw-eye in each end and thread it with picture wire or string.

Toy story

Visit the craft section of a specialist shop or a department store to find most of your requirements for this hanging. Felt fabric for the background is available by the metre; and you can also buy 20cm (8in) squares of the other colours you need for the smaller decorations.

Fake fur fabric is very popular at the moment, but make sure that you choose toy fur as it's much cheaper than the fashion fabrics. Toy fur also has a knitted background that means you don't have to neaten the edges and it shouldn't fray too badly.

If you're still hesitating, think how thrilled any child will be when they see this dog hanging on their wall. So don't delay – the children's shrieks of delight and its pride of place in the bedroom will justify the effort.

Measuring and cutting guide

Amount to buy

- **Felt background** 20 x 30in (8 x 12in) – Trim a 20 x 5cm (8 x 2in) strip off one edge for the loops. From the strip, cut five loops each 3 x 10cm (1¼ x 4in).
- **Felt for dog** You can buy felt in squares from craft shops. These should be sufficient for using on the dog (piece together two strips for the tail, if necessary).
- **Fake fur fabric** You will need 45cm (½ yd) of spotted fake fur fabric.

Make the templates for the dog

- Draw and cut a template out of paper for the various sections of the dog as described, then cut them out of the fabrics as follows: **Fake fur** – body, pouch, 4 feet and face; **White felt** – tummy and 2 eyes; **Black felt** – tail, nose, 2 ears and 2 pupils; **Beige felt** – cheeks; **Red felt** – tongue

- **Body** Cut a rectangle 18 x 30cm (7 x 12in). Mark a point 9cm (3½in) along one shorter side and draw a line joining this point  with the top left-hand corner (see diagram). Draw another line parallel to the first 6cm (2¼in) apart. Mark two more points – the first 8cm (3¼in) along from the top right-hand corner and the other 18cm (7in) up and 3cm (1¼in) from the lower left-hand corner. Join these two points with curved lines as indicated to represent the top of the body and the haunches.

- **Pouch** Cut a rectangle 12 x 19cm (4¾ x 7½in). Mark a point 4cm (1½in) along the lower short edge and draw a line joining this point with the top left-hand corner.

- **Tummy** Cut a rectangle of paper 6 x 20cm (2¼ x 8in). Mark a point 3cm (1¼in) along the lower short edge and draw a line joining this point with the top left-hand corner. Cut a fluted shape along the top.

- **Feet** Draw an 8cm (3¼in) diameter circle. Draw a line across the centre and mark in three scalloped shapes on one side.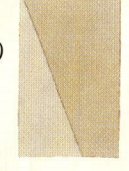

- **Face** Draw a 16cm (6¼in) diameter circle.

- **Cheeks** Draw an 11cm (4⅜in) diameter circle. Draw a line across one end of the circle (see diagram).

- **Ears** Draw a 14cm (5½in) diameter circle. Draw lines dividing it into four equal sections. In two of the sections, draw triangular shapes as shown for the ears.

- **Nose** Draw a 5cm (2in) diameter circle.

- **Eyes** Draw a 4cm (1½in) circle for the white part. **Pupils** Draw a 4cm (1½in) circle. Divide the circle in half and make a shaped section (as shown) in each half.

- **Tongue** Draw a 7cm (2¾in) square. Curve the lower edge of the square as shown.

- **Tail** Draw a bold, curvy shape following the outline of the dog's haunches (refer to picture opposite).

◄ *If you're forever tripping over small toys, then this simple wall hanging with ample pockets is just the thing to get them off the floor and keep a baby's room tidy. It's made from bright, primary colours and the pockets are held in place with rivets for extra strength*

Essentials

- Felt fabric in blue
- Fake fur fabric
- Squares of felt in black, white, beige and red
- 15mm (⁵⁄₈in) heavy-duty metal rivets
- Scissors
- Nail scissors
- Pencil
- Metal ruler
- Fabric glue
- Masking tape
- Paper for templates
- Pair of compasses

Making the wall hanging

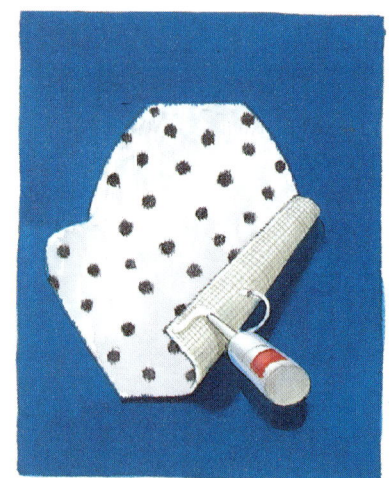

◄ *The little pockets on this wall hanging are ideal for tiny toys and teddies. Use fabric left over from making curtains, or choose two contrasting fabrics from a mix'n'match range*

1 ▲ Stick the body on the background Spread fabric glue in a broad band around the edges on the wrong side of the body, then carefully position it centrally about 14cm (5½in) above the lower edge of the felt background and press in position. Lift one edge of the dog's haunches and stick the tail in place on the lower left-hand edge of the body, tucking it behind the raised edge.

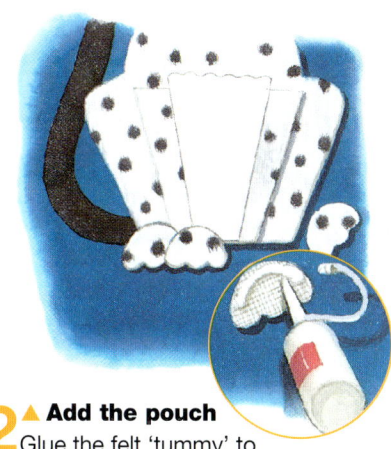

2 ▲ Add the pouch

Glue the felt 'tummy' to the centre of the pouch so that it slightly extends at the top edge. Aligning the lower edges, stick the pocket to the body, gently stuffing it with spare fabric so that it stays in shape while it's sticking. Position the feet along the lower edge, slightly overlapping the body, and stick them down.

3 ▲ Position the head and cheeks

Stick down the circle of fur fabric for the head, then position the felt ears, tucking them behind the head if necessary. Place the cheeks with the tongue poking out from underneath, and stick down. Attach the black felt nose.

4 ▲ Add the eyes

Stick the black sections of the eyes on to the white circles. Experiment with their

position in relationship to one another before you stick them down – you can alter the dog's expression in this way. Once you are happy with the effect, stick the eyes to the head.

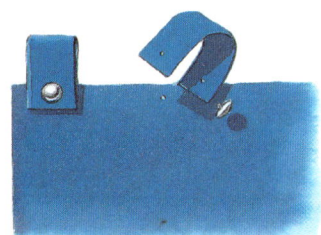

5 ▲ Secure the loops

Mark the position of the rivets for five loops along the top of the hanging – the corner ones should be 1.5cm (⅝in) in from both edges, with the others evenly spaced between. Use a pair of nail scissors to poke a hole through the felt. Fold the tabs in half and place either side of the top edge about 2cm (¾in) down, over the fixing points. Make small holes in the tabs to match those on the wall hanging. Secure each tab in place with a rivet through all three holes.

▲ *This charming wall hanging has a raised effect. You can create it making simple padded shapes and then sewing them on to the backing fabric*

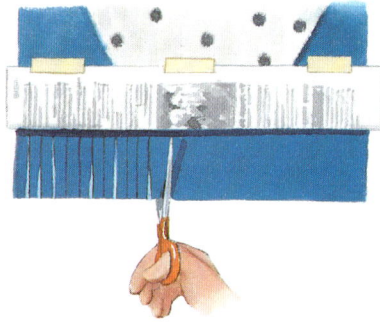

6 ▲ Fringe the lower edge

With the wrong side of the hanging facing, secure a strip of newspaper across the width with masking tape, about 7.5cm (3in) up from the lower edge. Using a very sharp pair of scissors, cut up to the newspaper strip at 1.5cm (⅝in) intervals to form the fringe. Finally, insert a rod through the loops to hang up the 'doggy' holder.

furry friends

For up-to-the-minute styling and a hint of animal magic, use fake fur prints to introduce a touch of the exotic

Indulge a passion for animal prints with fabulous fake fur. Hints of skin bring a new style dimension to upholstered stools or cushions; fluffy kitsch is blatantly over the top and can lend a 'fifties feel' to a living room or bedroom; while animal prints will add light-hearted realism to projects for children's rooms.

Furry dress and furnishing fabrics have a wonderful 'feel', but can be very expensive. So a better idea is to search out the craft department of your local store and look at the selection of fur fabrics for toy making. You'll find that their price is only a fraction of those charged for dress

and furnishing fabrics. Toy fabrics also have the benefit of a knitted (interlocked) backing, so that you can cut out shapes with sharp scissors without having to worry about neatening the raw edges.

Although fur fabrics aren't the easiest to work with, if you stick to small amounts in simple shapes and follow a few rules (see the checklist), then you just can't go wrong. Beware, though – fur fabrics do shed their hairs. Get rid of any loose fibres around the edges before sticking the shapes down. And if you get caught, simply remove any stray hairs from your clothes with a pad of sticky tape!

● See 'Spot the dog', p42, for a child's wall hanging with loads of animal magnetism

---

checklist
Fur fabrics

● **Fibre content** Fur fabrics are synthetic and require a certain amount of special handling. They also have a pile which usually runs in the same direction on all pieces. However, unusual effects can be achieved by running the pile in different directions and then brushing it.

● **Simple styling** Because fur fabric is quite thick, keep designs simple so that no complicated cutting and shaping is required.

● **Sew or stick** If you're sewing fur fabric, tack it in position first to stop it slipping around while you are stitching. Instead of sewing, you can also use fabric glue to stick it in place.

● **Variety of effects** Fur fabrics are available in most animal effects and also in a wide variety of colours from the natural ones shown here to bright pink and yellow.

● **Aftercare** Toy fur fabric should be washable, but check when you buy. If in doubt, sponge clean with a damp cloth and a small amount of dishwashing liquid.

---

1 Long-haired fur is really wild. Choose a pale golden colour for a look that says 'King of the Jungle'

2 You'll think you're seeing spots before your eyes with this dalmatian printed fabric in fashionable black and white

3 Stripy tiger-printed fabric is a popular choice for furnishing schemes with a retro feel

4 Teddy bears are an endearing favourite. Now you can cuddle up in fabric that emulates their plush fur

5 Sheepskin is noted for its warmth. The curly texture and creamy colour of this fake version is tops for style as well

6 Leopards never change their spots. Here's another jungle print that won't date and will stay looking great

Use an ivy stencil, available from craft shops or DIY stores, to create elegant table linen with a twist

Create a fresh, new look for your kitchen table with a tablecloth and napkins featuring an original stencilled border design. You don't even have to bother with making the cloth – simply find a colour or design that you like and you can stencil directly on to it. First you'll have to buy some liquid fabric paint, but this is widely available in specialist stencil shops or large haberdashery departments. And for extra advice and handy tips on getting the most out of stencilling, simply refer to the detailed information in 'Start stencilling', p42.

Choose checks

Plain fabrics are the obvious choice for stencilling, but checked fabrics look great in the kitchen and the straight lines make it easy to position the motifs. There are also plenty of checked styles to choose from, especially in the popular Indian Madras cotton ranges. Large, bold checks are particularly suitable, and the slightly off-beat pastel colours make a fresh background that's light enough to show off the design perfectly.

To complete the project you'll need a set of napkins, so go for matching plain or striped fabrics, then go to town with the decoration. Choose from a full trail of ivy or just a few leaves scattered in one of the corners.

Position perfect

You'll need to work out in advance where to position the ivy stencils on your tablecloth. Decide how far from the edge you want the border, then check how the motifs fit together at the corners.

join the ivy league

Depending on the length and width of your cloth, you'll need to calculate how to repeat the stencilled motifs. We've laid ours end to end, with no gaps between. But to finish a complete length with a full motif, you may need to leave some spaces between them.

Don't be daunted, though, by this small amount of preparatory work. It's often worth taking the time to practise on a spare piece of

▲ *For a fresh summer feel, random prints of lemons and limes all over the tablecloth make an attractive alternative to a border design*

fabric first, until you feel sufficiently comfortable with the techniques involved. In fact, once you get going, you'll find it difficult to stop stencilling – and the fabulous results will more than justify the initial efforts.

Essentials

- Bought, checked square or rectangular tablecloth and plain or striped napkins
- Ivy stencil
- Green fabric paint
- Tailor's chalk
- Spray adhesive
- Dish
- Sponge or stencil brush
- Kitchen paper
- Masking tape

▼ Here you can see an actual example of how two stencils fit together at the corner of your tablecloth. Following Step 2, make practise strips to position them first

Stencilling the tablecloth

1 ▲ Make mock stencils The easiest way to decide how to position the stencilled motifs at the corners and along the sides of the cloth is to first paint several stencils on to plain paper. Then cut out around the extremities of the motifs so that you make a border strip.

2 ▲ Position the corner Use two of the paper strips to fix the positioning of your corner design. Following the lines on your checked cloth, fit the first strip into the corner and hold it in place with masking tape. Then lay the next stencilled strip at right angles to the previous one. Fix the other corners in the same way, making sure that the motifs along each side follow through in the same direction.

3 ▲ Place the stencils along one side Now the corners are fixed, you can decide how to position the stencils along each side. Try placing the paper strips end to end to see if the design fits neatly to the next corner. If not, you will need to leave an equal gap between them. Mark their positions, following the step by step instructions to stencilling on p41. Continue around the cloth, marking the stencil positions along each side.

4 ▲ Apply the paint Once you are happy with the arrangement of motifs, you can begin stencilling. Fix the stencil in position with a light coating of the spray adhesive. Apply the paint by lightly dabbing the sponge or stencil brush over the cut-away sections of the stencil until you have an even coat. Leave the stencil in position for a few minutes until it's almost dry before moving it on to the next position. Once the complete design is dry, fix the paint to stop it smudging by ironing it with a warm iron.

TAKE ANOTHER LOOK

design ideas

Make a corner ivy trail
First, mark two stencil positions, the first one along one side edge of the napkin, with the end in the corner. Then, position the second stencil at right angles to the first (see Step 2 of the tablecloth design). Stencil the fabric in these two places only.

Work a reverse image
Check that the stencilled motif fits twice along the side edge that you want to stencil, then, starting at the corner, work the first stencil. Wash the paint off the stencil, turn it over and repeat the design, working towards the centre from the next corner. If there's space in the centre, you can add a single leaf to complete the design.

Stencilling the napkin

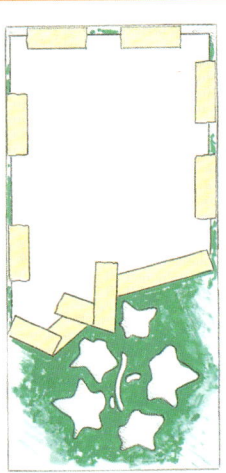

1 ▲ **Block off the stencil** Use a section of the main design to make smaller motifs to stencil in each corner of the napkin. Block off the cut-out section of the stencil that you don't require by taping over a piece of paper, or for smaller areas, use masking tape alone.

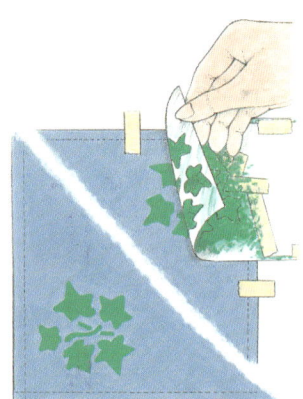

2 ▲ **Position the motif** Following Step 1 of the tablecloth, stencil a mock motif on to plain paper. Place it in each corner in turn, at a 45° angle to the point, and mark the positions with tailor's chalk.

3 **Stencil the motifs** Following the instructions for the tablecloth, work a motif in each corner, making sure that the same leaves point into the corner each time. Allow each motif to dry before moving the stencil on to the next position. Remember to fix the paint by pressing it with a warm iron.

the braided bunch

Trimmings add a dash of instant style. Give your plain cushions the star treatment with a length of spectacular braid or fringe

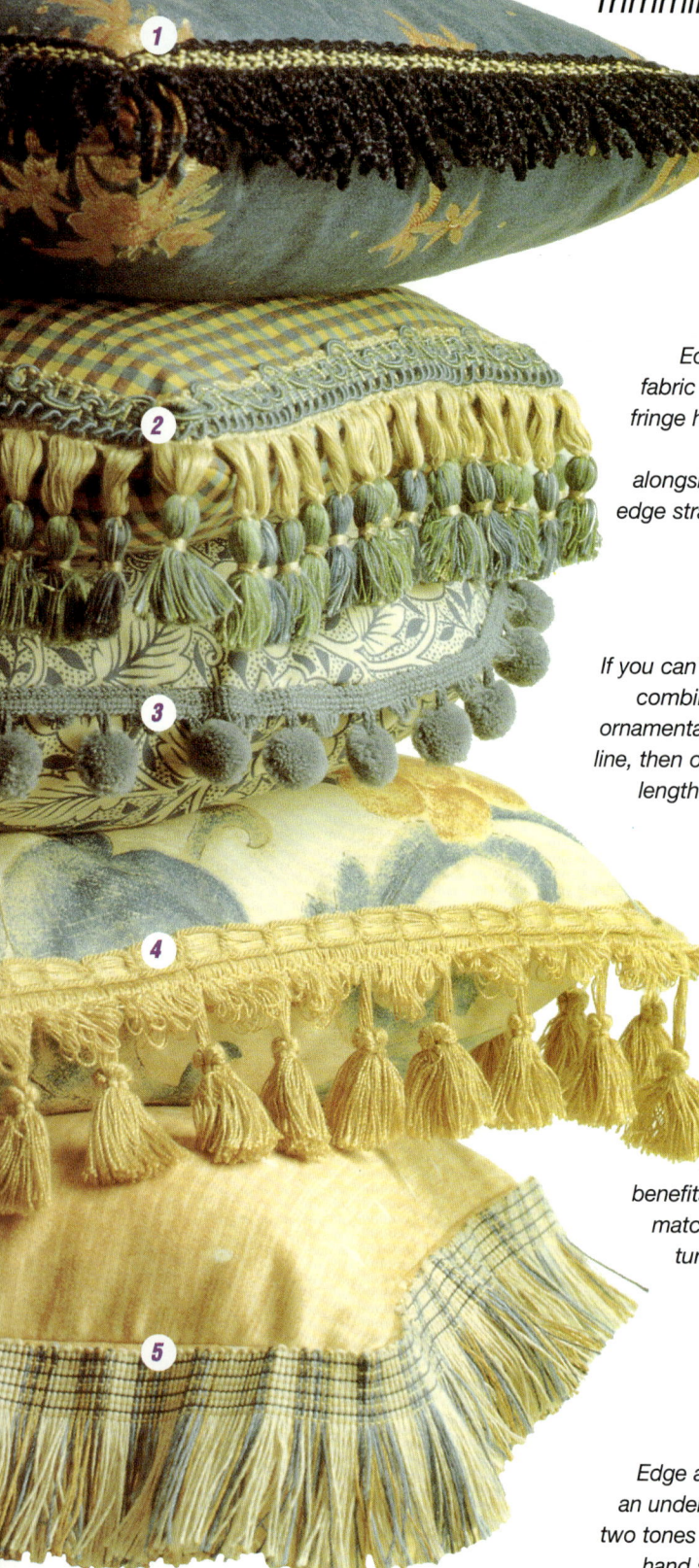

1 Distinctive edge
Echo the texture of dusty blue fabric with a deep twisted chenille fringe held on a gold braid. Line up the inner edge of the braid alongside the seamline to keep the edge straight and so the fringe over-laps the cushion edge; hand sew in place

2 Deep tassels
If you can't find a deep tassel fringing, combine two trims. Hand stitch an ornamental gimp trim along the seam-line, then overlay the outer edge with a length of luxurious long tassel trim

3 Blue pom-pons
Even William Morris-type prints benefit from an edging. Add a pompon fringe – this looks especially good on round cushion covers

4 Venetian edge
A bright Italian print benefits from a well-chosen trim to match its colour and style. When turning each corner, space the tassels evenly – if necessary, tuck under more or less of the braid at each corner point

5 Natural look
Edge a plain slubbed cushion with an understated linen fringe woven in two tones – to achieve the best result, hand sew around the cushion just above the seamline

For centuries trimmings have been used to enhance cushions in all sorts of ways. Now, decorative edgings are back with a flourish, so indulge yourself and create some sensational accessories for your own home.

With a host of different trimmings available – from richly-hued ribbons to deep fringes or long luxurious braids – you can add an extravagant edge to your cushions and bring the whole decor of a room to life.

Visit your local haberdashery department, rummage through your own sewing box, or seek out more unusual and exotic items by trying specialist shops and interior design outlets – you're bound to find plenty to inspire you.

A close attachment
To attach fringes and braids, simply measure around the outside edge of the cushion, adding 2cm (¾in), then cut this length of trim. Pin the trimming against the seamline around the sides of the cushion. Turn under the cut ends so that they butt together in the centre of one side and form a neat join. Hand sew the trimming in place with tiny slip-stitches, working along both edges of the braid, then slip-stitch across the joins to finish.

◄ Cushion corner

Cushions heaped high on the sofa spell a big welcome in any room. Mix together different fabrics and styles, giving each one a unique edge. Hand sew twisted cords around the seamlines, twisting them into knots at each corner; or add jaunty tassels and plain wide braids. With large groups of cushions, it's essential to harmonize colours and prints for an inspiring look

6 Cheery tassels

Tri-toned tassels in co-ordinating hues add pizzazz to a plain cushion. Simply hand sew the tassel fringe around the seamline. To help ease the braid around corners, gather up the edges and hand sew into gentle curves

7 Medieval message

Make a bold statement by adding large tassels at each corner of a subtle damask cushion. Use a slightly darker shade for best results

8 Tempting tartans

Clever sourcing of materials means a perfect colour match every time. This ruched fringe contains all the tartan hues and neatly divides the cushion in half

9 Classic edge

On large cushions, trimmings form a separate outline. Make guidelines using tacking, so that you can line up the braid edge and hand sew in place

10 Double vision

Use two rows of fringe for a wild-looking edge. Try saucy colour combinations like green and burnt orange fringes against a bright tomato red cushion

11 Weaver's world

Ornate fringes work well when they pick out one or two colours from a busy cushion cover pattern

▼ Plush textures

Cushions in rich fabrics like velvet are lent extra vitality with distinctive trims. First, stitch a wide ornamental trim along opposite sides, then outline it with an understated twisted cord. Finally, add an eye-catching tassel at each corner

castles in the air

Tab top curtains are hung from poles by simple loops, echoing the shape of castle battlements. Make this straightforward, unlined version for an eye-catching result

If you're after a pair of curtains with a difference, or if you've bought a pole you particularly want to show off, tab top curtains are the answer.

'Tab tops' is actually a reference to the way the curtains are hung, because their main feature is tabs which are folded over to make a series of loops, and sewn to the top of the drape. The tabs are then slotted on to a pole fixed to the wall, giving these curtains an individual look. The fact that they are not gathered makes them easy

Dusky-blue, floor-length tab tops form an elegant linen sweep, turning an ordinary window into a special feature

Measuring and cutting guide

- **To calculate the length**

  1 Fix the pole in place, making sure it is at least 8cm (3¼in) above the window top, which will leave enough room for the tabs to hang.

  2 Starting 3cm (1⅛in) below the pole, measure the finished length of the curtain.

  3 To this measurement add 11.5cm (4½in) for the hem and top turning – this is the <u>cut length</u> of the curtains. To this length add 10cm (4in) for the facings, then add the length of the tabs (see the final paragraph opposite). This is the <u>total length</u> of fabric that you need for the curtains.

- **To calculate the total area**

  1 To calculate the number of fabric widths needed, multiply the width of the window by one and a half, then divide this by the width of your fabric and round up to the nearest whole number.

  2 Multiply this number by the <u>total length</u> of fabric required for the curtains. This will be the total amount of fabric needed.

- **Cutting the fabric**

  1 Working straight across the fabric widthways, cut the number of curtain lengths you require to make up the width of your curtain.

  2 Cut the same number of 10cm (4in) deep facings to be joined along the top edge of each curtain length. Cut interfacing for each facing 1cm (⅜in) narrower than the facing all the way around.

- **Cutting the tabs**

  The width of the tabs will depend to some extent on the weight of the fabric used, the size of the pole, and the length of the curtain; but they are generally 5–7.5cm (2–3in) wide.

  1 Measure the curtain top for the number of tabs required, allowing a space of approximately two tab widths in between each one.

  2 For the length of each tab, measure around the pole and add 8cm (3¼in).

  3 For the width allow twice the finished width plus 2cm (¾in) for the seams.

▼ **Tab top curtains in classic cream lend a touch of elegance to any setting. Here they echo the neutral shades of the decor and help to create a sense of harmony**

to sew and perfect for fabrics with large patterns, since heavily gathered curtain styles have the effect of dulling the impact of bold designs.

Poles galore

Consider your choice of curtain pole. You can buy any sort to hang these curtains, from inexpensive wooden ones to the more ornate iron varieties. There are lots to choose from in the shops, and most DIY stores also stock a good selection.

Truly adaptable

These curtains are in fact truly adaptable and lend themselves equally well to formal or informal room settings, at any length from floor to sill. And tab tops can look particularly effective used for half, or 'café', curtains. Here the castle battlements effect of the heading is thrown into focus by light flooding through the window.

Any type of fabric can be used for tab top curtains, from light-weight muslins to heavy brocades. In this project we show you how to make a simple version, where the top edge is strengthened with a facing (a separate strip of material with stiffer, interfacing fabric attached) which encloses the tabs.

Making the curtains

1 ▶ **Neaten the curtain edges**
Where necessary, join the fabric widths using a plain seam and press the seams open. Fold 1cm (⅜in), then 2cm (¾in) to the wrong side down each side of the curtain. Press and then machine stitch the side seams, close to the fold.

2 ▲ **Stitch the hem** For the lower hem fold 2.5cm (1in) then 7.5cm (3in) to the wrong side and press, then pin in place. Fold the

corners of the hem under at an angle to form a neat finish. Starting and finishing at the side hem stitching lines, machine stitch along the hem, close to the fold. Then, using a needle and thread, hand stitch along the folded corners with small, neat stitches to secure the fabric in place (the stitches in the illustration are exaggerated in size so you can see them clearly).

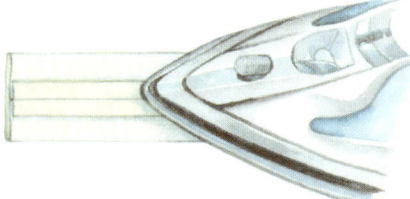

3 ▲ Make the tabs With right sides together, fold each tab in half lengthways and machine stitch a 1cm (⅜in) seam. Press the seam open, then turn the tab right side out. With the seam centred down the back, re-press the tab.

4 ▶ Position the tabs
Lay the curtain out flat, right side up. With cut edges together, place a folded tab to the top edge of the curtain at each end, facing downwards. Space the remaining tabs evenly between and tack in place.

5 Make the facing Where necessary, join the fabric widths for the facing using plain seams. Then, with the wrong side facing up, lay the interfacing fabric on top of the right side of the curtain. Fold a 2.5cm (1in) turning to the wrong side along the bottom edge of the facing, press, and secure the interfacing in place by stitching through both layers of fabric, close to the neatened edge (see the picture for Step 6 for further reference).

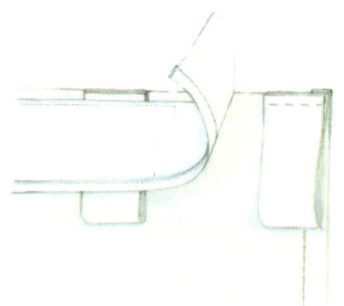

6 ▲ Stitch the facing and tabs in place With right sides together, cut edges level and side edges of the facing overlapping the side edges of the curtain, pin, tack and then machine

MAKE IT SIMPLE

no-sew tabs

For speedy results, tab top curtains don't always have to be stitched. Here are a few ways to cheat.

Bonding tape
Use iron-on bonding tape to secure the side and lower hem edges, and also to secure the hems on the tabs.

Eyelets
Eyelets are a speedy way of attaching the tabs to the top of the curtain and you'll find that most good haberdashery departments stock kits that also include a punch to secure the eyelets.

Arrow tabs
Alternatively, you can angle the end of the tab so that it points downwards in an arrow shape. Hold the tab in place with an eyelet through the point of the arrow. Finally, glue a button over the top of the eyelet for a stylish finish.

stitch the facing and tabs in place, taking a 1.5cm (⅝in) seam allowance. Trim the seam to remove the bulky excess fabric on the tabs.

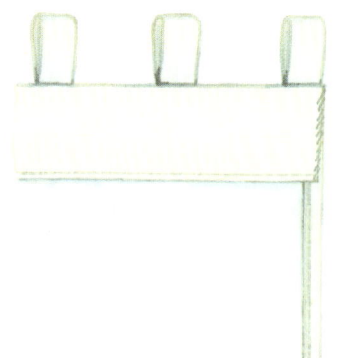

7 ▲ Neaten the facing Fold the facing over to the wrong side of the curtain and press in place, with the

seam along the edge. Turn under the cut edges of the facing at a slight angle, and slip-stitch to the side hem with small, neat stitches. Press the flap and the tabs and your curtain is ready to hang.

◄Shaker simplicity
A plain roman blind adds privacy to this glazed front door. Cream cushions soften an iron bench and complement the simple folk art feel

▼ Red hot
This out-sized curtain adds drama to a hall doorway. Swept up with a rope tie-back, the flamboyant deep red contrasts perfectly with the pale blue paintwork

first impressions

When decorating a hallway, fabric is often overlooked. But it can transform this space, bringing both texture and colour into the scheme

Your hallway is probably the first room visitors see in your home, so it needs to give a friendly welcome. Yet all too frequently this poor relation of decorating is seen as merely a transit area, and not as a room in its own right.

The hallway can set the scene for the rest of the home with complementary colours which lead the eye naturally into the areas beyond. Or it can stand alone as a bold statement using dramatic ideas.

Light lessons

If your hall is north facing, it will tend to feel cold and have less natural light. Choosing warmer colours – terracottas, rich reds and

► **Keep it simple**
Make a feature of a tiny hall window, without losing natural light, by using a simple blue and white fabric swag. Add a stencil on the writing desk for that clever finishing touch

golds, through to shades of peach and rose – and heavier fabrics, such as velvets, chenilles, tapestries or linens, will help to create an impression of comfort.

If the hall is south facing, it will get more sun and can take a cooler palette; try soft blues, aquas and greens teamed with chintz, cotton, sheers and voiles. Sunshine yellow and buttery cream work well in most hallways to lighten and brighten, but avoid large expanses of white. If you have a period house, look at the various ranges of traditional colours and fabrics to help create an authentic atmosphere.

Consider the view

Hallways often have little natural light so make the most of any windows. Roman blinds in voile or lace give privacy and stiffened organza, voile or muslin can be made into a simple fixed blind (use wooden dowel at the top and bottom to keep it straight).

Also, remember to think about what will be seen when doors are opened into the hall from other rooms. Consider using the same flooring throughout as a link, or perhaps the same colour woodwork.

Long narrow hallways can look rather gloomy and corridor-like, so try breaking up the space by

▲ **Lots of light**
Combine a number of elements for a light, airy feel. The plain simplicity of a wooden floor looks great with a rich, colourful rug and a decorative wrought-iron staircase

► **Mirror, mirror**
Create an illusion of extra space with clever use of a large mirror. Note the flattering effect of coloured fabric 'flags' suspended from the ceiling

hanging a curtain halfway along. This can be drawn to shut off other areas, or caught up on a tie-back to give visual interest to the hall. Add a large mirror to reflect any light.

Transformation tricks

A larger hall can have a double use. Stretch a sail of fabric to create a study area; or add an easy chair with unusual cushions and an

occasional table covered in a dramatic cloth, for a special place to read or write.

Use a curtain behind the front door not just to cut draughts, but as a decorating tool. A pretty voile or lace curtain will give privacy without taking away too much light. When draughts are a problem, use heavyweight fabrics and line them. And if the house

▼ Rich and warm
A wall hanging can add impact to a hallway. The terracotta and blue of this hanging contrast well with the golden tones on the walls and floor

▶ Closing off
Break up a long, narrow hallway by adding a curtain halfway along it. When drawn this gives extra privacy to the areas beyond

door is mainly glass, try lining curtains with a contrasting fabric which looks good from the outside.

If you want the curtain just to cover the door, use a special rod for a door curtain (known as a portiere). This makes the curtain automatically rise and fall as the door opens and closes, so your entrance isn't hindered.

An unusual fabric made up into a wall-hanging will add texture and warmth to an expanse of wall. Just use your imagination and try something different such as the colourful opulence of Indian sari fabrics for a bold impression.

Storage solutions

Organise some storage for the space beneath the stairs – shelves, hooks, boxes – slot all the clutter into place, then camouflage with a simple gathered curtain, or screen.

Make the most of the walls for storage. Get organised with key cupboards, shelves and wall-mounted tables. A vase of flowers, or a bowl of fragrant potpourri, are then all the finishing touches you need to transform your hallway into a warm and welcoming room.

◀ Create drama
A larger hallway can take a more dramatic scheme. This window seat echoes the bold colours and patterns of the room, while long dress curtains billow onto the floor from a gilded pelmet

Choose sheer muslin or a dramatic print to add a touch of glamour to your bathroom window with two of the prettiest draped and swagged blinds

bathing belles

◀ White linen

Turn your bathroom into a romantic haven with a sheer draped blind that lets the light in but keeps your bathing discreet

▲ Bathtime blues

Strong colours and patterns on these swags and tails add a touch of drama to an otherwise plain bathroom

Bathrooms are the one room in the house where privacy comes top of the list of requirements. This can be achieved with minimum fuss by using simple draped blinds.

There are a number of products on the market which will help you to achieve the desired effect but the simplest are drape hooks. Push a loop of fabric through the hook to the desired length and it does the rest. The drape above uses the hook traditionally at the top corners of the window while the blind, left, uses it at the side to reduce the length of the curtain.

For an instant uplift, drape your furnishings with a throw. Choose velvets, brocade and exuberant tassels for easy opulence at a price you can afford

lap of luxury

Today's 'must-have' accessory – a luxurious throw – can easily be yours if you're up to some basic stitching, have an eye for fabrics and a little time to spare. Throws are so versatile – use one to perk up an old armchair or sofa, add instant uplift to a room, soften the hard lines of sparse surroundings, or even as a comforter in the cold. And, a throw needn't be enormous (in case you've got some expensive fabric in mind) – just enough to cover the arm of a chair is sufficient.

Reverse the trend

For casual chic, choose a look that's uncalculated. Simply throwing, or draping, the fabric over furniture makes its own statement. Or, make a focal point of your furnishings with an arrangement where the throw takes centre stage.

If you want to do the minimum of sewing, a plain hemmed throw is straightforward to make. But a reversible one, such as

▶ *For extra richness, team your velvet throw with scatter cushions in brocade and tapestry fabrics*

◀ *Choose luxury fabrics, such as velvet and brocade, for their rich, jewel colours and opulent elegance. Team them with extravagant tassels*

Measuring and cutting guide

- **To calculate the velvet fabric**
  Throws can be any size, but they are generally square. To avoid joins, the width of the fabric dictates the size, eg if it's 115cm (45in) wide, you'll need to buy 1.20m (1¼yd) – the extra allows for straightening the edges (see Step 1).
- **To calculate the backing fabric**
  You'll need exactly the same length as the velvet. Use a brocade or woven fabric that's as wide (or wider) than it. If the backing fabric is a wider width than the velvet, trim the side edges so that both pieces match exactly.

cut edge

2 ▲ **Make a square** To find an exact square, take the cut straight edge and lay it along one side (selvedge) edge to form a large triangle. Pin at frequent intervals along both cut selvedge sides to secure the fabric, then trim off the excess fabric along the untrimmed edge. Keep any pieces of leftover velvet for pressing the throw later. Trim and square up the brocade fabric in the same way.

3 ▲ **Staystitch the corners and position the tassels** Determine the length of the tassels, then pin them in place in each corner on the right

ours, with two fabrics back to back, is only slightly more time-consuming and looks sensational. Further embellishment with trims and tassels completes the look and is simplicity itself.

Focus on fabrics

Your room and other furnishings set the scene for the type of fabric that you'll need. Soft wools and woven tweeds are best for country-cottagey settings, while we've chosen velvet for the opulence and the glamour statement it makes.

If you fall in love with a fabric, a throw is the ideal use for it as the drape will show off the design perfectly. Look for tapestries, appliquéd fabric, or 'craft' creations such as tie-dye or batik. If you just adore the fabric, you can keep it with you in any room of the house as you work, rest or play.

Essentials
- Crushed velvet
- Brocade fabric for backing
- 4 tassels
- Matching sewing thread
- Long metal ruler/wooden yardstick
- Tacking thread
- Safety pins
- Pins
- Scissors

Making the throw

1 **Trim the fabric** Cut the selvedges off the velvet so that all the edges are unfinished and the fabric will not distort. Now, using a long metal ruler or wooden yardstick as a guide, mark and cut a straight edge along the top of the piece of velvet (the nap, or pile, of the velvet should be running down the fabric). It's quite likely that the velvet may not have been cut straight when it was cut off the roll.

◀ *A beautiful woven throw, in reversible shades of lilac and lavender, adds casual chic to a stylish setting*

double up

For a quick, no-sew throw, choose a ready-quilted fabric. There's plenty to choose from – often a patterned fabric is backed with a plain colour (see the picture below).

1 Following Step 2 on p62, form the fabric into a square. Then, to neaten the cut edges, use straight binding in a wide width and matching colour. Attach the binding with iron-on bonding tape (fold the tape in half to fit over the edge of the throw and iron strips along each side).

2 Neaten the corners of the binding by folding it into crisp diagonal lines.

side of the velvet, with the tassels pointing into the centre of the throw. Secure the tassels with a safety-pin as shown to keep them out of the way while you are stitching the throw. Working 1cm (⅜in) from the cut edges, work a 5cm (2in) length of machine stitching (also known as staystitching as it adds stability) down each side at each corner. This prevents the fabric from stretching and holds the tassels in position.

5 ▲ Clip the corners and turn through Clip across each corner, cutting each side individually, taking care not to cut the staystitching or the excess cord on the tassels. Turn the throw to the right side through the opening in one side edge.

4 ▲ Machine the two fabrics together Place the brocade on top of the velvet, with right sides facing, and tack the fabrics together all around the edges. Machine stitch with the brocade side uppermost, taking a 1.5cm (⅝in) seam allowance and leaving a 30cm (12in) opening in one edge for turning through to the right side. Remove the tacking thread.

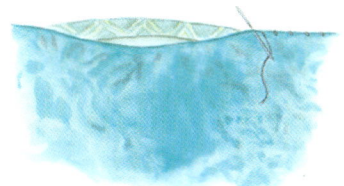

6 ▲ Slip stitch the opening Turn the seam allowance of both fabrics to the wrong side along the opening edges and tack the two pieces securely to hold them together. Neatly slip-stitch the opening closed: bring the needle out of one folded edge, across the gap and slide it through the opposite folded edge for about 6mm (¼in), pulling the needle out. Repeat in this way, across the gap.

7 ▲ Press the throw There's no need to press the throw all over – only press the edges, on both sides. To prevent damage to the velvet pile, protect it by placing a leftover piece of velvet over the area being pressed, with right sides together. Then iron on the wrong side of the spare fabric.

1 Fall for the film star looks of fabulous devoré with its rich swirling patterns in relief

2 Appreciate the dazzling way that light and shade play across the surface of crushed velvet

3 Bask in the glowing warmth of the rich, jewel colours and thick, smooth pile of cotton velvet

4 Velvets look exotic and fabulous in a variety of shimmering, multi-coloured printed patterns

5 Brush the pile of crushed velvet in a different direction and see how the colour changes

6 Exquisite 'gauffrage' is a technique for velvet that impresses textured patterns on to its surface

pile on the pleasure

Luxuriate in the rich warmth and sumptuous style of beautiful velvet – you'll be amazed at the choice

Despite its expensive image, you can easily bring a touch of exotic glamour to your furnishings with velvet accessories such as chair or bed throws, lustrous cushions and plump, soft footrests.

If your vision of velvet furnishings is heavy drapes that are dragged out in winter to keep out the draughts, then take a little time to catch up with the latest happenings. Velvet is a very 'in' fabric at the moment and if you visit your local department store, you'll be dazzled by what's available. Discover smooth cotton velours, slinky synthetics, crinkly crushed textures and elegant devoré (where the background pile is 'burnt' away, leaving the pattern in relief). There are masses to choose from and there's bound to be one you'll fall for.

Remember that a little fabric goes a long way, so if the cost of a metre seems daunting, small touches are perfectly acceptable. For further embellishment, team velvet with fabulous tassels, or a decorative braid, to complete a look that's unashamedly opulent.

◀ *Dress up a plain wicker chair with a velvet throw. Look out for a variety of different fabric effects – such as this tie-dye version*

● See 'Lap of Luxury', p61, for an excellent example of a velvet tassel-trimmed throw

checklist
Velvet fabrics

● **Fibre content** Natural cotton velvet is the most common form of furnishing fabric. Silk velvet is the most luxurious quality and its fabulous feel and drape (try using one for a soft throw) justifies the cost. Or, if it's value for money that you're after, then there are plenty of synthetic velvets that will fit the bill.

● **Sewing velvet** The fabric tends to slip around as you are sewing, so pin and tack first. It also helps to insert a piece of tissue paper between the two layers of fabric, with right sides together. Use the zigzag stitch attachment on your sewing machine for stitching stretch velvets as this gives additional elasticity.

● **Variety of effects** You only have to look at the fabric swatches on the opposite page to see a wide range of different effects on velvet. Other velvets to look out for are shimmering panné (a lighter version of crushed velvet) and the up-to-the-minute favourites with a novel appearance – tie- and dip-dyed varieties.

● **Nap (or pile)** A pile weave (such as velvet) has an extra thread which is drawn up into loops that are cut or sheared to create the distinctive appearance. If you're piecing velvet together, make sure that the pile runs in the same direction on all the pieces. The fabric has a different shade depending on which way the pile is running.

● **Pressing** Place a towel on an ironing board, then always press the velvet on the wrong side of the fabric.

● **Aftercare** Generally synthetic and stretch velvets are washable, while heavier varieties, such as cotton, should be dry-cleaned.

all on board

Forget boring cork pinboards – customize one to complement your kitchen instead and you'll be delighted with the results

Despite good intentions, it's so easy to mislay all those vital bits of paper – appointment cards, photographs, newspaper cuttings, recipes and so on – that accumulate in everyone's kitchen. A pinboard's the answer, and it's so easy to make a fabric-covered one to match your decor by nothing more than wrapping and sticking. A latticework of ribbons means you can just tuck anything behind the grid to keep it as good as new.

At base level

It's not always necessary to rush out and buy a new piece of MDF (medium density fibreboard) from your nearest hardware store either. First, check around the house in case you've something stashed away that'll fit the role – such as an existing pinboard that you could revitalize with a face-lift. Once the board is padded and covered with felt, then its origins are a well-hidden secret.

Felt or fabric?

The choice of background fabric is really up to you. Bright felt is eye-catching and suits an uncluttered setting. But if you hanker for co-ordination, then go for a fabric that matches your furnishings – maybe a print for the background, with a plain border decorated with a stamped or stencilled pattern using a repeat design.

Measuring and cutting guide

- **To calculate the felt background**
  To work out how much felt you need to cover your board – the one shown here is 60 x 50cm (24 x 20in). Measure it both ways, then add an extra 10cm (4in) in each direction.

- **To calculate the checked borders**
  You need two kinds of checked fabric for the top/bottom and side borders. For the top border, measure the length across and add 10cm (4in) to wrap around the back. Decide on the width of the border, (ours were 11cm (4¾in wide) then add on 8cm (3¼in) for turnings. Double these amounts to account for the bottom border. Repeat this exercise to work out the amount of fabric required for the side borders.

- **Wadding**
  Cut to the exact size of the pinboard.

- **Calico backing**
  You will need to add 5cm (2in) to the lengthways and widthways measurements of the board.

- **Ribbon**
  Starting from each corner, mark the outer edges of the board with pins at intervals (our were 7cm (3in) apart). Cut pieces of string and lay them diagonally across the board between the marks, to form a grid. Add up the total length of string for the amount of ribbon to buy.

Essentials

- 9mm (³⁄₈in) medium density fibreboard(MDF)
- Felt fabric
- Scissors
- Cotton fabric in each of two different checks
- Calico for backing fabric
- Mediumweight polyester wadding
- 1cm (³⁄₈in) wide satin ribbon
- 2 small screw eyes
- Cord for hanging
- Staple gun
- Bradawl

Making the pinboard

1 ▲ Prepare the padded background Lay the felt down on a clean, flat surface. Place the wadding on top of it, in the centre, then put the board exactly on top of the wadding.

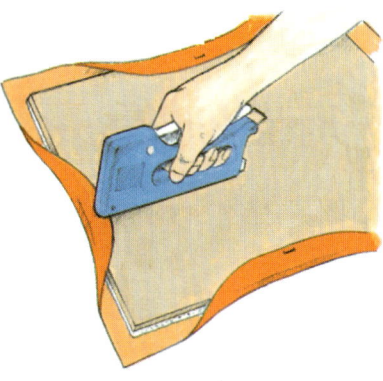

2 ▲ Secure the felt Using a staple gun, fix the fabric in the centre of one side to the back of the board, about 3cm (1¼in) from the edge. Pull the felt taut and fix it again at the centre of the opposite side. Fix the centres of the two remaining sides. Working from the centre of each side towards each corner in turn, add further staples at 10cm (4in) intervals.

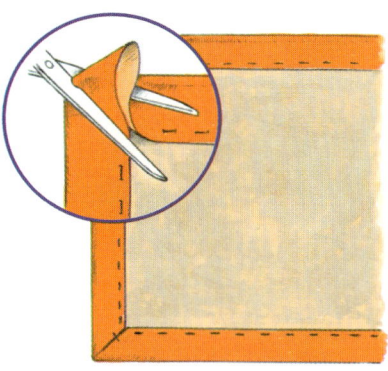

3 ▲ Neaten the corners Fold the fabric at each corner into a point, cut off the excess to leave a neat edge and staple down. For an extra-smooth background, add further staples between those already inserted.

4 ▲ Attach the ribbon lattice Using the string that marked out the lattice, cut the ribbon up into

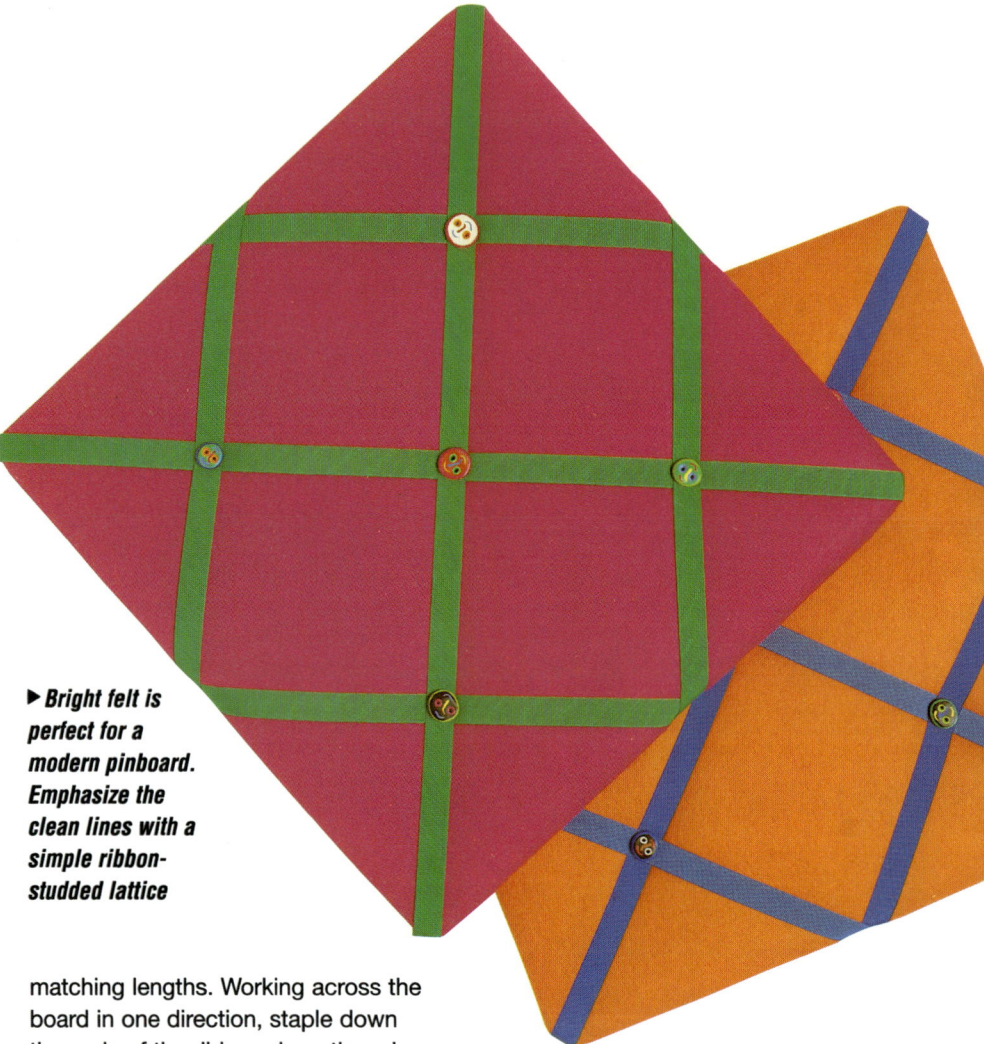

▶ *Bright felt is perfect for a modern pinboard. Emphasize the clean lines with a simple ribbon-studded lattice*

matching lengths. Working across the board in one direction, staple down the ends of the ribbon along the edges of the board, making sure that you pull them taut as you are working. Then, work across the board in the opposite direction, adding the second lot of ribbons. Remember to weave them under and over the ribbons already in place to form the latticework grid.

5 ▲ Position one set of borders Neaten the long edges of the border strips by pressing under 4cm (1½in) to the wrong side. Position the

wrong side of one long strip against one long edge of the board, wrapping the ends around the back. At the right-hand side of the board, add one of the short strips, placing the top edge over the existing strip and wrapping the ends onto the back of the board as before.

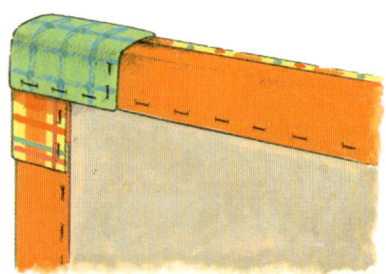

6 ▲ Secure the ends On the back of the board, staple the ends of each border in place to secure them. Place the staples at regular intervals and parallel with the cut or folded edges of the fabric.

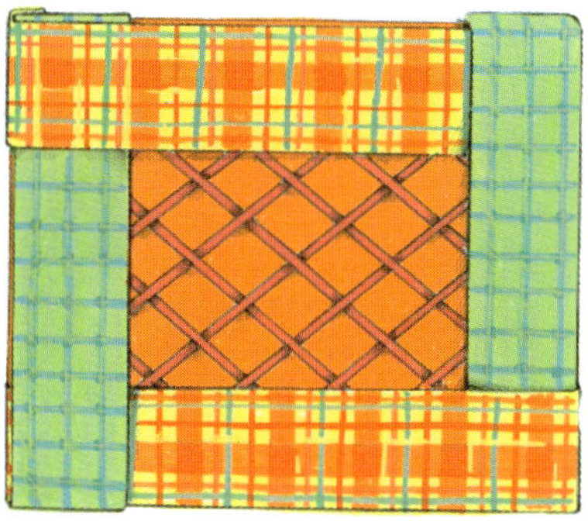

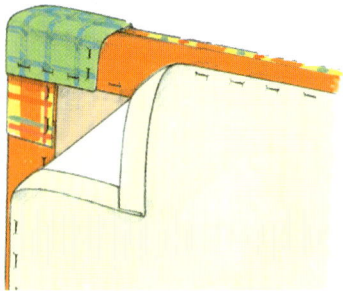

7 ▲ **Complete the borders** Turn the board around so that the other long edge is at the top. Position the other set of border strips along the uncovered edges. At the bottom right-hand side, slip the new strip under the first one, and at the top left-hand side, overlap the strip as shown. Staple all of the strips securely on the back of the board.

8 ▲ **Neaten the back** Neaten the calico backing fabric by pressing under 2.5cm (1in) around the cut edges to the wrong side. Staple the backing in position around the edge of the board to hide any untidiness.

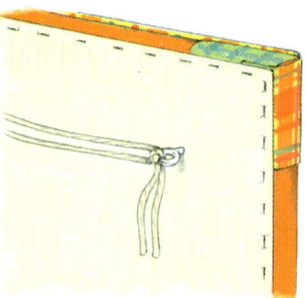

9 ▲ **Position the cord** Using a bradawl, mark the positions of two screw eyes about 10cm (4in) down from the top and 40cm (16in) apart, making sure they are level. Insert the screw eyes, then tie a double length of cord through them to hang the board.

TAKE ANOTHER LOOK

lattice looks for a screen

Use the same methods described here to cover a larger piece of board with a background fabric to form a full-size screen that will look good in any room in the house. Lattice it with broad multi-coloured ribbons and use the screen to display your Christmas cards. Lavish a border of fresh greenery across the top edge to set the festive mood.

For a change of scene once Christmas is over, add different ribbons and use the screen as a mega pinboard for family snapshots, or holiday postcards.

bathroom bound

Transform your towels with borders. A variety of co-ordinated shapes and styles will add extra zest to your bathroom

It's easy to give your bathroom a lift with colour co-ordinated towels in fresh citrus tones. Plain and shaped bound edges give them an up-market designer look for very little outlay. All you have to do is buy a couple of towels and stitch on a binding made from plain cotton fabric in a contrasting colour. The stitching is also worked in a different colour to add to the bold theme.

Alternatively, buy a patterned fabric and choose a plain cover for the binding, matching it to your existing bathroom accessories. However, when you're mixing fabrics in this way, remember to use only washable and shrinkproof fabrics for the bound edges.

◄ *Go for a rustic look in your bathroom. Try a waffle-weave towel with a zigzagged border depicting a traditional French scene in shades of deep pink or blue*

A variety of styles

From a straight zigzagged panel to fancy, shaped edges, there's plenty of choice for edgings and bindings to suit your tastes.

If you're a confident stitcher, then you'll be able to attempt some of the fancier shapes such as our pointed edge towel. The straight border is the easiest to work. It looks as if it is set into the fabric, but is actually just zigzag stitched in position on top of the towel. We've used plain colours for our towel borders as this way the stitching is more distinctive.

For an up-to-the-minute look, you can decorate your borders with metal eyelets, or punched holes bound with buttonhole stitch. Just choose which style of towels is best matched to your bathroom and follow the steps for each.

Making the zigzag-stitched border

Essentials
- Bought hand towels
- Contrasting cotton fabric for border, binding or panel
- Matching sewing thread
- Sharp scissors
- Water-erasable pen
- Pins
- Hole punch and eyelets

1 ▲ Cut the band to size Using a pair of sharp scissors, cut a rectangle of cotton fabric to exactly the same width as your hand towel and 9.5cm (3¾in) deep. Pin, then tack the band in position a short distance away from the edge of the towel.

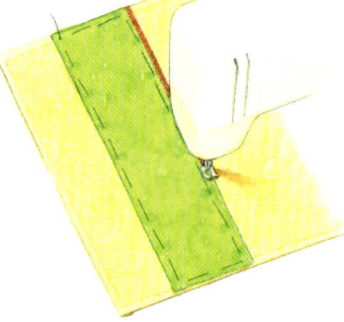

2 ▲ Stitch the band on to the towel Set your machine to a close zigzag stitch and carefully sew all around the band, making sure that the stitching covers and neatens the cut edges. Thread any loose ends through a needle and secure them back into the zigzag stitching.

Making the pointed border

1 ▲ Cut the border fabric Cut a rectangle of the cotton fabric the same width as the towel and 15.5cm (6¼in) deep (this includes 1.5cm (⅝in) extra along one long edge for the seam allowance). Make sure all the edges are straight.

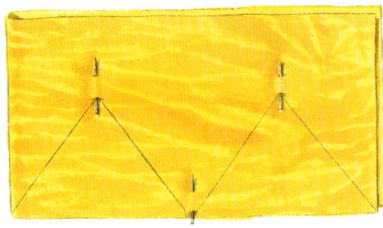

2 ▲ Mark the points To make symmetrical points, fold the border fabric in half widthways with wrong sides facing. Mark the upper and lower points of the border (measuring accurately so that they're even) with pins placed through both layers. Using a ruler and water-erasable pen, join the marked lines to form the points.

3 ▲ Attach the border Mark a line on the towel, 13cm (5¼in) up from one short edge. With right sides together, place the border fabric

▲ Select a style of border to match the character of your bathroom: our citrus colours look bright and zingy in a fresh, modern setting.

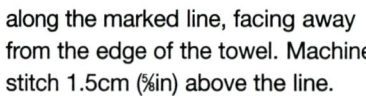

along the marked line, facing away from the edge of the towel. Machine stitch 1.5cm (⅝in) above the line.

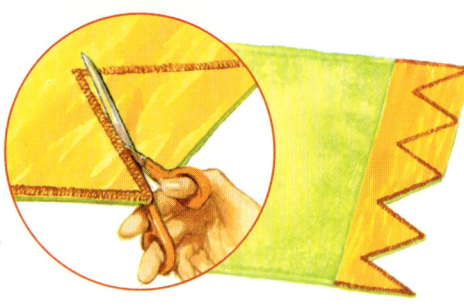

4 ▲ Stitch the points Flip the border over into place so that the right side is uppermost and the edges of the towel and border are level; tack the two layers together. Set your machine to a zigzag stitch with the widest width and almost no length (test it first on a spare piece of fabric). Join the layers by carefully stitching down the short sides of the border and along the pointed edge, following the 'V' marks you made earlier.

5 ▲ Neaten the edges Fasten off the thread ends. Cut away the excess towel and border fabric, close to the stitching, using very sharp scissors. Take care not to cut any stitches as you work.

6 ▲ Decorate the border Insert a metal eyelet at the uppermost point of each 'V'. Most good haberdashers stock a kit including a punch and eyelets. Following the directions, make a hole with the punch then fix the eyelets securely in place.

do it right

Here's some advice for tackling basic DIY to help you put the projects you've made in place

Build your confidence where simple fixing jobs are needed for home furnishing. Equip yourself with your own tool box complete with a set of basic tools, including today's essential power drill. Then here's how to use them to fix the projects you've made in position around the house.

Measuring

For measuring, choose a strong and accurate retractable steel tape. A hooked end enables the tape to be anchored in location. Look out for tapes that can be locked when extended and then released. Lengths are usually marked in both metric and imperial measurements.

You can buy metal rules in sizes from 150-1000mm (6-39in). They provide an ideal hard edge for cutting against with a craft knife.

A 'T' or try square is an L-shaped tool with a fine, straight steel blade fixed at 90 degrees into a straight handle. It's ideal for measuring and for checking that joins meet at perfect right angles.

Spirit level

Use this to check that a surface is level both horizontally and vertically. The outer casing is usually made from either metal or plastic. Inside is a glass tube filled with coloured liquid containing an air bubble. The tube is marked with two fine lines. Adjust the surface until the bubble is centred between these two lines, then you can be sure that it's level. Sometimes a spirit level has two tubes so that you can measure the horizontal levels and vertical lines at the same time.

Saws

Saws can loosely be divided into three categories: large flexible saws, stiff-backed saws and speciality saws. With each saw the more teeth per cm, the finer the cut. The most common type of flexible saw is the panel saw, used to cut large pieces of wood. The most popular of the ridged saws is the tenon saw, used for more accurate cutting such as trimming a curtain pole.

The junior hacksaw is a useful all-purpose saw for cutting wood, plastic and metal. If you're making a specific item such as a pelmet board, most DIY stores or wood yards supply pieces cut to size.

Screwdrivers

There are two basic types of screwdriver and both come in a range of sizes. Use a slot-headed screwdriver with the traditional slot-head screws, and a cross-head (Phillips) screwdriver for cross-slot screws which have a cross cut in the top. It is important that the size of the screwdriver blade exactly matches the slot in the screw head.

Combination pliers

Use square-nose pliers to grip, cut and bend metal or to remove pins, etc. Use the cutting edges which are set into the shank for stripping electric flex or cutting wire.

Bradawl or gimlet

A bradawl is a short metal spike set into a handle, with which you can begin a hole in wood for screws or hooks. A gimlet is similar, but has a screw effect.

Fill a tool box with some handy items and you'll be set to tackle those simple DIY tasks involved in putting up your projects

Hammer

The larger the hammer, the easier it is to drive in nails. The claw hammer has a hammer head on one side and a claw head on the other for pulling out bent nails. A lightweight pin or tack hammer has a smaller head and is used for jobs such as hammering in tacks and upholstery nails.

Craft knife

This is a sturdy knife fitted with retractable blades. Most craft knives are multi-purpose and come equipped with a variety of blades, including saw blades, so they can be used for several jobs.

Drill

An electric drill can be used for all drilling jobs involving walls or wood. The best buy is a mid-range drill. Its main features are a hammer action (essential for drilling into solid walls) and different speeds, so that you can begin slowly and then increase speed. Speed variation is a help when drilling through a variety of different surfaces.

Mains-power drills plug into a main electrical socket so an extension lead will be needed for most jobs, as drill leads tend to be short. A drill with a 400-500W motor can manage most household DIY tasks. Cordless drills are powered by a rechargeable battery pack in the handle. They are less powerful than mains drills but more convenient as there are no trailing wires. Cordless drills can also be used outdoors and safely in damp conditions.

The nose of the drill is called the chuck and holds the drill bit firmly in place. Loosen and tighten the chuck with a key which fits into evenly-spaced holes round its base. The trigger switch turns the drill on and off and controls the speed. Use both hands to operate the drill. Hold the rear handle with one hand and grip the front of the drill or front handle with the other

hand, supporting the weight. While drilling keep the drill steady and at right angles to the surface and keep the pressure constant.

Drill bits

These are the cutting tools of a drill and fit into the chuck. You must match the drill bit to the surface. Use a masonry bit which has a hardened tip for cutting into tough material such as solid walls. A twist bit is for drilling into wood or plasterboard walls and ceilings.

Wall plugs

Hammer wall plugs into drilled holes in walls to provide a good grip for screws. When the screw is fitted inside, the wall plug expands to fit the surroundings, holding the screw in position. The size of wall plug needs to match the drill bit and the screw size. There are various types of wall plug from plain and heavy duty plastic, to collapsible plastic anchors, metal strings and gravity toggles which hold screws in hollow and unstable walls.

Screws

Screws are generally steel and are sold by length – from 6mm (¼in) to 150mm (6in) – and gauge (the size of the screw). Gauges number from 1-20 and the higher the number, the thicker the screw. Gauges 6, 8 and 10 are used most frequently, so keep a good stock of them.

6-gauge – use these for fixing lightweight items into wood

8-gauge – use these for fixing mediumweight items into wood and walls

10 & 12-gauge – use these for fixing heavy-weight items into walls

in pole

Use the skills described here to put up curtain poles and tie-back hooks and even to hang a picture

checklist
Safety tips

- **Storing tools** Keep all tools clean and dry and together in a solid tool box or hang them securely on the wall of a work room or in a dry garden shed.
- **Check for electrical cables** Before you drill into an internal wall, use a cable detector, a simple metal detector which emits a high-pitched sound as it passes over wiring in the walls. Check the position of cables that run up to light sockets and switches and between any lights. Pipe detectors, which detect copper and metal pipework in walls and under floors, are also available.
- **Changing bits** If you want to change the drill bit on an electric drill, turn off the drill at the mains socket and remove the plug before making the adjustment.
- **Maintenance** Always clean your tools after use and regularly check the cable on the drill and any extension leads for signs of wear and tear.
- **Face facts** Wear safety goggles to protect your eyes when drilling into walls. A face mask prevents you breathing in any harmful dust.

position

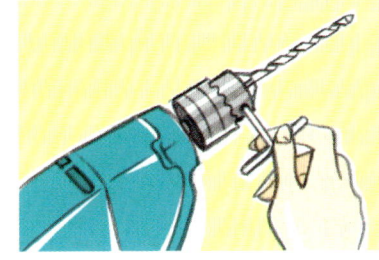

1 ▲ Mark the position of the hole with a soft pencil. Use a hammer and nail to provide a starter hole for the drill bit. This prevents the plaster from cracking. Select the correct type of drill bit to match the surface and fit firmly into the drill.

2 ▲ Measure the length of the screw against the drill bit, measuring up from the tip. Mark with a strip of tape.

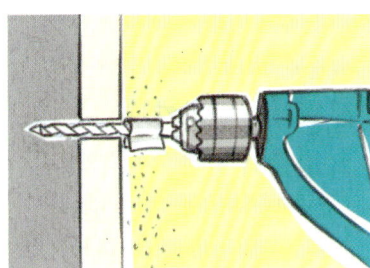

3 ▲ Hold the drill firmly at right angles to the wall. Drill in short bursts, until you reach the marking tape. On hollow walls be prepared for the drill to suddenly break through the wall into the cavity behind the surface.

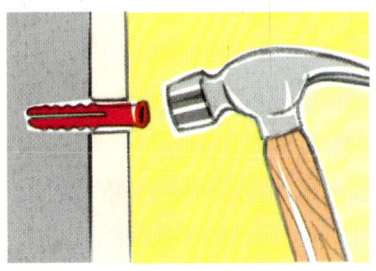

4 ▲ Hammer in the correct size and type of wall plug, until it is flush with the surface. On hollow walls you

must use a plastic anchor plug which has special holding 'wings'. Now screw the fixing in place in the centre of the rawlplug.

How to insert a screw into wood

Use this method when you are fixing blinds (such as roller blinds) into the window recess, or attaching cleats and tie back hooks where you need to screw directly into the window frame.

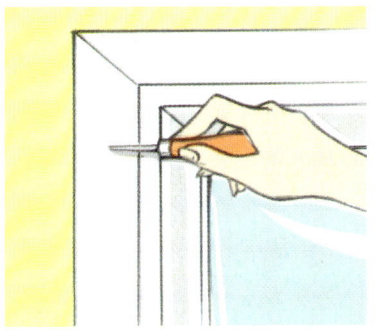

1 ▲ Mark the position for the screw with a soft pencil. Use a bradawl to provide a starter hole for the screw.

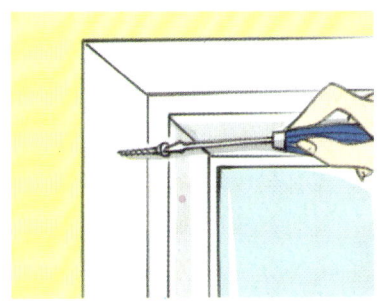

2 ▲ On soft woods, such as pine, you do not need a wall plug, simply screw directly into the wood. The screw will cut a hole as it progresses.

3 On hard woods, mahogany for instance, use a fine wood bit and an electric drill to make a starter hole about half the depth of the screw. In addition to making it easier to insert the screw, this will prevent the wood from splitting. You can tell a hard wood by its dark natural colour, eg front doors and some window ledges. Soft woods are light in colour, eg window frames, and need painting to protect them.

How to drill a hole in walls

This method should be used where you are attaching tracks and curtain poles above a window, or for any job that requires a strong fixing. All outside walls of your house will be solid (on older houses you may find some internal walls are too). When you drill into a wall, red dust denotes brickwork and grey dust breezeblock.

Most modern houses have hollow internal walls made from plasterboard fixed over a wooden frame. Tap the wall to find the hollow sections. When hanging heavyweight items you must screw into one of the timbers that make up the frame. Check which surface you will be drilling into before you start and use the correct drill bit, wall plug and screw fixing as described on the previous page.

cover your tracks

Create your own room with a view by adding a stunning scalloped pelmet to finish off your window with pizazz

Crown the soft layers of your window dressings with a simple, fabric-covered pelmet, boldly scalloped at the lower edge. Select a fabric for the pelmet that contrasts with your curtains to create an eye-catching, layered effect that's easy to achieve.

Use pelmets to hide curtain tracks, cover up roller blind fixings or to stop the light from coming in at the top of the window. Shaped pelmets can also soften the hard, rectangular appearance of the window itself, especially in a room where the window is very dominant.

Hidden values

Clever use of a pelmet can affect the apparent height of your ceiling. By positioning the pelmet higher than the top of the window, you will make the window look larger than it is, and seemingly raise the height of the room. But a deep pelmet set at a normal height will lower the top edge of the window to create a cosier feel in a tall room.

There's just a couple of simple DIY steps to follow at the start of the job. To support the fabric you will need to make a pelmet board out of timber (use a type of manufactured wood called MDF

which is available from DIY stores). The pelmet board is similar to a shelf fixed above the window. Curtain tracks can then be attached to the underside of the pelmet board, or to the window frame, and will be hidden from view.

Shape and style

Just about any type of main fabric can be used for the pelmet, except one that is very sheer. The lining fabric for the reverse side of the pelmet should be a good-quality plain cotton in a complementary colour. No sewing is required. Just use iron-on bonding material to stick both the main and lining fabrics onto buckram, which is a coarse linen stiffened with glue. This can be bought from good department stores.

The actual shape of the scallop edge will have a huge influence on the overall effect, so you should test out a few variations first. Cut shapes from paper, then tape each one in turn over your window and choose the one that looks best.

▼ *A deep pelmet with a bold plaid brightens a plain kitchen window. Trace around the edge of an up-turned bowl or saucer for regular small scallops*

▲ *Make a marriage of styles for this pelmet fitted flush with the window frame. The plain simplicity of the raffia-covered pelmet contrasts with the exuberance of generous raffia rosette trims on the scallops*

Essentials
- Wood, screws and two angle brackets for the pelmet board
- Large sheet of paper for the template
- Pelmet fabric • Lining fabric
- Buckram (or other pelmet stiffening)
- Iron-on bonding material
- Iron-on hemming tape • Scissors
- Touch-and-close fastening
- Pressing cloth • Drawing pins

Measuring and cutting guide

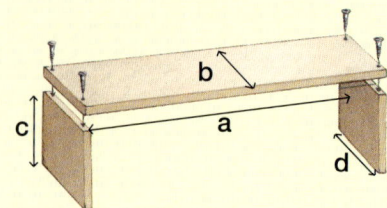

- **To calculate the pelmet board**

  1 Measure the width of the window from the outer edges of the frame. If the curtain track extends beyond it, add extra at each end.

  2 The result is the required width (a) of the pelmet board. Depending on the depth (b) needed to cover the curtain track or the roller blind fitting, use 4-by-1in, 5-by-1in, 6-by-1in or 7-by-1in timber (ie 4, 5, 6 or 7in-wide timber by 1in thickness) for the pelmet board.

  3 The timber verticals (c) at the sides of the pelmet board should be about 5cm (2in) shorter than the pelmet drop.

- **To calculate the width of the pelmet fabric**

  The width of the pelmet equals that of the pelmet board (a), **plus** the depth of its sides (d). Make the pelmet template first before calculating the materials required.

- **To make the template**

  1 Draw the pelmet width and depth on to paper.

  2 Estimating the number of scallops across the front, draw

  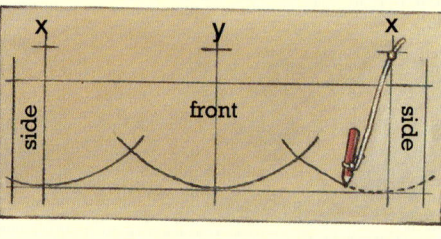

  vertical lines at both corners (x) and at the centre of each scallop between the corner points (y).

  3 Tie a length of string near a pencil tip; attach it to each vertical, the same distance from the lower edge. Experiment with this distance – closer to the lower edge gives a tighter scallop, further away gives a wider arc. Draw the arcs to intersect as shown.

  4 Cut out the template. The amount of fabric, buckram and lining required is the size of your finished template plus 2cm (¾in) all around. Double this amount for the bonding material.

Making the pelmet

1 ▲ **Make the pelmet board** Calculate the size of the top of the pelmet board following the 'Measuring and cutting guide'. Cut the timber to the required size. Then, cut the two sides and screw them to the top (see diagram in 'Measuring and cutting guide'). Screw the angle brackets to the underside of the board, level with the back edge, then screw the board in place above the window.

2 Prepare the iron-on bonding material Place the cut template on to the smooth (paper) side of the iron-on bonding and draw the outline with a pencil. Cut out a rectangle around the shape. Prepare another piece of bonding material in the same way.

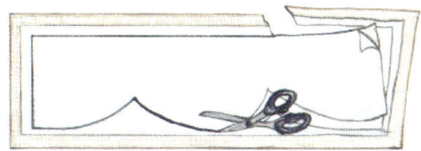

3 ▲ Press the bonding material on to the buckram Place the glue side of one piece of bonding material on the smooth side of the buckram. Press with a dry iron, according to the instructions.

4 ▲ Cut out the buckram Cut the buckram and binding material along the pencil line, then remove the paper.

5 ▲ Fuse the pelmet fabric to the buckram Using the buckram as a template, trace the pelmet shape on to the fabric and cut out 2cm (¾in) from the outline. Place the wrong side of the fabric centrally on top of the side of the buckram with the bonding material, and press in place following the instructions.

6 ▲ Secure the seam allowance in place Press the pelmet fabric seam allowance to the wrong side of the pelmet, clipping into the corners and notching the curves. Following the manufacturer's instructions, fuse the seam allowance to the buckram with the hemming tape.

star-stamped pelmet

STAMP IT

Brighten up a plain ready-made pelmet and roller blind with a star-stamped pattern using a rubber stamp, available in craft shops and DIY stores. We've used gold paint on dark blue fabric to resemble a midnight sky.

1 Stamp stars in a regular pattern all over a scalloped pelmet. For lots of inspired information, see 'Stamp of approval', p20.

2 Make a plain blind in matching fabric and decorate the lower edge with a line of stars.

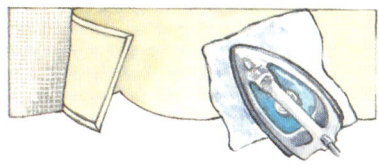

7 ▲ Line the pelmet Trace and cut out the lining as given for the pelmet fabric and secure the seam allowances as given for Step 6, pressing a little more than the seam allowance to the wrong side. Fuse the second piece of bonding material to the back of the pelmet fabric, remove the backing paper and press the lining fabric in position.

8 Attach the touch-and-close fastening Stick the looped-sided fastening along the top of the pelmet fabric, 1cm (⅜in) from the edge. Stick a strip to each side, close to the edge.

9 ▲ Attach the pelmet to the board Stick a strip of the hooked side of the touch-and-close fastening along the edge and top of the sides of the pelmet board, finishing close to the wall. Firmly press the looped fastening on the pelmet in place to complete the finished look.

curtain control

Eye-catching hold-backs add a dramatic flourish to a window dressing

Make the most of the metres of lush fabric falling from your curtain rails and poles. You can transform the look of your room simply by sweeping a curtain back and hooking it behind a well-positioned hold-back. The resulting curve of the curtain's leading edge will soften the sharp edge of the window frame. And at the same time it will draw the eye to the appealing flow of fabric pleats radiating from the point at which the curtain is caught back.

Modern moves

Window treatments have come a long way since the days of buckram-stiffened, crescent shaped tie-backs and heavy cords with giant tassels. And although these Victorian curtain restraints may still suit some room schemes, today there is a variety of contemporary alternatives from which to choose. Some manufacturers of modern metal curtain poles are now making metal hold-backs that mix and match with their stunningly crafted finials (the ornamental ends of the pole).

One thing to remember: when choosing a hold-back, keep in mind the type of look you want for your room – formal or informal, dramatic or understated. And don't forget to choose a style that complements the curtain heading.

◄ Chain mail

Chain is an original alternative to the classic cord tie-back. It is useful for curtains that are too heavy to hang around hold-backs. Metal paint can be applied to chain to achieve a colour that co-ordinates with curtain fabric and walls

◄ Fabulous florals

Sumptuous furnishing fabrics look good with traditional-style brass claw hold-backs. Reproduction brass claws are available from furnishing fabric departments

▲ Bathroom style

A simple wooden knob can be used as a hold-back, and painted to match an unusual curtain such as this one, which is made from a fringed bedspread

◄ Bold as brass
A gold scallop shell hold-back makes this rich royal blue curtain, trimmed with small gold shells, the dramatic focal point of the room. An elegant effect is achieved by placing the hold-back high on the wall and lifting the over-long curtain up on to it

Drape it!

Make sure that your hold-back is seen in all its glory. Its true role is to scoop back a curtain, making the most of its fullness and creating a soft, gentle line. So that you have the right proportions of draping curtain in relation to the position of the hold-back, do some simple measuring before you begin.

1▲ Measure with string Fix both the track or pole and the hold-back before you decide on the length of the curtain. To gauge the amount of fabric you need, tie string around the pole to replicate the leading (front) edge of the curtain.

2▲ Calculate the amount of fabric Drape the string around the hold-back, then down to the floor, allowing extra for pooling on the ground if required. Measure the string – this is the finished length of the curtain. Don't forget to add extra for hems and heading finishes.

► Layered look
These large shield rosettes are inspired by smaller and more traditional versions. They have been cleverly positioned at different levels to emphasize the two layers of curtains. Notice how using a lighter fabric for the outer curtain creates depth between this and the darker one underneath

Warm and inviting, the influences of the folk art look are worldwide, evoking memories of home comfort and your favourite things

home on the range

If the home is truly where the heart is, then the classic motifs of folk art design are perfect for a decorating look that is warm and inviting. Folk art can be cosy and comforting in its appeal. It can also come right up to date offering a simplicity that's completely contemporary.

Every country has its folk art tradition, from the red and white gingham checks and painted

◄ Rag doll Buy traditional folk art rag dolls for a true Shaker look. Tucked under a quilt or hung by ribbon or sat on a cushion, they will add instant appeal to a room

▲ Blues feel Mixing country checks and florals, this strong blue and ivory scheme combines folk art simplicity with a cheerful jumble of favourite things

furniture of Scandinavia, to the Shaker furniture and Amish quilting of America – perhaps the ultimate folk art melting pot.

The basis of style

The classic elements however are similar the world over. This is a no fuss style. At home in a country cottage or modern house alike, the look is based on a muted palette of soft reds, blues, and earth colours, toned with white, ivory or cream.

◀ **Choose checks**
Cushions in home-spun checks can add a folksy feel to any room. Mix check sizes in a single colourway, add embroidered naive motifs, and fill small pillows with lavender

▼ **Heart and home**
The heart is a traditional folk art motif. Here it is used for bright, lively patchwork-effect bed linen to give a look that's young and contemporary

Walls are left plain, or decorated with folk art stencils – hearts, flowers, simple geometrics and naive animal designs work well. Wooden furniture is left natural, or given simple paint effects such as gentle distressing. Add basic accessories, such as wicker baskets, Shaker-style boxes, decoy ducks, or rag dolls, to pull the look together.

Quite a quilt

Perhaps the epitome of the look is the patchwork quilt. Pieced together from scraps of fabric, there are literally hundreds of traditional designs. In turn-of-the-century America, quilts were often made in 'sewing bees', as the women of the neighbourhood gathered to sew and chat, perhaps making a special quilt for a future bride's bottom drawer.

Quilts look great on beds, even better thrown over sofas or piled

▼ Shaker-style
Home-spun checked bed linen, on a very plain wooden four-poster bed, recreates the classic simplicity of the American Shaker look

▲ Kitchen class
Simple checks add to the down home appeal of this kitchen. Fabric gathered below the work tops cleverly conceals what's behind while co-ordinating with the curtains

◄ Amish appeal
Deep colours and strong traditional geometric designs typify the work of the Amish quiltmakers. With its intricate quilting patterns, this quilt would make a striking wall hanging

high on chairs or blanket chests. Turn the best bits of worn old quilts into cushions or stuffed toys.

Some quilts, like those created by America's Amish people (for whom quilt making is one of the few outlets for creative expression allowed by their religious beliefs), are works of art in their own right. They make unusual and striking wall-hangings, particularly in a more contemporary setting.

Sweet dreams

Bring folk art into the bedroom with gingham or homespun check bed linen. Embroidered motifs on white cotton bed linen are characteristic of Scandinavian and Eastern European traditions. American four-poster beds are lighter than European ones, with much simpler hangings. Window treatments should be similarly plain. Hang simple tab-top curtains from plain wooden or metal poles and edge a striped or plain fabric with gingham to add interest.

Rag rugs can add a folksy note to the kitchen or bedroom. Thin strips of fabric are hemmed and plaited together to make long pieces, which can then be coiled into a circle or oval rug and stitched in place. (There are instructions for making a plaited bathroom mat from towelling in 'Step on it', p132.)

Scents of success

In the kitchen, add gathered gingham check or muslin curtains behind glazed cupboard doors to give a folk art look. Use checks or stripes for table linen. Edge natural linen cloths with strips of cheerful homespun fabric.

Finally, to complete the scene, don't forget the evocative scents of traditional folk art – spicy cinnamon, orange, lavender and rose pot-pourri. Make simple heart shaped muslin or gingham bags and fill with lavender, rose petals, herbs or spices. Then hang in cupboards, place on pillows or dangle from door handles, using narrow ribbon or jute twine.

dine in style

Give your dining furniture a quick make over using draped and layered fabric with a bright Mediterranean feel

For that extra special meal, or if you simply fancy a change, drape your dining chairs in layers of brightly-coloured fabric or large square tablecloths. Use plain weave fabrics such as cotton or linen, so that the covers don't slip off the chairs. There's no sewing involved and the fabric can be used over and over again.

Follow the look through by using several large tablecloths in layers on your table. Either line up the corners or, for a more dramatic effect, offset them.

▲ Table treats
Tablecloths in rich shades of blue and orange make quick covers for dining chairs

▶ Blue mood
For a very modern look, layer tablecloths on your table in the colours of your décor

bolstered up

Do away with traditional padded bolsters with tightly fitting, piped covers and flat ends. Instead, zoom right up-to-date with these romantic, new bolsters that are much more informal, and easier to make. Even when the cover needs to be removed for cleaning, the gathered ends can quickly be undone, because there is no need for complicated fastenings or zips.

Sympathetic styling

Depending on your choice of fabric, bolster cushions can blend in with existing soft furnishings, or provide bold, focal points in your room. Go for extravagance with rich-looking velvets, brocades and tassels; or you may prefer the Scandinavian simplicity of gingham fabric and striped ticking.

Floral designs are ideal for cane furniture in a conservatory, or comfortable sofas, while plain linens or glazed cottons give a more formal look to a living room. Single colour and printed fabrics

Cylindrical bolsters have long been used to cushion chaise longues, divans or day beds. But they have now come into their own as versatile accessories, which can be adapted to suit any contemporary setting

can be combined to make a patterned cushion with plain ends, or vice versa. Striped fabrics are particularly suited to the curved contours of a bolster, and the cover can be cut in two ways so that the stripes run either lengthwise, or around the cushion pad.

For an individual look, customize a bolster by sewing on bands of silky braids, cord or bobble fringing, and finish off the ends with tassels, bows or buttons.

Fill for the future

Standard-sized filler pads for bolsters can be bought from good furnishing suppliers and department stores. Or, if you want to make more of a statement, look out for the large continental-style bed bolsters which are increasingly available in this country. A pad stuffed with feather and down is a worthwhile investment – it's long-lasting and will maintain its shape despite repeated use. However, for people who suffer from allergies or prefer a lower-cost option, pads with foam or fibre fillings are easily available, at a snip of the price.

▼ *Enjoy a touch of classic French elegance with the rural scenes of toile de Jouy fabric – it's ideal for a bolster. Trim the gathered end with cord and two-colour tassels to match the material*

Measuring and cutting guide

The measurements given are for a standard-sized 45cm (18in) bolster, 18cm (7in) in diameter. Scale the figures up, or down, if your pad is a different size to the one given here, using the diagram on the right as a guide.

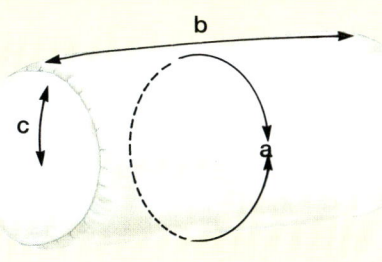

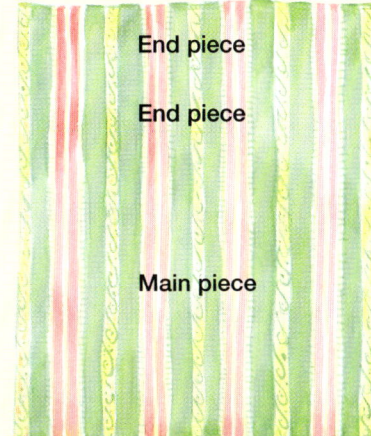

End piece

End piece

Main piece

- **To cut the bolster fabric**
  From a piece of fabric measuring 61 x 72cm (24 x 28½in) – or the size calculated following the diagram above – cut the main and two end pieces of the bolster as shown in the diagram.
- **Main piece**
  Cut a rectangle 61 x 48cm (24 x 19in) or **a** (width) x **b** (length), plus 12mm (½in) all around for the seams.
- **End pieces**
  Cut two strips 61 x 12cm (24 x 4¾in) or **a** (width) x **c** (length), plus 12mm (½in) for seams all around.

Making the gathered-end bolster cover

1 ▲ Sew the cover With right sides facing and cut edges matching, pin and tack the two long edges of the main piece together to form a tube. Machine stitch, taking a 12mm (½in) seam allowance. Press the seam open and turn the tube right side out.

end piece

2 ▲ Prepare the ends Pin and tack the short edges of one end piece, with right sides facing and taking a 12mm (½in) seam allowance. Machine stitch and press the seam open. Press a 12mm (½in) turning to the wrong side around one cut edge. On the right side, hand sew a line of 1cm (⅜in) running stitch close to the fold, using a double length of strong thread and keeping the stitches even. (These threads will be used for gathering up at a later stage.) Prepare the other end in the same way.

◄ **For an inviting 'come into my tent' look, scatter cushions and tied bolsters, in contrasting fabrics, on to a draped sofa. Use ties in a matching fabric for total co-ordination**

3 ▲ **Attach the ends** With right sides facing, slip one end piece over the main piece so that the cut edges line up as shown. Match the seams, then pin and tack together. Machine stitch 12mm (½in) from the edge. Sew on the other end in the same way. Press the seams open and turn back the ends so that the right side is showing.

4 ▲ **Sew on the braid** Cut two pieces of braid to fit around the circumference of the bolster, plus 2cm (¾in) extra. Fold under 1cm (⅜in) at each end. On the right side of the work and starting at the centre seam, pin one length around each end of the cover, to hide the joins. Adjust the folded ends, so that they butt neatly together, and tack down. Secure the braid in place with tiny hand-sewn stitches, or by machine, depending on its thickness.

5 ▲ **Finish off** Insert the bolster pad and draw up the gathering threads at both ends. Tie the surplus threads tightly and push to the inside. Sew a tassel securely to each end.

TAKE ANOTHER LOOK — sunflower stencilled bolster

Use a striking sunflower stencil, available from most craft shops or DIY stores, to decorate plain cotton fabric for a fabulous bolster. If you need further information on how to stencil, see the detailed instructions in 'Start stencilling', p40. There's also more about fabrics and paints for stencilling in 'Cut-out creations', p119. For details of how to make the bolster, see the box below.

STENCIL IT

MAKE IT SIMPLE — tie-end bolster

1 ▲ **Sew a simple tube** For a simple bolster with tied ends, cut a length of fabric two and a half times the length of your bolster pad and the same circumference as it, plus an extra 12mm (½in) on all four sides for the seam allowance. Form the fabric into a tube by sewing the long edge, and hem the two open ends as shown.

2 ▲ **Tie the ends** Using contrasting fabric cut two strips 6 x 75cm (2¼ x 30in). Fold in the cut edges on the long sides for 1cm (⅜in), and then fold the strips in half again with the right sides showing. Turn in the ends to neaten them, then machine stitch along the side and ends. Slide the bolster pad into the cover and tie the ends as shown.

Before you start making curtains of any type, you must first decide on their length and fullness and accurately calculate the amount of fabric needed

Whatever fabric you choose for your curtains, the most important thing to do first is to calculate accurately the amount of fabric you need. It is also best to buy all the fabric for your curtains at one time. If not, there could be variations in dye from roll to roll. This may not show on a small fabric sample, but it's often very noticeable when the completed curtains are hanging.

First decisions

To calculate accurately just how much fabric is required for your curtains, you should first decide on the type of pole or track you are going to use and how high it will sit above your window. See the panel on poles, tracks and heading tapes for advice on which one will best suit your needs.

Next decide on the amount of fullness you require. This is largely governed by the type of heading tape that you use as certain tapes need a specific width of fabric to achieve the desired effect.

Finally, decide on the finished length of your curtains. And when choosing both length and fullness, remember to consider the overall proportions of the room and the size of the window concerned. A large, sweeping bay window would suit long, heavily gathered curtains while a small bedroom window would be better dressed with shorter, less gathered drapes.

Curtain width

Generally, curtains are gathered at the top to create some fullness in the width. This means that the

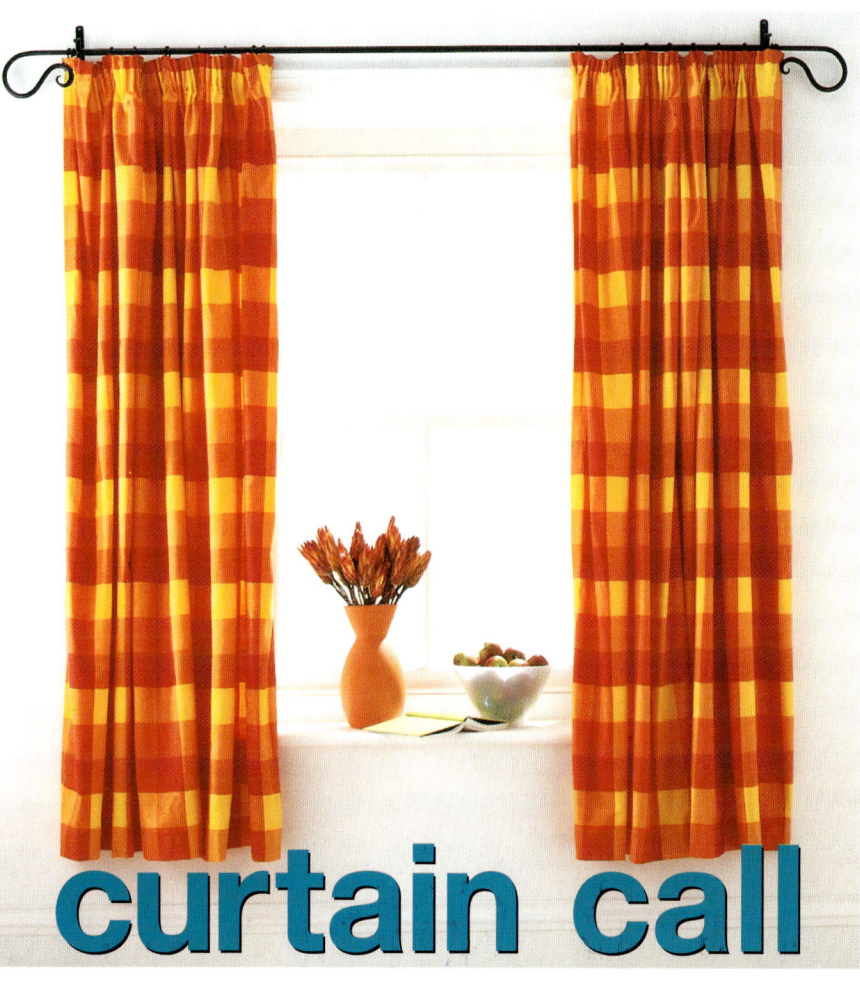

curtain call

Measurements for curtain length and width

- **Length A:** sill-length curtains should hang about 1.5cm (⅝in) above the sill
- **Length B:** below-sill curtains should hang 5–10cm (2–4in) below the sill and clear any radiators by 2cm (¾in)
- **Length C:** floor-length curtains should hang 2.5cm (1in) above the floor
- **Length D:** excess-length curtains have fabric cut deliberately long
- **Width:** curtain poles and tracks can extend to either the width of the window, or beyond to make a window appear wider than it is

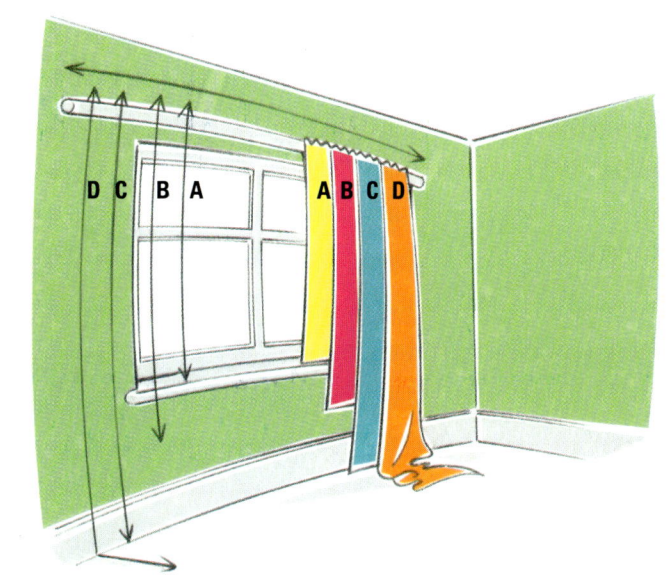

fabric is much wider than the window – usually you need to allow for fabric that is twice, to two and a half times, the width of the curtain pole or track.

To calculate the finished width of the curtains, simply measure the length of the pole or track from which they are going to hang and multiply this figure by 2 or 2.5.

Now divide this amount by the number of curtains you intend to hang to determine the finished width of each one. If you have an overlap track, allow for the width of the overlap – on one curtain.

Curtain length

Next, decide on where the curtains are to finish. You may want them to fall to the window-sill, just below the sill, or to the floor. **Sill-length curtains** should hang about 1.5cm (⅝in) above the sill to give clearance. **Below-sill curtains** should hang 5–10cm (2–4in) below, but must clear any radiator by at least 2cm (¾in). **Floor-length curtains** should finish 2.5cm (1in) above the floor. If you want to create an opulent effect – for example in a bedroom or living room – you can make the curtains extra long so that the fabric 'pools' on the floor.

Once you have decided on the desired length of the curtains, you will need to allow extra fabric for turnings and hems. Add about 10–15cm (4–6in) for the bottom hem, depending on the weight of the fabric and the chosen length of the curtains. For sill-length and floor-length curtains, deduct the amount you wish the curtains to clear the sill or floor by.

For the top heading, allow between 2.5–15cm (1–6in) of fabric, depending on the type of curtain heading tape and curtain style you have chosen. If you are in any doubt, follow the manufacturer's instructions provided with your heading tape. See 'Castles in the air', p54, for information on measuring tab top curtains.

▶ *Floor-lengths curtains form an elegant sweep in this bedroom and make the perfect frame for a long window*

▼ *Iron or wooden curtain poles with fancy finials (the decorated end section of the pole) make a dramatic impact against a plain-coloured wall*

Calculating total fabric

With the length of your curtains finalised, fix the track or pole in place on your wall at the required height above the top of the window (see 'Do it right', p73, for tips on how to do this).

Then, to work out how many drops of fabric (finished curtain length by fabric width) are needed, divide the desired *total finished width* of both curtains by the *width* of your chosen fabric. Round up the final amount to the next whole number, and this will give you plenty of fabric for the seams and side hems. Divide this figure by the number of curtains you have decided on to find the total number of drops in each curtain – if you have a part width, this will go to the outside of each drape.

The number of drops multiplied by the total length of each curtain will give you the amount of fabric you need to buy.

Poles, tracks and heading tapes

Many tracks and poles are sold in kit form with clear instructions for easy installation. When you choose a track or pole, make sure you select one that is strong enough to support the weight of your curtains, and one that suits the style and size of the window. Remember to allow for extra space on either side of the window – about 10–20cm (4–8in) – so that your curtains do not block the light coming through the window.

Basic curtain track
This is a strip of plastic or metal with runners that slide across the length. The curtain hooks simply slot into the eye at the bottom of each runner. The curtain track can be concealed completely if you thread the hooks into the lower pockets of a deep heading tape.

▶ *Tracks come in various forms and widths to suit different weights of curtain*

Patterned fabrics

If you are using patterned fabric, then you will have to allow for matching the pattern – both when you join widths at the seams and also across pairs of curtains when they are drawn together. If you are making more than one set of curtains for a room, the pattern should appear in the same place across all curtains.

On a large pattern repeat, the bottom of the repeat should coincide with the hemline. This way, any half patterns will fall at the top of the curtain, so that, when the curtain is gathered into the heading tape, the pattern will be less noticeable.

Generally, you will need to buy extra fabric if it is patterned. To calculate how much you will need, measure the depth of the pattern repeat – that is, the distance from the top of one motif to the top of the next identical one. Add this measurement to the total calculated length and multiply by the number of drops as usual. To save wastage, especially on expensive fabrics, you can calculate your curtain length (including turnings) to accommodate exact pattern repeats.

To make sure that you cut all the lengths of patterned fabric at the same point, place the first cut length alongside the second and subsequent lengths, with patterns matching, before cutting out. Note that some repeats may not align exactly across the width to create a more random-looking pattern, so careful planning is essential.

Cutting out

The easiest way to cut out curtains is to lay out the fabric on a large table or on the floor. Fabric should always be cut on the straight grain. Use a large set square, long ruler and tailor's chalk to mark the cutting line. And double check all the measurements before cutting out. Also make sure to mark the top of each curtain drop so that they can be joined with the straight grain or pile running in the same direction.

Any small left over pieces of fabric can be used to make curtain tie-backs, while larger pieces can be used for cushion covers.

▲ Finials and poles come in a variety of styles and finishes, from traditional to modern, to suit any home

▼ Heading tapes gather curtains by varying amounts, from tight pleats to box pleats

Tracks comes in various lengths, widths and finishes for lightweight, medium or heavyweight curtains. Both the plastic and metal varieties are good options for large bay windows, as they can be bent to fit around corners.

Corded tracks

If your curtains are particularly heavy, or made from a pale-coloured fabric that is likely to get dirty quickly, you can choose a corded track. This type of track allows you to draw the curtains open and closed, without touching the fabric, by using a set of pull-cords. You can buy the track with a built-in cording set, or alternatively, buy a set separately and fit it into your existing track.

Curtain poles

Metal or wooden curtain poles come in various thicknesses, so choose one appropriate for the weight of your curtains – heavy curtains on a fine pole may cause the pole to bow in the middle. The rings, which fit over the pole, have small screweyes from which the hooks hang. Because there are so many styles of curtain pole, ranging from antique brass, modern iron to painted wood, you should be able to find one that co-ordinates perfectly with your decorative scheme.

Expandable rods

Sprung-tension rods, which are suitable for nets or sheer curtains, can be fitted between flat-facing walls in a narrow recess or across a window inset. Heading tapes for nets are quite sheer and have loops that thread over the curtain rod, or you can attach rings to the top of the curtain.

Fine rods and curtain wire

Rods and curtain wire can be threaded directly through a cased heading, making heading tape unnecessary. The rods are narrow and made of metal or plastic, while the curtain wire has a metal eye at each end and is expanded to fit between metal hooks.

Heading tapes

A popular way of gathering curtains is by fixing a heading tape to the top of the curtains. You can buy ready-made heading tapes with printed stitching lines for ease of attaching the tape to your fabric. These tapes will gather curtains by varying amounts, ranging from tight pleats, to chunky box pleats, to simple folds. Gathered curtains hang from plastic or metal hooks slotted into the heading tape, then through screweyes in the curtain rings or track gliders.

one layer's enough

Curtains needn't be a major production – make them unlined and they will be easy, quick and inexpensive

Unlined curtains can be stylish and lightweight alternatives to the more traditional lined drapes – and they are easier on your pocket. Make them whatever length you like, and they're sure to become a focal point of your room.

Practical choice

Unlined curtains, which are easy to wash, are just perfect for those rooms such as kitchens and bathrooms where fabric is likely to attract steam, dust and food smells.

Measuring and cutting guide

See 'Curtain call', p91, for more information on calculating your curtain size.

● *To calculate the width*
Choose your heading tape. Multiply the length of the curtain track or pole by the amount of fullness needed for your chosen tape, then add 4cm (1½in) for each side hem. Divide the total by the width of the fabric and round up to the nearest whole number. If each curtain has more than one width, add 3cm (1¼in) for each seam.

● *To calculate the length*
Measure the finished (hanging) length of your curtain, adding 4cm (1½in) for the top hem and 10cm (4in) for the bottom hem (total length).

● *To calculate the total fabric*
Multiply the total length by the number of widths needed. You may need extra length on each width to match a pattern.

Making the curtains

And they are equally at home on any window where the aim is to let some degree of light through, rather than blocking it completely: soft evening light seeping through the single layer of fabric can create a serene atmosphere in any room. One word of warning, though – remember that strong sunlight, say in a south-facing room, will fade your curtain fabric if you don't have linings.

Suitable style

Printed cotton fabrics are a good choice for your unlined curtains and these are available in a wide range of colours and patterns, usually at a price that's affordable. Look out for other heavyweight voiles or natural bleached cotton in textures and fancy weaves.

Choose a suitable heading tape for the style of curtain that you want and get cracking! If you go for a plain fabric, then you can get started straight away. But if you opt for a pattern, then it will take a little more thought. You will need to allow extra fabric for matching the pattern over the width of each curtain, and for when the pair of curtains are drawn together.

▼ *Use unlined curtains as an up-to-the-minute alternative to traditional nets*

1 ▲ **Prepare the fabric** Cut the first width of fabric to the correct length, making sure that you don't cut through large motifs, if possible. Cut further widths so that the pattern matches at the lower edge, including widths for the second curtain. You can use the off-cuts for matching accessories.

2 ▲ **Trim the selvedges** When you have cut the fabric to the correct number of widths, trim away all the selvedges at the side edges – these may shrink at a later stage, when the curtains are washed.

3 **Join the widths** It may be necessary to join widths of fabric together for each curtain. Place the fabric lengths with right sides facing, pin and machine stitch them together, taking a 1.5cm (⅝in) seam allowance.

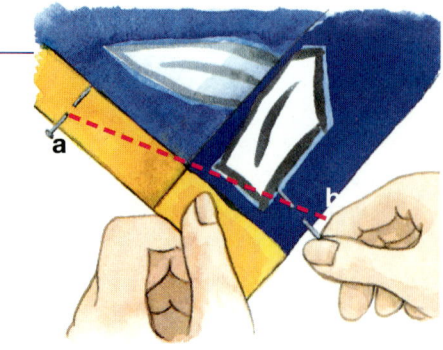

4 ▲ **Neaten the seams** Using a pair of pinking shears so that the fabric does not fray, trim the seam allowance (so that a minimum is visible through the curtains when they hang). Press the seam open. If you don't have pinking shears, you can zigzag stitch the allowance together, then trim and press the seam to one side.

5 ▲ **Mark the hems** Turn in the side seams for 2cm (¾in), pin and press. Remove the pins. Turn up the bottom hem for 5cm (2in), pin and press. Remove the pins. Place one pin 10cm (4in) above the bottom folded edge (a) and another pin 4cm (1½in) in from the folded side edge (b).

6 ▲ **Fold the corner** Fold in both of the hems to form a diagonal line between the two pins. Remove the pins and press the corner in position.

▼ *Mix'n'match striped unlined curtains with patterned Roman blinds in the same colours for greater control of light*

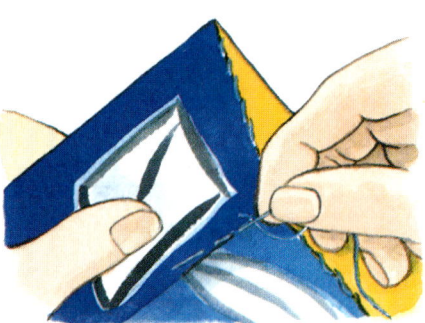

7▲ Mitre the corner Turn in the side hem again to form a double 2cm (¾in) hem, then fold up the lower hem again to form a double 5cm (2in) hem. With the corners in a diagonal line, pin and tack the hems in place.

8▲ Secure the hems Using matching thread, slip-stitch the hems and the diagonal folds together to hold the corner in place.

9▲ Prepare the heading tape Fold down 4cm (1½in) along the top of the curtain and press in place. Cut heading tape to the same width as the curtain, plus an extra 4cm (1½in). Turn 2cm (¾in) of one short edge of the tape to the wrong side and ease the cords free. Starting at the neatened end, pin and tack the tape 2.5cm (1in) from the top of the curtains, leaving 2cm (¾in) free at the opposite end. Tuck in and pin the extra tape level with the side.

MAKE IT SIMPLE

instant curtains

Here's a window treatment that you can put together in a moment. You don't need any sewing skills at all and it looks fantastic.

The basis of this amazing design is an Indian-print bedspread in fine cotton (you'll need one for each curtain). Search out examples in rich, bright colours that will look dazzling with the light shining through.

Team up the prints with a gleaming brass curtain pole and decorative clips which are available from department stores. For a finishing flourish, drape two long strips of the same fabric in a fancy swag arrangement.

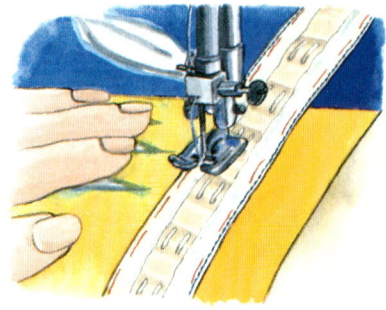

10▲ Machine the tape in place Make sure the cords are free at both ends to avoid catching them in the stitching. Stitch the tape along one short edge, one long edge, then the second short edge. Stitching in the same direction, stitch the second long edge, also stitching the short edges a second time.

11 Gather the tape Tie one pair of the heading tape cords (at what will be the centre front edge) in a knot to prevent them from being pulled out. Draw up the free cords at the outer edge of the curtain to the required width and so that all the gathers are at the centre front edge.

Tie the cords at the outer edge in a knot (but do not cut off the surplus) and distribute the gathers so that the fullness is even before hanging the curtain. Prepare and gather the second curtain to match. To avoid the surplus cords showing at the outer edge, double them over and loosely knot them. Loop the extra cords through a curtain hook a little way along the heading tape or secure with a safety pin.

window shopping

Treat yourself to a drift of new fabric to make easy unlined curtains – it's an inexpensive way to jazz up your windows

When selecting your fabric for unlined curtains, consider the effect of the light streaming through them, be it Mediterranean sunshine or from your own back yard! Depending on the amount of light you want to let into your room – heaps for a breakfast room, but less for a bedroom – choose your fabric with care. Lightweights will give an airy, even breezy, effect, whereas heavier-weight fabric will give a warmer, more substantial feel to a room.

Remember, also, that strong sunlight has an adverse effect on most fabrics – they will fade fairly quickly. So it's probably wise not to buy very expensive fabrics and to treat unlined curtains more as a short-term style feature. Then, once you're bored with the look, or the fabric has perished, you'll be happy to replace them.

- See 'One layer's enough', p94' for information on easy-to-make unlined curtains

▲ *To soften the effect of graphic styling, such as a chrome venetian blind, yet retain the contemporary feel, choose brightly coloured curtains in bold checks*

checklist
Unlined curtain fabrics

- **Fibre content** Fabric for unlined curtains can be virtually any fibre – synthetic, natural or a mixture – as long as it's not too heavy so that some light shows through.
- **Pattern pointers** If you choose a patterned design, you may need extra fabric to match the pattern. Take your window measurements with you when buying the fabric and the staff in furnishing fabric departments will be able to advise you on pattern repeats. For much more information on how to calculate and measure curtain lengths and widths see 'Curtain call', p91.

- **Tidy seams** One of the disadvantages of unlined curtains is that the seams are visible on both sides of the curtains (ie through the windows as well as through the fabric). Keep the seam allowances tidy by trimming them with pinking shears or by placing them together and working over the edges with zigzag stitching.
- **Variety of styles** Unlined curtains are suitable for most heading styles. You can use conventional heading tapes (see 'Curtain call', p91), or try contemporary tab tops (see 'Castles in the air', p54, for instructions about making these).

1

2

3

4

5

1 Tiny printed shapes against a bright background give this cotton a Provençal feel

2 A solid ribbed cotton in deep blue brings to mind heavenly fields of scented lavender

3 For a restful, natural effect, try a soft cream fabric with unwoven runners that let the light in

4 Bring the feel of a Bedouin tent to your living room with this bold, densely-striped fabric

5 Country style is the order of the day with this closely woven hemp – perfect for heavy drapes

crowned in glory

A cloud of white muslin cascading over your bed is truly luxurious and a dream that's easy to fulfil

A coronet, draped with muslin, around the head of a bed adds an enticing softness to the appearance of a bedroom. The dreamy-white effect is elegant, yet cosy at the same time. And although this type of bed canopy requires masses of fabric so that it falls easily into graceful drapes, you'll find they're still inexpensive to make.

Because canopies are such a popular style feature, they're often available in furnishing stores (look out for mail-order furniture catalogues if you're unable to visit a shopping centre). It's worthwhile buying a plain canopy and then, if you have a little time to spare, you can customize it to fit in with your bedroom decor.

There is one thing you should do before you start this project though – seek advice from someone about finding a joist in the ceiling and the best method of attaching a hook to it for mounting the canopy. A sheer coronet isn't very heavy, but the hook must be screwed securely into a joist to avoid damaging the ceiling.

Custom made

It's so easy to give your canopy a touch of individual styling. Just changing the colour is the simplest option – and the lightweight fabric means that the dye takes in just 15 minutes. Or, sew on a braid down the front opening edges.

We've chosen two other options to decorate our canopies. The first involves adding a trimming made with beads – there's a tremendous variety to chose from so you can be really outrageous. Or secondly, stencil a simple motif on to the fabric (perhaps to match a border used elsewhere in the room). Buy a stencil design that complements your style or make your own from a piece of manilla card.

◀ Filmy white muslin looks dreamy in a cottage bedroom. Add a draped string of large beads in colours to match the rest of your bedroom decor

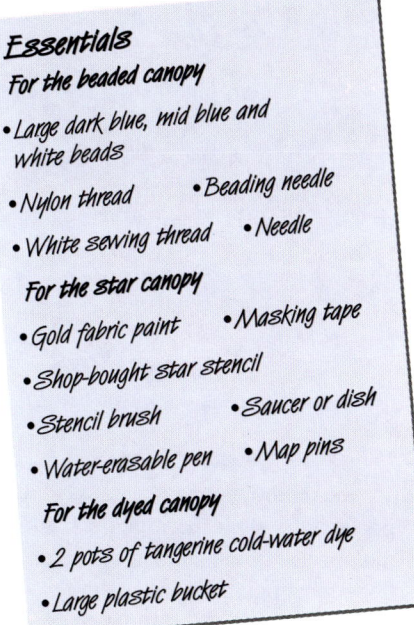

Essentials

For the beaded canopy
- Large dark blue, mid blue and white beads
- Nylon thread
- Beading needle
- White sewing thread
- Needle

For the star canopy
- Gold fabric paint
- Masking tape
- Shop-bought star stencil
- Stencil brush
- Saucer or dish
- Water-erasable pen
- Map pins

For the dyed canopy
- 2 pots of tangerine cold-water dye
- Large plastic bucket

Making the beaded canopy

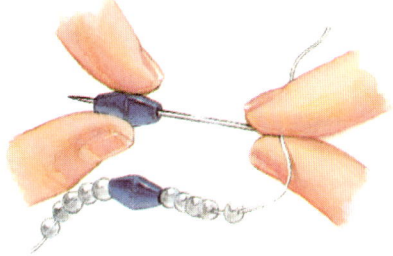

1 ▲ String the beads Lay your chosen beads out and move them around until you achieve the desired pattern. Thread your beading needle (a long fine needle which passes easily through the holes in beads) with a long length of nylon thread. Slip the beads onto the thread in the correct order.

2 ▲ Decorate the canopy Starting and ending at the back of the hoop where the join will not be seen, stitch the bead string securely onto the canopy in neat swags as shown.

Making the star stencilled canopy

1 ▲ Prepare the canopy for stencilling Using a water-erasable pen and the stencil as a guide, mark the position of the stars (a dot in the uppermost point) on your canopy. Stretch a small section of fabric on to a firm, clean and protected surface (otherwise the paint will go through the layers). Secure it in place for stencilling with a few map pins.

2 ▲ Stencil the stars Pour a little of the gold fabric paint into the dish. Using the paint sparingly, stencil a star at each marked point on the canopy (see 'Start stencilling', p40, for more details). When the stars are dry, re-stretch another section of the canopy and continue stencilling.

Sweet dreams will follow naturally beneath a spangly drift of golden stars

Mosquito net canopies can be dyed in any colour to match the rest of your bedroom furnishings. Use a cold water dye specifically for synthetic fabrics

Dyeing the canopy

1 ▲ Dye the canopy Weigh the canopy dry (without the hoop) and, following the manufacturer's instructions, add the correct amount of dye and salt to a large bucket. Add the canopy and leave until it is the required depth of colour. Rinse well and hang it to dry.

◄ Stars and hearts

Combine fabric and wood to create a Shaker style box. Draw hearts in two different sizes on to the drawer fronts. Cut out the hearts and sew or stick a button, then glue the motifs to each drawer front. Outline each heart with white painted dots and add a few stencilled stars

▼ Curtain call

Washable felt is an excellent fabric to use for appliqué hearts on soft furnishings such as curtains. First, make a paper template and cut out the hearts from felt of a contrasting colour to your curtain fabric. Position the hearts randomly along the edge of your curtain, pin them in place, then embroider around each one using fine tapestry wool. Alternatively, glue the hearts in place and then use a permanent fabric pen to draw on stitching lines

the heart of the matter

Spread a little love around your home by introducing stylish heart motifs in all sorts of ways

Hearts add instant appeal and never go out of fashion, so it's an easy theme to extend around the home. Cut out heart shapes and appliqué or glue them on to other fabrics. Sprinkle hearts across large soft furnishings, or work them singly on to napkins for a quirky touch at meal times.

We've made cutting out a heart easy for you. Over the page you'll find three popular heart shapes –

including rounded with gentle curves and long and thin – in different sizes for you to trace and use as templates. If you prefer a different shaped heart, make your own template first. Fold a sheet of paper in half lengthways. Using the fold of paper as the central divide, draw half a heart shape on the paper. Keeping the paper folded, cut out around the outline, then unfold the paper and check your pattern.

Make it!

Brightly-coloured gingham hearts will update your storage system in next to no time. Firm canvas makes a strong background and there are plenty of storage systems to choose from in the shops or mail-order catalogues. Choose a neutral colour such as cream, then you'll be able to go to town with multi-coloured hearts.

1 ▲ **Cut out the hearts** Using our handy templates as a guide, draw a heart pattern to fit the size of the storage pockets and cut out the required number of motifs in gingham fabrics with different-coloured checks.

2 ▲ **Attach the heart motifs** Alternating the colours, position the hearts centrally on to each pocket of the storage unit. Simply stick the hearts in place with fabric glue. Alternatively, you can use iron-on bonding material.

▶ Lover's linen

Simple white napkins can be transformed with the addition of a single heart stencilled in red. Following our simple guide on the opposite page, cut a small heart from a sheet of thin card or acetate. Mark the position of your heart on the napkin with a water-erasable pen or tailor's chalk and then stencil the motif (see 'Start stencilling', p40, for further information)

▶ Light relief

A plain lamp can be brought to life by decorating the shade with a series of appliqué hearts. Draw up a heart pattern that will fit comfortably around the shade. Choose two pastel shades of gingham fabric that tone with your other soft furnishings, and, using pinking shears, carefully cut out two heart motifs from each fabric. Then simply fix them in place using fabric glue

Pick brightly-striped canvas and create a quick-to-make hammock for lazy days in the garden

swing high, swing low

Hammocks fulfil the dream of lazily rocking in the shade during long summer days in the garden. If you have two well-positioned trees or posts, you can easily string up a hammock between them. Because it involves the minimum of stitching, you can make the hammock in a week-end – allowing you to spend leisurely, carefree days swinging in the balmy air. And, once summer's over, you simply roll it up and store it away ready to use again next year.

Make the hammock from sturdy canvas which is strong enough to withstand a short rain shower as well as cleaning with a damp cloth. Ropes running down each side casing provide support as well as shaping, while the end ropes loop through eyelets, connecting a wooden batten at each end. Extra rope lashes the hammock to the supporting trees.

Strength from stitching

Canvas is an ideal fabric for a hammock. It doesn't fray so the edges can be cut and left without neatening, but you will need to practice your machine stitching. Fit a heavy-duty needle, then thread and test the machine tension on a spare piece of canvas before you begin to stitch.

Turning a double hem at the hammock ends gives extra strength. But if your machine is hesitant about stitching through three layers of canvas, you can turn under a single hem instead. You'll find strong natural rope between 6mm and 1cm (¼-⅜in) thick at specialist shops such as ship chandlers, while large eyelets are easy to find in kit form in haberdashery departments.

Measuring and cutting guide

You will need a piece of canvas measuring 105 x 230cm (42 x 212in) for our hammock

- **To make it wider**

  Hammocks are usually between 80-120cm (32-48in) wide. Add 5cm (2in) to the chosen width for side casings.

- **To make it longer**

  A hammock is usually 200cm (80in) long, but if you prefer, measure your height and add approximately 50cm (20in). Add 30cm (12in) to the chosen length for hems.

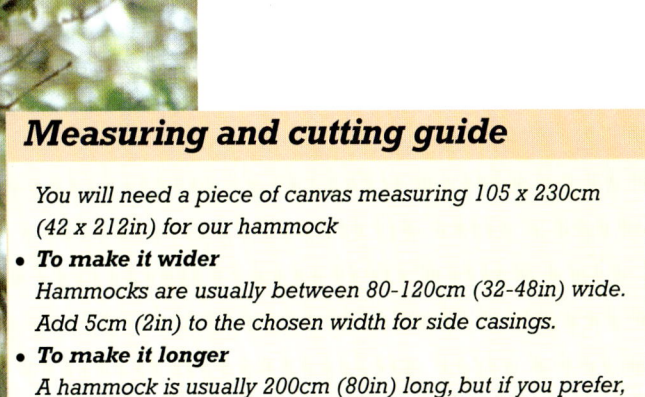

Essentials

- Striped canvas fabric, at least 115cm (45in) wide
- Two 105cm (42in) lengths of 5 x 2.5cm (2 x 1in) wooden battening
- Electric drill and twist bit
- Coarse and fine sandpaper
- Matching thread • Paper clips
- Strong rope • Whipping cord
- Two 7.5cm (3in) diameter metal rings
- Large eyelets and fixing tool
- Clear household adhesive

Making the hammock

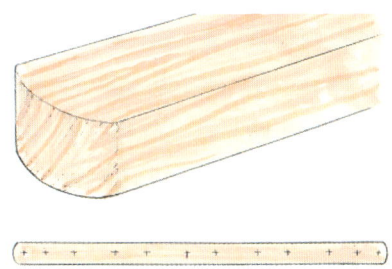

1 ▲ **Prepare the battens** Round off the sharp corners of the 5 x 2.5cm (2 x 1in) battens with coarse sandpaper and then sand down the edges with a finer version until smooth. Mark positions for the rope holes. Place the first two 2.5cm (1in) from the outer ends and the next two 6cm (2⅜in) further in. The remaining holes are spaced in pairs 8cm (3¼in) apart, with 12cm (4¾in) between each set.

2 ▲ **Drill the holes** Rest the batten on a spare piece of wood and, using a drill with a twist bit, drill a clearance hole at each rope position through each batten. The size of the drill bit will depend on the thickness of the rope – see 'Do it right' p73.

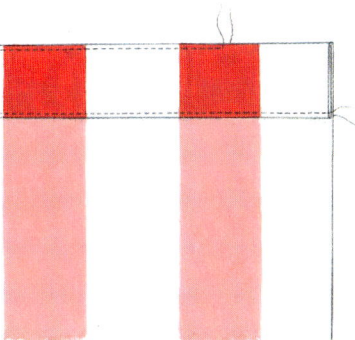

3 ▲ **Cut out the canvas** From the canvas, cut a rectangle 105 x 230cm (42 x 212in) for the hammock. Turn under a double 7.5cm (3in) hem at each end of the canvas. Hold in place with paper clips (the canvas is too thick to hold with pins). Machine stitch across the hems, close to the hem edge. Stitch across the hems again close to the outer folded edge.

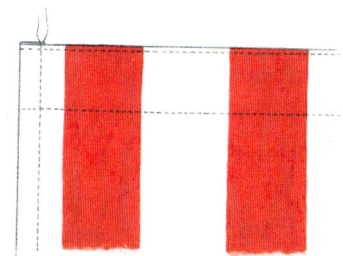

4 ▲ **Form the casings** Turn under a 2.5cm (1in) hem to the wrong side along each long edge to form the casings for the side ropes. Machine stitch the hems in place close to the raw edge. If the double hems are too thick to stitch over, slip-stitch this part of the casing by hand.

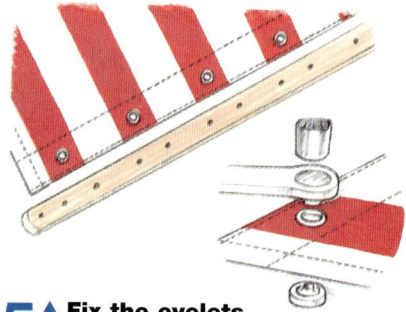

5▲ Fix the eyelets
Using the tool supplied, insert the eyelets in the double hems to correspond with the marked end positions on the battens and half way between the drilled pairs of holes.

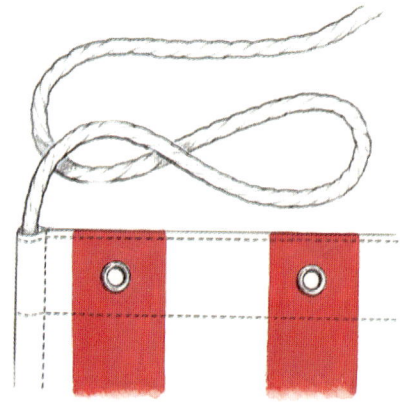

6▲ Thread the casings Cut two 380cm (150in) lengths of rope. Attach a large safety-pin as a guide to one end, then thread each length of rope through the casing on either side of the hammock, leaving an equal amount free at the ends.

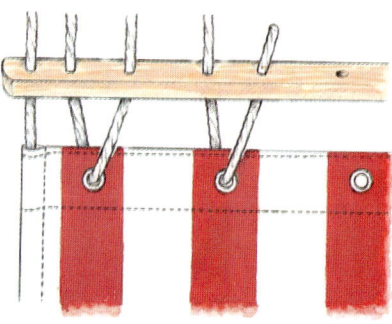

7▲ Thread the eyelets Cut ten 180cm (71in) lengths of rope. Thread each length through an eyelet, leaving an equal amount on each side of it. Continue threading the rope through the pairs of holes in the batten, noting that the side casing ropes go through the holes in each end as shown.

▲ *Instead of hanging your hammock out in the open between two trees, choose a veranda for a peaceful place to relax*

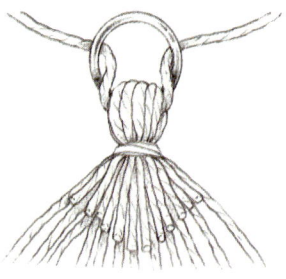

8▲ Gather up the ropes Lay the hammock out flat and position the batten a short distance from the edge of the canvas. Gather the ropes together in a triangular shape and pass through one metal ring, bending back about 10cm (4in). Hold with an elastic band. For tying around the tree, cut two 152cm (60in) lengths of rope and thread through the looped rope ends.

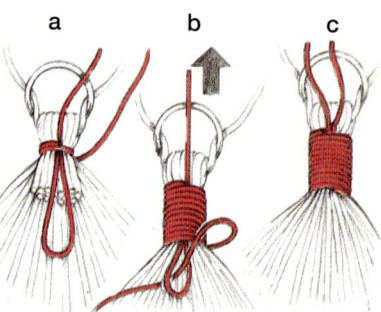

a   b   c

9▲ Bind the ends Make the loose rope ends equal. Using the thinner, whipping cord, first form a loop about twice the length to be bound (a). Continue binding over the rope end (including the loop of whipping cord). Then, to finish off, thread the working end of cord through the protruding loop (b) and pull the other free end to draw up the loop (so that it's hidden) and working end to the top edge. Knot the loose ends together (c) and seal the whole binding with adhesive.

snuggle up

The bed linen you choose sets the scene for the kind of bedroom you create, from cosy romantic retreat to stylish contemporary chic

One of the fastest, and cheapest, ways to give your bedroom a change of scene is with new bed linen. Even if all you do is to add some extra pillows and cushions, or change the colour of your linen, the bedroom will have an instant fresh focus.

The bed is usually the largest item in the room, so the bedding you use will set the mood. Blue linen always looks good in the bedroom, but try using flashes of pink, yellow or green, perhaps with a contrasting pillowcase, throw or cushion, to warm up the scheme. Warmer colours, yellow or pink, work well in a dark or north-facing bedroom. Mix them with white or cream for a soft, cosy feel.

Making a statement

If your walls are fairly plain you can use plenty of pattern on the bed linen to make a real statement. Don't feel you have to co-ordinate perfectly, try different patterns using the same colour family as the unifying theme. Or stick to one type of pattern – checks, stripes or florals – but use contrasting colours. Small flower prints give a country look, white and gingham a stylish Shaker feel. Bright citrus shades look fresh and contemporary, pure white or ivory can be crisp and smart, or

▶ *Citrus chic*
A smart, button-down checked duvet cover and pillowcases make for a chic, crisp feel

▼ *Cushion extra*
Pile up cushions and pillows in mix-and-match stripes and checks to create a dramatic contemporary look

Turquaz

Malabar

romantic and luxurious, with the addition of frothy lace trimmings.

For a traditional English country look, dress up a plain cream or white duvet cover with antique pillow shams, and bolsters or cushions made from floral fabric remnants, or antique linens and lace. Finish with decorative buttons or ribbon ties, then layer on a quilt or coverlet.

Lots of layers

If you can't find the colour of bed linen you want, try dyeing ready-made plain white linen, or make your own from sheeting. You can add trimmings, buttons, quilting and appliqué to give an individual touch.

The layered look is both fashionable and practical. Adding or shedding layers is the best way to keep warm in winter or cool in summer. After the domination of the duvet, blankets, quilts, even old-fashioned comforters, are making a welcome comeback. Layer the pillows too, with extras like big, square continental pillows, bolsters, and cushions, all adding to a cosy, luxurious feel.

Buy the basics

Duvets come with a variety of fillings from goosedown to polyester. Most have a tog rating which denotes its warmth, and the higher the tog, the warmer the duvet. The latest in duvet design is wool filling, said to make it cosier. You can wash a single polyester duvet in an ordinary washing machine, but anything else needs a launderette or specialist cleaning.

Blankets come in all the colours of the rainbow and in fibres such as wool, wool/mohair mix, cotton waffle, even thermal fleece. Electric blankets should be fitted with a 3-amp fuse and have BEAB approval. Check frequently for signs of wear, make sure it is not creased or crumpled and always switch it off after use.

Another alternative is to buy a quilted bedspread, comforter or coverlet. Use it as a lightweight

▶ A touch of luxury

Crisp cotton bed linen looks, and feels, luxurious. Edge plain pillowcases with lace or broderie anglais, mix with new and antique linen finds

Sanderson

Sanderson

◀ In the pink

Create a layered look with stripes and florals, linked by shades of pink, for a soft, English country feel

▶ Colour flash

Dress up plain blankets with pillowcases, or cushions, in flashes of pattern and colour for a look that's bright and modern

Kingfisher/Forbo Lancaster

Anna French

▲ Summer bright
Use furnishing fabrics to make bedspreads and cushions. Here a bright, summery floral print co-ordinates with the window dressings

◀ Smart layers
Combine a striking blue and white colour scheme with the layered look to great effect

Nimbus

cover in summer, or an extra layer in winter. You can get many different patterns from traditional patchwork quilts, to Jacquard coverlets, and bedspreads made in fabrics to match your furnishing scheme.

Anti-allergic bedding helps alleviate the problem of dust mites, which can cause allergic reactions including asthma and eczema. You can buy mattress and pillow protectors and anti-allergy duvets and pillows from most major stores.

Linen low-down

If you decide to make your own bed linen, check that the fabrics you choose are suitable for the job. They need to withstand frequent washing, and to feel soft enough next to the skin. Furnishing fabrics are generally better for quilts, comforters and cushions, rather than duvet covers, sheets or pillowcases. Sheeting usually comes in 180cm (70in) and 230cm (90in) widths to make single and double bedding.

Several fabrics are suitable for making bed linen. Pure linen looks luxurious, is cool in the summer, strong and very durable, but it can be expensive and is hard to launder as it creases badly. Pure cotton is easier to care for and feels good, but will still need plenty of ironing. Egyptian cotton has longer, finer fibres than plain cotton and feels more luxurious.

Cotton percale has extra fine threads and is very soft to the feel – most commercial bed linen is made from cotton percale. Cotton flannelette has a warm fluffy surface making it feel cosy for the winter. But probably the best choice is cotton polyester – it's non-shrink, hard wearing, inexpensive, very easy care and, with a high proportion of cotton, feels nicer against the skin.

● **For information on how to make your own matching duvet and pillow set, see 'All tied up', p22. Also, see 'Home on the range', p83, for a folk art quilt.**

on the ball

Give your surroundings a lift by stitching playful bobble trims, available in all shapes, sizes and colours, on to curtains, cushions and lampshades

▲ Conservatory comfort

A buttercup yellow bobble trim on a cushion, with matching green bobbles on the throw, looks fun. The bobbles also have a softening effect against the harsh lines of striped and checked fabrics

▶ Baby bobbles

Babies' and toddlers' rooms are an ideal setting for bobbles; they add a touch of fun to the scene. Extend their use around the room to create a theme, stitching the same bright trim to a roller blind, shelf edge or lampshade

◄ Sheer chic
Add a white bobble trim to white curtains and throw the whole lot into contrast against a background of royal blue. The curtain trim is echoed by the pom-pon-sized 'bobbles' on the throw

▲ Clever cushions
A plain room based around neutral tones comes alive with the tiniest hint of bobbles. Don't overstep the mark though – match the trim to the fabric colour for an integrated effect

Make a bold statement by introducing bobbles in all sorts of clever and quirky ways around the house. Hang them from hard edges, or dot them over softer surfaces and you'll produce a jaunty effect with real designer appeal. Feast your eyes on these examples of how to use bobble trims to good effect.

Try a trim

Bobble trim is available in a fabulously wide range of colours, styles and sizes. Some bobbles are fluffy and made like small pom-pons, while others are solid and are produced from textile-covered beads. The heading to a trim can be a simple, delicate string, a narrow tape, or a wide, elaborate braid.

When choosing a bobble trim, be brave – don't shy away from the larger, more generous bobble sizes. Smaller ones may well end up looking mean and fidgety, while larger bobbles will make a bolder and simpler visual statement.

In most cases, the best colour to choose for a bobble trim is one that closely matches your fabric. The bobbles then become a subtle extension to the main design. Contrasting bobbles can look good on bold and bright designs, although it's a good idea to hide the contrasting heading, so that only the bobbles are visible.

Stitching on bobble trim can be done in a flash. Simply use a matching thread and work running stitch, alternately taking a long stitch under the trim, catching the base fabric, and then taking a short stitch on top of the trim to hold it down.

◄ Free fall
Stitch a trim inside a curtain seam and the bobbles will fall magically down either side of your window

Make it!

Some of the most stylish bobble trims around (such as the lampshade on the right) feature pom-pons, which are so simple to make yourself. For bold bobbles, use knitting or tapestry yarn which has masses of colours to choose from. Or, for a finer effect, look out for sewing silks in jewel colours.

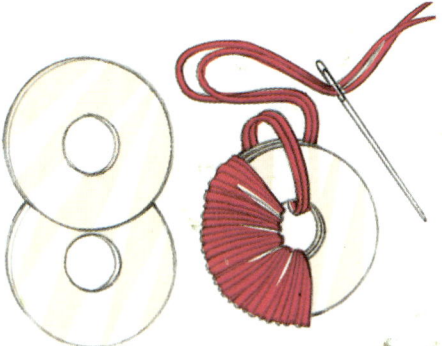

1 ▲ Cover the cardboard rings

Cut two firm cardboard circles the diameter of the pom-pon. Cut a central hole through the circles. Place the card rings together and wind the yarn round the cards, gradually filling the centre. Thread the yarn into a needle to fill the hole completely.

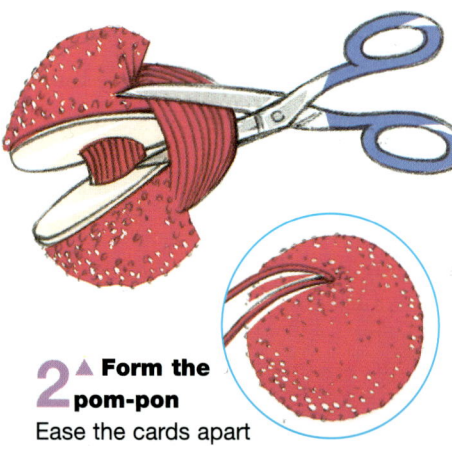

2 ▲ Form the pom-pon

Ease the cards apart and cut all the strands around the outer edge between the two circles. Tie a double strand of yarn very securely around the centre of all the strands, leaving a long end for attaching the pom-pon. Gently remove the cardboard circles. Fluff up the strands of yarn and trim the ends all over to form a neat bobble shape.

◄ Lamplight
For a bold, jaunty room, trim a jazzy lampshade with large pom-pon bobbles. We tell you how to make them on the left

► Mobile shapes
Bobbles on lampshades are especially striking. Here, a string of beaded shapes in graduated sizes are thrown into relief by the light shining through

a meal in Provence

Bring the warmth of a Mediterranean summer's day into your kitchen with colourful accessories made in traditional Provençal fabrics

For a French country kitchen look bursting with sunshine, go for the versatility of Provençal prints. The charm of this style comes from the riotous mix of patterns, both in colour and scale, within a dining setting. As well as cushions and tablecloths, make a range of matching accessories for an exuberant look.

Traditional Provençal fabrics are printed cottons with a country style charm all of their own – ideal for kitchens and informal dining areas.

Some of the patterns date back to the 19th century, but their fresh bright colours are as appealing today as they were back then.

Quick quilting

The trick to creating an authentic French country look is to make lots of accessories from wadded and quilted layers of the Provençal prints. It's common to find contrasting prints on either side of the 'sandwich', and the complete effect is drawn together with a bright outline of either wide or thin bias binding.

One idea for your table setting is to include co-ordinating tablecloths, napkins and placemats; choose fabrics in colours to match your existing dining accessories.

Bags for bread

However, to really enter into the Mediterranean spirit, why not make bread holders to complete the look? Nothing reminds us so much of France as food, especially their breakfasts with delicious baguettes, croissants and brioche.

The wall-hung bread bag is large enough to contain four long French bread sticks, but would be equally useful as a bag for napkins, tea towels or even cutlery. The croissant nest and the rectangular bread basket, meanwhile, will be centre stage for any family breakfast or brunch.

Essentials

- Fabric in two Provençal prints
- Lightweight polyester wadding
- Bias binding • Tacking thread
- Matching sewing thread
- Paper and pencil • Needles
- Ruler • Scissors
- Dressmaker's fading pen

Extras for the bread bag:
- 40cm (16in) length of 1cm (³⁄₈in) diameter dowelling
- 2 small brass screw-in eyelets

Making the croissant nest

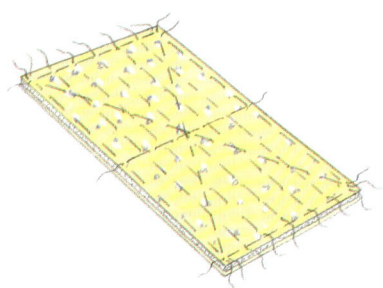

1 ▲ Prepare the quilting Sandwich the wadding between the two pieces of Provençal fabric with the right sides facing outwards. Using long tacking stitches, and keeping the layers flat, tack through all the fabrics diagonally from corner to corner, then from side to side and top to bottom, working through the centre point. Sew several more lines, parallel to the long edges, then tack around the outside edge.

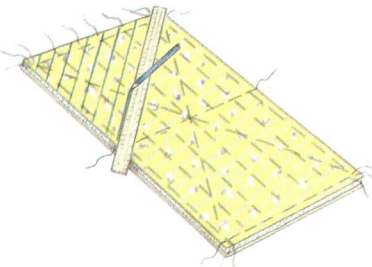

2 ▲ Mark the grid Draw a line diagonally across one corner, then mark a series of lines parallel to this, 4cm (1½in) apart, across the top of the fabric. When you have finished, draw a second set of lines at right angles to the first, so that the whole top is covered with a regular diamond-shaped grid.

3 Stitch over the lines Set the stitch length on your sewing machine to a medium length, and thread the machine with matching thread. Machine stitch along the marked lines, working each line of stitching in the same direction. In this way you return to the same edge to start stitching each time, instead of working back and forth.

Fabric cutting guide

Croissant nest

Two contrasting Provençal fabrics	50cm x 1m (19½in x 1yd)
Lightweight polyester wadding	50cm x 1m (19½in x 1yd)
25mm (1in) bias binding	3m (3½yd)
12mm (½in) bias binding	1.6m (2yd)

Bread basket

Two contrasting Provençal fabrics	20 x 30cm (8 x 12in)
Lightweight polyester wadding	20 x 30cm (8 x 12in)
12mm (½in) bias binding	2m (2¼yd)

Bread bag

Two contrasting Provençal fabrics	75 x 80cm (29½ x 31½in)
Lightweight polyester wadding	75 x 80cm (29½ x 31½in)
12mm (½in) bias binding	3m (3¼yd)

▶ Nestle your warm, buttered croissants in a basket made from two Provençal prints. The quilted wadding will prevent them from going cold, as well as add a touch of French flair to your breakfast table

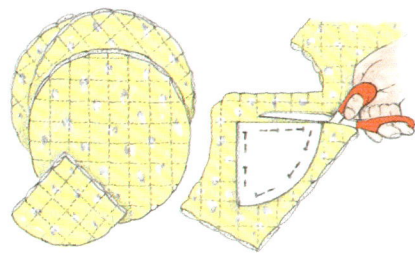

4 ▲ **Cut the fabric** Draw a 30cm (12in) diameter circle on a piece of paper, using a dinner plate. Cut this out, and use it as a template to cut three circles of quilted fabric. Next, fold the paper into four, and cut two quarter-circles from the remaining fabric.

▲ Now that you can quilt (following Steps 1–5), add a cheerful touch to your table with these mix and match table mats. Bound edges complement the rest of the range

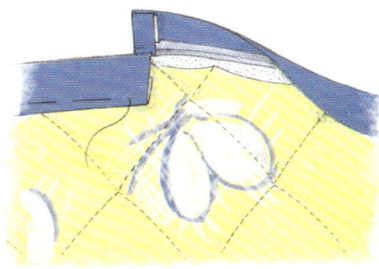

5 ▲ **Neaten the edges** Fold the wide bias binding in half and slip it over the cut edges of the circles and quarter-circles. Tack it in place, easing it around the curves. Make a neat, overlapped join by folding under the last 6mm (¼in) of binding, and wrapping it over the start point. Machine stitch close to the inside edge, making sure that you sew through all the layers.

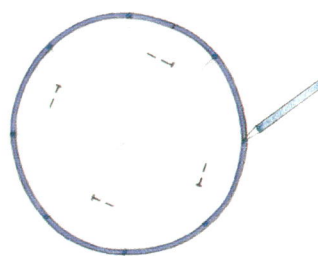

6 ▲ **Mark the divisions** Fold the template again, so that it now has eight equal segments. Using this as a guide, mark the centre point and eight divisions around the circumference on two of the fabric circles. Draw a line on one of the two quarter-circles to halve it.

7 ▲ **Join the circles** Place one of the marked circles on top of the unmarked one, with the same pattern facing upwards. Pin the edges together at every other mark, then secure with a few over-stitches. Pin the third circle on top of the second, with the same pattern facing upwards again, matching the marks. Oversew just these top two circles at the intervening four marks. Secure all three together at the centre point, working through all thicknesses.

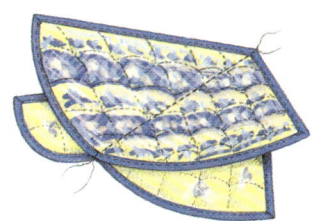

8 ▲ **Make the centre** Pin the marked quarter-circle to the unmarked one, with the same pattern

facing, and machine stitch them together along the centre line. Cut the narrow bias binding into eight 20cm (8in) lengths. Turn in the ends, then fold the binding in half lengthways, with wrong sides facing. Machine stitch along the edge and ends to make the ties. Sew one to each top corner of the quarter-circles.

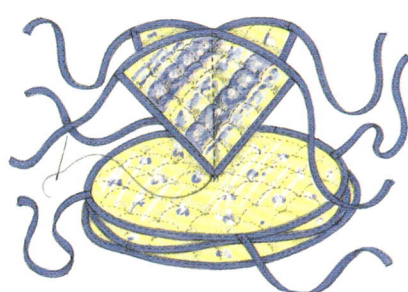

9 ▲ **Finish off** Sew the remaining four ties to the stitched points on the top circle. Place the quarter-circles on the top circle so that the ties line up, then sew the bottom point firmly to the middle, through all the layers. Fasten together by making the ties into bows, so that the quilted layers are drawn up to form individual compartments for your croissants, or bread rolls.

Making the bread basket

1 Quilt the fabric Prepare the layers of Provençal fabrics, sandwiched with polyester wadding, and quilt them, as described in Steps 1–3 of 'Making the croissant nest'.

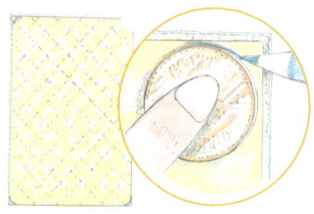

2 ▲ Curve the corners Draw around a large coin in each corner, and cut along the marked line to curve the corners. Neaten the cut edges with bias binding, as described in Step 5 of 'Making the croissant nest'.

3 ▲ Add the ties Cut the remaining bias binding into eight 15cm (6in) lengths. Turn in the ends, then fold the binding in half lengthways, with wrong sides facing. Machine stitch along the edge and ends to make the ties. Attach a tie, 5cm (2in) from each corner. Make two ties at each corner of the basket into a bow, so that the quilted Provençal fabric forms a basket-shaped container for your bread.

Making the bread bag

1 Prepare the fabric Cut the Provençal fabric and wadding into two rectangles, one 40 x 45cm (16 x 18in), the other 40 x 75cm (16 x 29½in). Mark, tack and quilt the fabric as in Steps 1–3 of 'Making the croissant nest'. Curve all the corners of the larger piece, and the bottom two corners of the smaller piece, as given for Step 2 of 'Making the bread basket'. Neaten the top short edge of the smaller piece with bias binding – see Step 5 of 'Making the croissant nest'.

2 ▲ Join the pieces Place the two pieces together, with wrong sides facing, and matching the bottom, curved-corner edges. Pin and tack together, then machine stitch, leaving a 12mm (½in) seam allowance. Trim the allowance back to 3mm (⅛in). Cover the cut edges with bias binding, making the join at the centre of the bottom edge.

3 ▲ Make the casing for the dowelling Fold the top 13cm (5¼in) of the back piece forwards, to make a flap. Pin along the fold, then mark a line 2.5cm (1in) down from the fold. Stitch along this line to form a casing.

4 ▲ Finish off Fix a screw-in eyelet to the centre of each end of the dowelling, then slide it inside the casing. Press the remaining bias binding in half lengthways, with wrong sides facing, and machine stitch together close to the edge. Tie one end to each eyelet, then ensure the casing covers the dowelling by slip-stitching it to the tie.

◄ *Hang up a bag and fill it with delicious French bread for sunny mealtimes. This olive and vine design evokes the true spirit of Provence*

cut-out creations

You don't have to be an expert to print fabric with your own range of exciting stencil designs

Stencilling fabric is so easy, and the results are nothing less than impressive – as seen in 'Start stencilling', p40, where you'll also find step-by-step instructions for getting the best results.

You can buy a variety of stencils in craft shops that will add a touch of flair to all sorts of fabric items around the home. But for added originality, you can also design and cut your own stencils from oiled manilla stencil card or acetate film. Card is the easiest to cut, but as film is transparent, it can be quicker to use when positioning a repeating stencil on the fabric.

Apply paint to the fabric with a sponge, brush, or spray depending on the effect you want to achieve and the fabric surface. The trick is to choose the right paint for the fabric and then use the correct applicator for the paint.

Sources of inspiration

Look all round you for designs – the ideas are limitless. Choose strong, easily identifiable outlines. Simple shapes are just as effective as more complex designs when grouped together. Glean floral patterns from wallpaper or gift wrap. Choose groups of flowers and leaves or large single blooms. Use individual flower motifs as a single striking design on a cushion cover or as a repeated pattern over a length of fabric. Clusters of tiny flowers look charming as a border along the edge of a valance, tablecloth or curtain. Animal or large geometric shapes are the best children's motifs.

Look at picture books, pick a favourite image and stamp it with your own individuality. Or make geometric stencils with the use of a set square and a pair of compasses. Simply use them to create a collection of interesting shapes. And, once you've chosen your design, enlarge or reduce it on a photocopier to fit your fabric area.

Choosing fabrics

The best fabrics for stencilling are the smooth-surface, closely woven natural variety, such as cotton, linen, muslin, calico and silk. These fabrics are predominantly used in soft furnishing projects anyway.

Stencilling is the ideal opportunity to turn an inexpensive natural fabric into a designer original.

Stencilling synthetic fabrics often proves disappointing as the fabric resists the paint, so producing pale uninteresting colours. It's best to avoid water-repellent and oily fabrics as they have difficult surfaces, while you must stretch and tape down flimsy material to prevent it from moving during the stencilling.

Heavily textured fabric gives a broken outline. So anticipate this problem when choosing your stencil and incorporate the effect into the design – go for a bolder motif which will be enhanced by an uneven surround.

Always wash and dry the fabric before you begin to remove any

treatments, then iron it smooth. When stencilling a ready-made item, such as a cushion cover, slide a sheet of card between the two layers of fabric to prevent the paint from seeping through onto the bottom layer.

Choosing fabric paints

Stencil paint must be thick enough to be absorbed by the fabric, without running. There are several permanent water-based fabric paints on the market and they come in a huge range of colours, as well as in black, white, gold and silver and in several finishes. Choose from matt, opaque, transparent or pearlized.

You can use fabric paint on most fabrics (check the instructions before you begin stencilling though, to avoid mistakes). They are fixed in place by ironing over paper. Once dry these paints leave the fabric soft and pliable ready for stitching, and you can launder them in the usual way.

You'll also find ranges of stencil paints and sticks in the shops, specifically designed and manufactured for use on fabric. Check any instructions supplied with these products before you begin. As these paints are produced for stencilling, they are ideal, being semi-dry and easy to apply.

Essentials
- Pencil
- Tracing paper
- Felt tip pens
- Fine permanent marker pen
- Stencil card or acetate film
- Cutting board
- Craft knife or scalpel
- Masking tape
- Carbon paper

Applying the paint

The drier the paint, the easier it is to apply to a fabric. To give some control, pour only a small amount of paint into an old plate or saucer. Then dip the sponge or brush into the paint. Dab off any excess paint on to a sheet of absorbent kitchen paper before you begin to work on the fabric. Use a quick dabbing movement to apply the paint through the stencil. Avoid brushing the paint as this causes it to seep under the edges and gives an indistinct outline.

Sponges
A sponge gives a soft, speckled finish when it's dabbed over the design. Sponges are a quick and easy way of applying several different paint colours, one on top of the other. You can also apply graduations of the same colour.

Brushes
Stencil brushes have stiff, square-cut bristles. You can buy them in a variety of sizes, so pick one that's suitable for the size of the stencil. Wash brushes between coats of different coloured paint and dry them with kitchen paper.

◄ *Gather together a selection of equipment, including paints in various colours, brushes and sponges, for your stencilling projects*

Marking out the stencil

1▲ Break down the outline Cover the image with tracing paper and break its outline down into a number of segments that create the design. Keep the shapes fairly bold and simple with a minimum of 3mm (⅛in) between them.

2▲ Preview the result To gauge the result, fill in the sections of the re-drawn stencil with felt tip pen in your chosen colours – this is how the stencil will look on the fabric.

3▲ Mark out the design Cut a piece of card or film at least 7.5cm (3in) larger than the design all round. For card, trace the design using carbon paper. Firmly secure the design and carbon paper to the card using strips of masking tape. Use a fine-

Cutting out the stencil

1 ▲ Secure the uncut stencil
Tape the uncut card or film to a cutting board using strips of masking tape. The best cutting surface is an artist's cutting mat which doesn't mark. It's available from specialist art and craft, or stationery, shops.

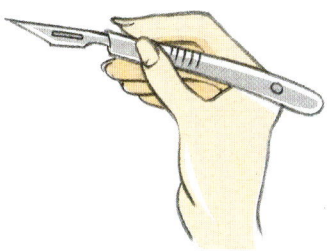

2 ▲ Hold the knife correctly Hold the craft knife or scalpel firmly in the same way as a pencil. Begin by cutting out the smallest shapes first as large cut areas will weaken the stencil and make it harder to cut out the intricate pieces afterwards.

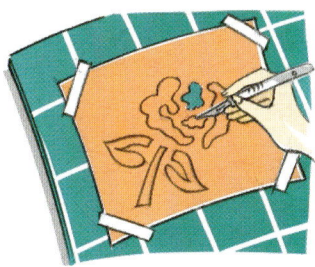

3 ▲ Cut out from the centre
Work from the centre of the design outwards, keeping firm, even pressure on the knife. Work in a smooth, continuous movement, with the blade of the knife coming towards you, and slightly manoeuvre the board to achieve an uninterrupted and continuous line. Rest your little finger on the board beside the knife to help guide it as you work.

tipped, hard pencil to go over the outline. For acetate film, simply trace the design outline straight on to the film using a fine permanent marking pen.

▲ *A simple leaf makes a distinctive motif on a patchwork quilt. Stencilling on plain and patterned squares adds variety*

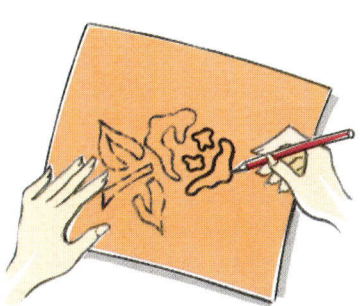

4 ▲ Complete the outline
Remove the design and carbon paper (if used). Go over the shapes with a fine permanent marking pen, neatening any outlines where necessary on the design.

checklist
Successful stencil cutting

- **Keep the knife sharp** To avoid snagged edges, change the blade of the knife often. If you have any dots or small holes, cut these last with a hole punch.
- **Knife angles** When cutting out stencil card, angle the knife away from the design as you work to gently bevel the edges. This will help prevent the paint from seeping under the rim of the stencil.
- **Corrections** If you make a mistake, seal the stencil on both sides with clear adhesive tape and cut out again. Any rough edges can be smoothed out later with fine abrasive paper.

1 *The bountiful harvest is evident in these stripes of different widths. Wheat sheaves, olive branches and ears of corn have a rural appeal*

2 *A rich, stylized floral pattern, set against a gold background, will add warmth and brightness to furnishings in a cool, north-facing living room*

3 *The warm, rusty red of this fabric's background typifies the feel of a French farmhouse kitchen. Quilting adds weight to the fabric and enhances its patterns*

4 *Broad panels of alternating sunflowers and olive branches, work well when interspersed with a small print in the same colours*

5 *Paler shades and small repeating patterns, such as this, blend with other larger, more-intricate ones to maximize the impact of Provençal fabrics*

● See 'A meal in Provençe', p115, for kitchen accessories with a French twist

French fancies

Evoke the taste and style of French country living, using cotton fabrics adorned with Provençal prints

Traditional Provençal motifs range from small, repeating patterns to large-scale, all-over fruit and floral designs. Other distinguishing features include vertical stripes in varying widths, each with their own distinctive pattern. It's easy to capture the intensity of Mediterranean sunlight in your home with the deep, earthy shades of the landscape – gold, blue, green, dark red, cream – used in colourful abundance.

Provençal prints are often associated with the heart of a French home – the kitchen. But with a little imagination, their beautiful variety works wonderfully in most living areas.

▶ A tablecloth with subtle fruits and flowers against a forest green background looks dramatic in a French country-style dining room

checklist
Provençal fabrics

● **Fibre content** Provençal designs are always printed on cotton. The fabric weight varies from mediumweight for curtains and accessories, to heavier furnishing fabrics for loose covers and more substantial projects.

● **Wash and wear** The woven cotton construction of Provençal prints makes them ideal for flinging in the washing machine – essential for tablelinen that is frequently stained. As the fabric will crease as it dries, always press it with a steam iron on a hot setting.

● **Neat seams** One of the drawbacks of woven fabrics is that they tend to fray easily unless the seams are neatened. A simple, no-sew solution once a seam is stitched is to trim any seam allowances with pinking shears. For a more-durable finish, oversew the two edges of the allowance with the zigzag attachment on your sewing machine.

5

big screen attraction

Whether a decorative cover-up for unsightly clutter, a clever room divider, or an optional window covering, a fabric screen can be a valuable addition to any room

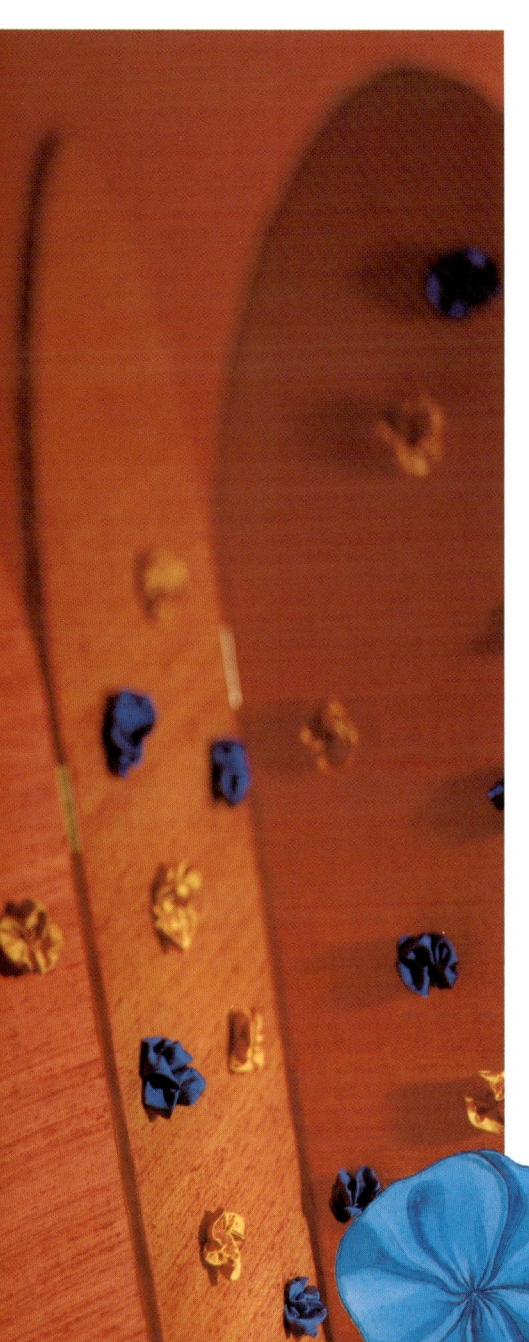

◀ *Jazz up a plain coloured screen with colourful rosettes made from silk ribbons*

▶ *Be bold and brave when choosing fabric for your screen. A flamboyant pattern and a rich colour that enhances, rather than blends into, the decor will turn your screen into the talking point of any room*

If you're stuck for a way of dividing your living space into two separate areas, forget about making structural changes and go for a more flexible option with a fabric screen. You can separate your sitting room from a dining area, for example, or a living room from a work space, simply by installing a screen. Screens can also provide an attractive cover-up for concealing children's toys, a messy desk or a laundry area.

Bargain hunters might want to try and track down a simple wooden frame in a junk or antique shop. Alternatively, you can use a modern ready-made chipboard or MDF (medium density fibreboard) blank screen as these have smooth edges that are easy to work with. It's also worth remembering that in nearly all cases, the easiest way to cover a screen is to separate the panels and cover them individually, then join them together again.

Effective touches

For the most striking results, choose a screen with a distinctive outline, such as one that has a pointed, rounded or scalloped top edge. You can even use two fabrics – one on either side of the screen – to give two contrasting aspects in a single room. Try covering separate panels in different but cleverly co-ordinating, fabrics for variety.

To give the screen a luxurious padded look, each panel is covered with a thin layer of interlining or lightweight wadding, with the outer fabric then tacked or stapled on top. For the final touch, finish the edges with a matching or contrasting braid.

Measuring and cutting guide

- **To calculate the amount of fabric**
  Modern screens usually have three panels and are approximately 150cm (60in) high. The panels measure about 40cm (16in) across the centre. This narrow width means that you can cut the front and back pieces from one width of soft furnishing fabric. To find out how much fabric you need, measure the panel length, adding 20cm (8in) for overlapping allowances and cutting out. Then multiply this figure by the number of panels in your screen. If you want to match a fabric across the whole screen, add one extra pattern repeat to each length when measuring.

- **Interlining**
  You'll need the same amount as for the fabric, minus 10cm (4in) since there are no overlaps.

- **Decorative braid**
  Its finished width should be slightly narrower than the depth of the panel. Measure the side and top edges of one panel, add 4cm (1½in) for neatening, and multiply by the number of panels.

- **Ribbon rosettes**
  You'll need approximately 50-60cm (19½-24in) of 4cm (1½in) wide ribbon for each rosette.

- **Fabric rosettes**
  You'll need a 17.5cm (7in) circle of fabric for each rosette.

Essentials
- Screen
- Paper for the pattern
- Smooth, thin curtain interlining or lightweight wadding
- Fabric
- Strong fabric adhesive
- Bradawl   • Braid   • Needle
- Wide ribbon, or oddments of silk fabric in several colours
- Sewing thread to match the ribbon rosette or fabric

Covering the screen

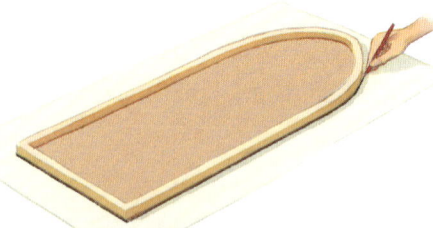

1 ▲ Make a paper pattern
Remove the hinges and separate the screen into individual panels. Cut a large piece of paper about 10cm (4in) longer than the panel. Place the panel on the paper and draw around it. Remove the panel and mark an allowance of 2.5cm (1in) all around the outline. Cut on the outside line.

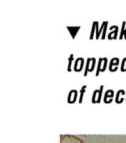

2 ▲ Cut out the fabric and interlining Pin the pattern on the fabric following the straight grain. Cut out one piece for the front of each panel on the outside line, then follow the same procedure for the back. Cut away or turn under the 2.5cm allowance on the paper pattern, then use it to cut out two pieces of interlining for each panel.

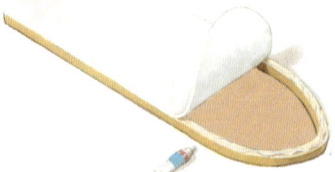

3 ▲ Attach the interlining Place one piece of interlining over the back of the panel, level with the outer edge. Turn back the edge of the interlining and glue in place all around the outer edge of the panel. Smooth it in place as you go, making sure it is taut. Attach the interlining to the front of the panel in the same way. Repeat with the remaining panels.

4 ▲ Cover the back Centre the first piece of fabric over the back of the first panel. Take the allowance over the base edge and temporarily hold it on either side of the centre with a couple of tacks (only hammer the tacks in half way). Smooth the fabric over the panel and temporarily fix the allowance in place on either side of the centre top edge in the same way. Repeat on each side edge. Check that the fabric is straight, then fully hammer the tacks in position into the panel edge.

▼ Make a real feature of your scallop-topped screen by adorning it with a row of decorative plates

5 ▲ **Shape the top** Continue to fix the allowance along the base edge, spacing the tacks or staples approximately 5cm (2in) apart. Pull the fabric taut and fix it around the top edge of the panel, working from the centre out to the sides. Snip into the allowance, or form small pleats to allow the fabric to lie flat around the shaped top.

6 **Stretch the fabric** Now tack the allowance down each side edge, working from the centre out to the top and base edges, stretching the fabric so that it lies straight and taut over the panel. Tuck under the extra fabric at each base corner, trimming off excess material as necessary, and tack in place.

7 **Cover the front** Turn the panel over and cover the front, tacking or stapling the front allowance over the back all around the edge of the panel. Make sure that you position the tacks between those already hammered in and that the fabric lies taut and straight. Repeat Steps 4–6, to cover each of the remaining panels.

8 ▲ **Add the braid edge** Beginning at one corner of the base edge, turn under the edge of the braid for 2cm (¾in) and stick it in place. Stick the braid along both side edges and around the top, covering the tacks and the fabric edge. Finish off at the base of the second side by turning under the cut edge of the braid and stick it in place. Add the braid to the remaining panels in the same way.

clever cover-up

TAKE ANOTHER LOOK

STAMP IT

Your screen doesn't need to be a big project. Make a small one with three panels to stand on a table and serve as a desk tidy. Then, when you've finished work for the day, you can hide all your clutter behind it.

First make up the screen, using a plain glazed cotton fabric. Then, with the panels complete, you can see where to position the stamped motifs. You might like to try a fleur de lys stamp, available in most craft shops,

stamping the pattern first in a dark colour, and then overstamping in a lighter tone (silver was used here). When stamping the first set of motifs, stick down a piece of masking tape to mark where the bottom left corner of the holder falls for each motif.

Allow these motifs to dry, then start on the second round of stamping. This time, off-set the design by stamping in a lighter colour, up and slightly to the right of the position marked with tape.

9 **Re-assemble the panels** Use the bradawl to pierce the braid and the underlying fabric at the hinge positions. Lay the panels right side up and side by side. Carefully fix the hinges back in place, making sure the panels align or the screen will topple over.

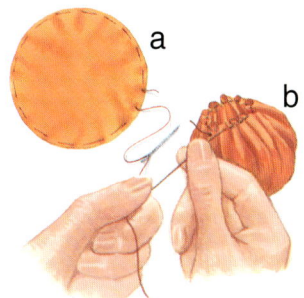

a

b

10 ▲ **Make the rosettes** Cut out a 17.5cm (7in) circle of fabric. Thread a needle and knot the thread at

the end. Work running stitches around the outer edge (a) and pull up the gathers to form a puffy ball shape (b). Work a few stitches on top of one another to secure the shape, then take the thread through to the front of the fabric and make a small stitch. Working from the right side, scrunch up the fabric and fasten it with tiny stitches, creating a crushed and puffy effect. Fasten off the thread. Make several rosettes in different-coloured fabrics and stick them randomly over the front of the screen.

blind
date

Screen off the outside world with new variations on a design classic – you'll find these blinds surprisingly straightforward to make

With ordinary blinds, the norm is to roll them up during the day to keep the windows entirely free. But shaped-edged blinds are a different story. We think you'll want to keep them at least part-way pulled down whatever the hour, to show off their interesting edges. But blinds in general have other advantages. For example, awkward shapes, such as a three-sided bay, can be hung with a series of narrow blinds – a much easier solution than curtains.

And depending on the fabric you choose, a blind can be used to block or filter daylight. A dark colour in a close weave will help to stop light seeping into a bedroom, particularly if it is hung behind curtains. For privacy, or to hide an unattractive view, a pale, thinner fabric allows the sun to shine through, and makes a modern alternative to nets.

Splash out

Roller blinds use much less fabric than curtains, which means you can splash out on an expensive material, or a dramatic print which may look overwhelming if gathered and draped. Linens, ticking and woven stripes, or ginghams are all suitable.

The selection will depend on your other furnishings, but choose a fabric that will not fray easily, or be too bulky when rolled up.

Using fabric stiffener

Before it is mounted, you should spray the blind with a special stiffener, to give it body and prevent fraying. If possible, do

this outside, following the manufacturer's instructions. Some materials may shrink slightly when they are treated, so spray a piece first to test its suitability, and adjust the final measurements accordingly.

Fitting is easy

All the necessary components for mounting roller blinds can be bought in kit form. The pole, or roller, comes in various sizes; buy one that is longer than you need, and cut it down. One end is fitted with a round metal cap, containing the spring-loaded mechanism that works the blind. The second cap is fixed in place with a special round pin. You'll also find two special brackets: one has a slot for a spring, the other has a socket in which the pin rotates. The wooden lath which weights the blind, the cord, cord holder and 'acorn' are also provided.

◄ *Roller blinds are very effective for dressing narrow windows and side panels. Experiment with shapes for the lower edge before you start. Either use a small section of the larger blind, or make a simpler, complementary scallop*

Measuring and cutting guide

a

b

- **To calculate the width**
  Width = length of finished pole, or roller, minus 2.5cm (1in) or, plus 4cm (1¼in) if using a fine fabric
- **To calculate the length**
  Length = 20cm (8in) longer than drop to be covered
- **To position the blind**
  Before cutting out the fabric, fix the brackets in place. Their position depends on the shape of your window; it should be fitted within a recess, close to the glass (a), or flush to the frame of a window that is not recessed (b). In this case, add an 5cm (2in) all round.

Making the blind

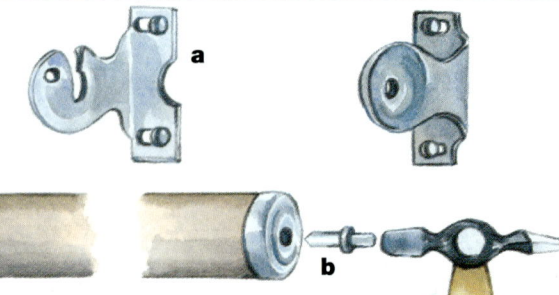

1 ▲ Fix the brackets and roller
For a recessed window, screw the brackets to the wall 4cm (1½in) from the top of the recess – make sure that they are level – with the slotted bracket (a), on the right-hand side. For other window types, mount the brackets on the frame, or on to a batten above the window.

Using a metal ruler, measure the distance between the brackets and deduct 2.5cm (1in). Saw the pole to this length. Hammer the second metal cap carefully in place, without putting any pressure on the spring. Check that the roller fits correctly, and will turn smoothly when in use.

◄ *Red and white gingham brings a freshness to a kitchen. If you have a piece of furniture with a shaped edge, such as the dresser in the picture on the left, echo this in the shape of your roller blind*

2 ▲ Cut the fabric The blind must be cut square along the grain (ie at right angles to the woven side edges), or it will not hang properly. Use a metal ruler and a set square to draw the exact shape on to the wrong side of the fabric. Centre the pattern, or ensure that the stripes or checks are straight. Make a 2cm (¾in) single seam along each side edge, if needed, and zigzag stitch along to cover the cut edges.

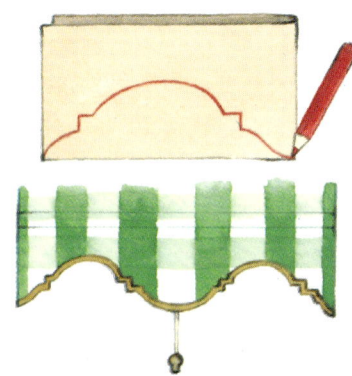

3 ▲ Cut out the template
Cut a strip of paper to the exact width of the blind and the depth of the finished edging. For an arabesque shape (like ours), fold it in half and draw on one half section of the design. Cut along the line and open out.

Essentials

- Main fabric
- Lining fabric for shaped edge
- Matching sewing thread
- Fabric stiffener
- Roller blind mounting kit
- Rawlplugs or wooden batten and screws
- Hacksaw   • Hammer
- 6mm (¼in) tin tacks (if not supplied with kit)
- Dressmaker's pencil
- Bias binding or decorative braid
- Iron-on bonding material

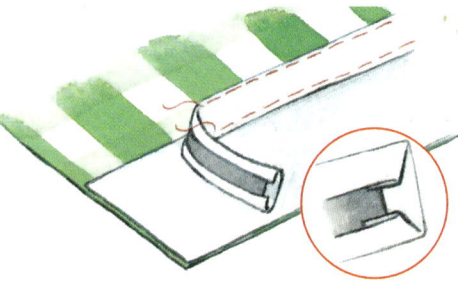

4 ▲ Add the facing Cut the lining fabric and the iron-on bonding material to the same size as the border. Using a cotton setting, iron the bonding material to the wrong side of the lining; peel off the backing. Place the lining along the bottom of the blind, with wrong sides facing, and iron it in place.

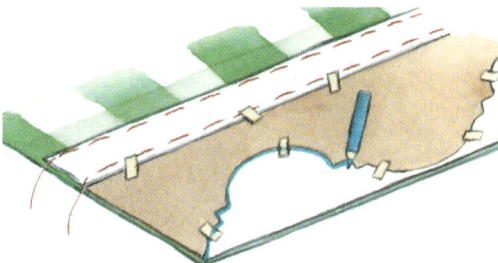

5 ▲ Make the casing Cut a 6cm (2¼in) strip of lining, 2.5cm (1in) wider than the blind. Press under 12mm (½in) on each edge and machine stitch to the wrong side, so that it covers the top edge of the facing. Leave the short ends open.

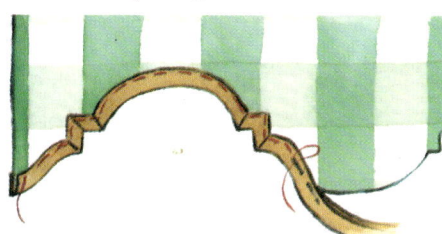

6 ▲ Cut the edging Tape the template to the wrong side of the lower edge, and draw around it with a dressmaker's pencil, or fading pen. Cut carefully along the marked line.

7 ▲ Bind the edge Enclose the cut lower edges with a bias binding strip – choose a matching or contrast colour. Alternatively, sew on a decorative border,

TAKE ANOTHER LOOK

pointed hem

Create a heavenly effect with this starry fabric blind. The fine, slightly sheer fabric looks wonderful against a night-time sky.

1 Make up the blind following Steps 1, 2 and 5. At this stage, press the blind well and spray to stiffen it.

2 Following Step 3 make a template for a dramatic deep-pointed edge. Now that the fabric has been stiffened, you can cut it without any danger of fraying.

3 For a fabulous finishing touch, add crystal teardrop beads to accentuate the points, and help to weigh down the points.

as a finishing touch. First pin, then sew the binding in position. Make neat corners along the shaped edge by folding the binding into diagonal lines.

8 ▲ Fix the blind to the roller Place the blind, right side up, across the roller with the round pin on the left. Tape the top edge along the marked guide line on the roller, with the ends against the metal caps, then hammer in the tacks at 2.5cm (1in) intervals. Cut the lath (the weighting batten at the lower

edge) 2cm (¾in) narrower than the blind, and slip it in place. Press the blind well and spray it with stiffener.

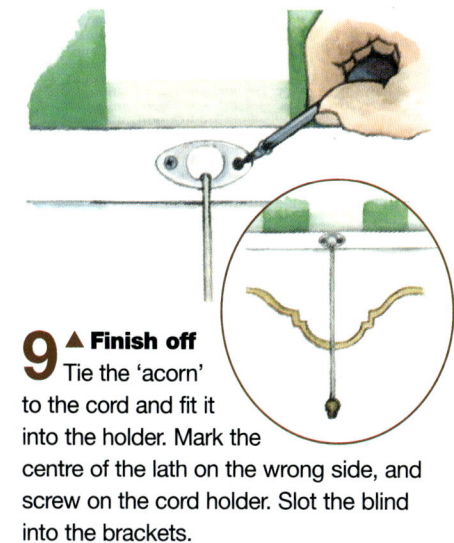

9 ▲ Finish off Tie the 'acorn' to the cord and fit it into the holder. Mark the centre of the lath on the wrong side, and screw on the cord holder. Slot the blind into the brackets.

step on it

Brighten up your bath time with this vibrantly coloured,
springy mat. Make it with a minimum of fuss and stitching

Give your bathroom an instant update by making a modern version of an old-time favourite – a rag rug. Plaiting (or braiding) is the simplest of three methods that can be used – and not only is it satisfying to do, but it's very quick and easy too.

In the past

Rag rugs date from the Shaker people of 18th-century America. Shaker style is now a popular minimalist – almost stark – look of simple wooden furniture and plain interiors. Shaker people traditionally used whatever was at hand to make these economical floor coverings, so you are echoing their thriftiness in making your own rug. Use a rag rug in a room which has its own simplicity, such as a bedroom, bath or shower room. Or, instead of towelling, use woven fabrics and work a rug in bright colours and patterns to complement a country style interior.

A modern concept

Towelling is perfect for a bathroom mat; it's absorbent, easy to work with and soft on your feet. Then you can fling it in the washing machine and hang it on the line to dry. Although, in the true tradition of the craft, you should ideally tear up your old towels for the braiding ribbons, it's more effective to buy towels, or towelling fabric, in the colours you have chosen to suit the look of your bathroom.

You'll love today's braided mats for their textured appearance, colour effects – and the speed at which they can be made (just allow yourself some free time at the weekend and relax with some peaceful plaiting).

Experiment by mixing different fabrics together, but make sure that they're all the same weight and pre-shrunk before you begin the plaiting. Or, try a different effect with clever colour tricks – shades of a single colour and similar tones, such as all pastels, or various bright colours. Using printed fabrics along with plain ones adds another dimension – see the next page.

Essentials

- 3 towels, each about 85 x 150cm (33 x 60in)
- Scissors
- Pins
- Darning needle
- Matching strong sewing thread

Making the oval mat

1 ▲ Cut the strips Buy the towels in three complementary colours. Trim off the woven edges and any bands that sometimes decorate the ends of towels. Cut strips about 7.5cm (3in) wide along the length of each towel. Fold each strip into three lengthways, tuck under the cut edge on the final fold, and secure it with a running stitch that just catches into the folded fabric, but doesn't go right through the strip.

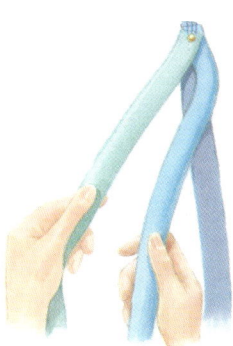

2 ▲ Prepare to plait With the neat, folded edges underneath, place strips in each colour, one on top of the other, and secure them with a few large stitches. Attach the strips at the central point with a drawing pin to a pinboard, or piece of hardboard, so that your hands are free for plaiting.

▲ *Give your feet a treat with a super-soft, braided bath mat in three zingy colours to match your existing towels and bathroom accessories*

3 ▲ Plait the strips Make sure that the strips don't twist; always work with the neat, folded edges of the strip underneath. Bring the left-hand strip into the centre, then bring the right-hand strip into the centre. Continue in this way, bringing alternate strips into the centre, to form the plait. Keep the plait flat and even throughout.

4 ▶ Start to coil

Pin the working ends of the plait together to stop it unwinding. Thread a darning needle with a double length of strong thread. Remove the drawing pin and start to coil the plait around on itself, tucking under the flat section at the start of the plait as you set the shape. Initially the coil will look slightly rectangular at the centre, but shape it into an oval by winding longer flat strips at the sides with rounded ends.

5 ▲ Stitch in place

You'll need to stitch the plaits to secure them as you go along. Place the mat on a flat surface and work on the wrong side. Hold the coils in place with large slip-stitches worked through several layers of the fabric. Watch the tension of the stitches: too tight and the rug won't lie flat, too loose and the plaits won't be held firmly together.

6 ▲ Join in extra lengths

Make sure you are joining only one new length at a time – if necessary trim the lengths to be sure of this. Position your new strip so the join will lie underneath the plait. Turn under the raw edge of the new strip and place it over the old strip. Secure it with a few tiny slip-stitches along the top.

TAKE ANOTHER LOOK

using woven fabrics

Create a colourful rag rug like this one out of woven fabrics instead of towelling. It will make a homemade statement that blends with both a traditional or modern bathroom.

The rags can be easily plaited into circular or oval mats. You are spoilt for choice as far as colours are concerned because there are so many fabrics – both printed and plain – available in the shops. In this instance, you'll be able to re-use old fabrics such as printed furnishings and dresses (look for bargains in charity shops). Pick colours which will harmonize with your room scheme.

Starting a circle

First make your plaiting strips – here left-over dress fabrics replace the towelling. Secure the thread at the end of the plait. Run the thread through each plait in turn, then back to the starting point. Pull tight to form a coil, then continue from Step 5 in 'Making the oval mat'.

7 ▶ Finish off

On one of the long sides of the oval mat, taper the plait into the side, so that the end is hidden underneath. Neaten the cut ends of each strip by turning under 1cm (½in) and oversewing to the previous row, on the wrong side. Neaten any loose threads on the wrong side of the mat.

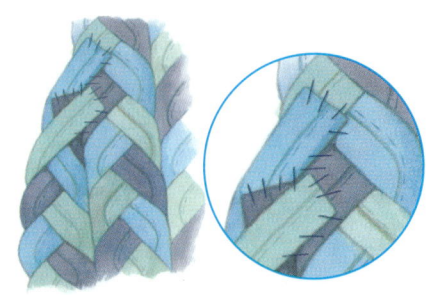

a room for living

Today's living room needs to be multi-purpose, yet retain its essence as a space in which to relax and unwind

The living room can have many roles – it can be a place for entertaining friends; for quietly watching TV or listening to music. Some living rooms have to double as dining room, study, children's playroom or home office. When planning your living room, it's important to look carefully at how you, and your family, use the room and what kind of activities will take place there now, and in the future.

Making plans

Make a scale plan of your room, with paper cut-outs of the furniture you need to fit in. Try alternative arrangements of seating, tables, storage. This will give you an idea of what is physically possible before you start to buy new furniture or move things around.

If you need a multi-purpose room, think about how you can

Crown

Dulux

◄ Sunny style
Fabrics in strong, modern colours, a checked blanket draped over a chair as a throw, and appliqué cushions give this living room an up-to-date but comfortable feel

▲ Natural focus
A contemporary scheme takes the fireplace as its focus. In calming natural colours and fabrics and with single chairs grouped facing the 'fire', it is ideal for relaxing

define the different areas. Storage or shelving units can help to screen off a section used as a study or home office.

Even how you treat the floor can visually separate the different areas of a dual-purpose room, for example using durable wood, cork, lino or vinyl in a dining area, with softer carpet or rugs in the sitting area. If the children play in the room by day, have plenty of large baskets, boxes, or cupboards to stow away the toys when you want to transform the room back into a grown-up space.

Comfort zone

If a room is to be relaxing, comfort needs to be at the top of your list. When you are buying a new sofa or chair check that the arms and back are the correct height for you and make sure the seat depth and height don't leave you with your feet dangling uncomfortably off the ground. You can buy sofas in three basic sizes: two-, two-and-a-half- and three-seaters. Make sure that the size you choose works with the size of the room.

Consider two smaller sofas instead of a traditional three-piece suite. Think about what kind of seating arrangement – L-shaped; facing sofas; or a mix of occasional chairs and a sofa – suits the room. If the sofa has to double as a bed for guests, buy a specific sofa bed. Check that the opening mechanism is easy to operate and that it is comfortable both as a bed and a sofa.

Smarten up a favourite old sofa with a new cover, or transform it with a stylish throw. Blend new and old furniture with toning upholstery fabrics.

Create a focus

Grouping furniture around the fireplace gives a room a natural, and traditional focus. But if you don't have one, you can still create a focal point with perhaps a special picture, a clever window treatment, or even a dramatic house plant.

The way you store the natural clutter of a living room can also provide a focus for the room, with

Laura Ashley

Ikea

▲ Mix and match
Give a traditional seating option of sofa and two chairs a modern country feel with different, but complementary, upholstery fabrics. Cushions help to pull the colour scheme together

◄ A place for everything
This living room doubles as a library with impressive wall-to-wall shelving. The chair offers a comfortable place to sit and read, listen to music, or watch TV

▶ **Simple storage**

Simple white shelves provide stylish storage in this contemporary living room. A checked sofa and rattan chairs continue the informal feel

Ikea

▼ **Fill the alcoves**

A good way of making use of the alcoves flanking a fire-place, these built-in shelves can house books, magazines, ornaments, CDs, videos and stereo system

▶ **Studious corner**

A small desk and chair, tucked into the corner of this living room, offers a quiet place to sort out the household accounts, or write letters

stylish contemporary, or antique free-standing storage shelves and bookcases, or built-in cupboards.

Good lighting works wonders for atmosphere. Aim for several sources as you may need soft background lighting for watching TV, plus more specific task lighting for more close-up work. Think about adding table lamps, up-lighters, wall lights, and dimmer switches, which will allow you to adjust the light level.

Elizabeth Whiting & Associates

A living style

Resist the temptation to make the living room into a showroom. If you have one basic room, go for an informal approach which suits your main lifestyle. Add character with accessories, cushions and throws to ring the changes. And to keep the look fresh change your accessories with the seasons – warm colours and rich textures in winter, cooler colours and lighter fabrics for the summer.

- **For step-by-step instructions on how to create a dramatic mood with lighting in your living room, see 'Natural shades', p35.**

Elizabeth Whiting Associates

all taped up

For perfectly hung curtains every time, make sure that you use the right heading tape for the look you want, the fabric and the weight of the curtains. There is a wide range to choose from and they all give your curtains a professional – and speedy – finish

Tracks, poles and heading tapes all play a part in the effect your curtains have on your room. Heading tape is a strong strip of fabric in varying widths with integral drawstrings for pulling up the curtain to the required width. There's a wide variety of tapes to choose from and most fabric shops will help match the tape to your fabric weight.

When stitching the tapes in place make sure that all the 'pockets' are correctly positioned for your track or pole. Pull up the drawstrings evenly but do not cut them off. Tie them securely and loop out of sight. Insert hooks every 8-10cm (3-4in), or as needed for the pleat, and your curtains are ready to hang.

Standard Tape

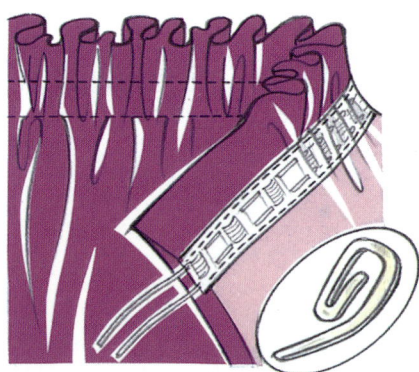

The cheapest and simplest form of heading tape, standard tape merely gathers the fabric. It works best with lightweight, unlined curtains in kitchens and bathrooms. As it is not decorative, it is the choice for under pelmets where it won't be seen. Just 1½ to 2 times the track length is needed with this tape.

Triple Pleat Tape

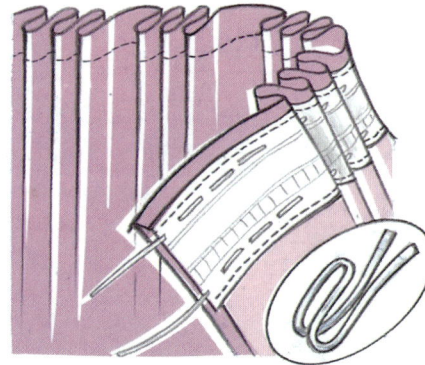

This tape pulls up into evenly-spaced groups of three pleats. Stitch the tape in place from where the two curtains individually meet so that the tops match across each curtain. Allow twice the track length for each curtain.

Pencil Pleat Tape

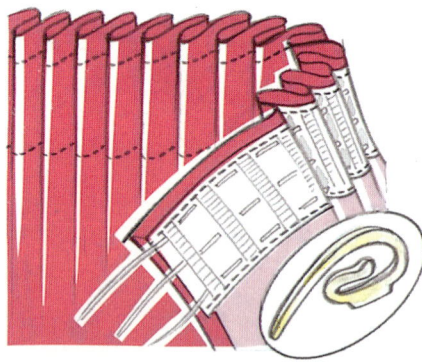

This is possibly the most popular of all the curtain heading tapes. It pulls the fabric up into neat, evenly spaced pencil pleats. It is available in a variety of widths and is suitable for use on most fabrics, and on lined or unlined curtains. Between 2¼ and 2½ times the track length is needed for this tape.

Goblet Pleat Tape

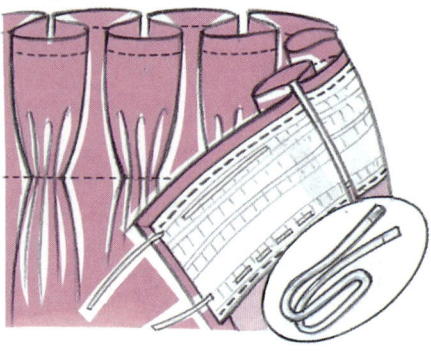

When fitted with this tape, and with the strings pulled up, the curtain heading forms deep pleats with open tops, which look a bit like goblets. The effect is fairly formal. You will need about 2¼ times your track length for this tape.

Box Pleat Tape

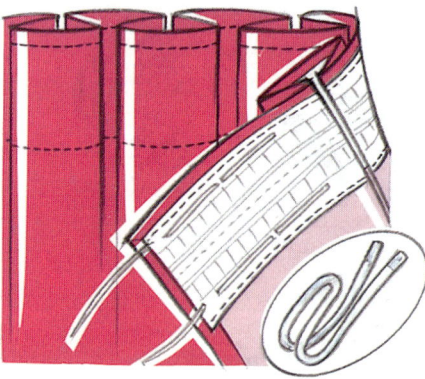

When this tape is pulled up, the curtain folds into neat box pleats. The pulled-up heading must match across adjoining widths, so allow for this when calculating fabric amounts. You will need roughly 3 times the track length.

Cordless Triple Pleat Tape

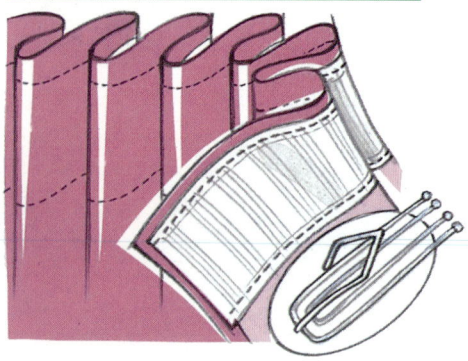

There are no cords with this tape as the hook creates the pleat, so you can position your pleats as you want. You'll need twice your track length of fabric.

it's a wind-up

These sumptuous padded tie-backs are a breeze to make. Simply wind three fabric tubes around one another to make a decorative plait

Curtain tie-backs not only add a touch of class to a room, they are practical too. By holding the fabric back from the window they let in the maximum amount of light, create an attractive line for the curtain and can be made in any number of styles.

Padding it out

Plaited tie-backs are made from padded tubes of fabric and make an interesting alternative to more traditional styles. Part of the charm of the plaiting technique is that you can use the same colours or patterns for all three strands, pick out a single shade in the curtain fabric for one strand only, or mix and match.

You can create a variety of effects using tie-backs, depending on where they are positioned and how much fabric there is in your curtains to gather up. Use heavy tie-backs for curtains with plenty of body and less obvious styles if your window is on the small side, or if your curtains are only very slightly gathered.

▶ *Highlighting the main colours from your curtain fabric in the tie-back plait creates an integrated look*

Measuring and cutting guide

- *Each tie-back requires three tubes and each tube needs to be cut 10cm (4in) wide by 1.5 times the finished length of the plait.*
- *To calculate the length of your plaits, measure the distance from the wall hooks (for securing the tie-backs by the rings at their ends) around the drawn-back curtains with a flexible tape measure. Adjust the drape to your liking and then add an extra 5cm (2in) to allow for the seams.*

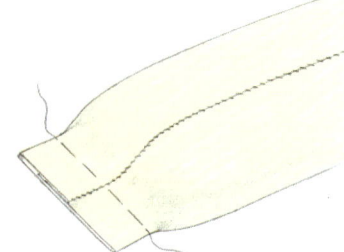

3▲ Finish the edges On the remaining long edge of the lining, turn under 1cm (⅜in) and slip-stitch to the roll (work small, neat stitches across the gap, sliding the needle through the folded edge). Tack across both ends of the roll, using neat stitches.

Essentials

- *Main fabrics*
- *Matching sewing thread*
- *Lining fabric*
- *Lightweight wadding*
- *Length of fine cord*
- *Large-eyed blunt needle or bodkin*
- *Four small brass curtain rings*
- *Scissors*
- *Pins*

◄ *Three Provençal fabrics in contrasting colours and patterns lighten the effect of this heavy navy blue curtain*

Making the tie-backs

1 Cut the materials Cut the main fabrics to the calculated sizes, following the guide above, then cut three lining strips 15cm (6in) wide and the same length as the main fabrics. Cut three strips of wadding 12cm (4¾in) wide and 4cm (1½in) shorter than the main fabric.

4▲ Attach the cord to the main fabric Secure a length of cord to the right side of the main fabric by hand stitching it to one short end, making sure it is slightly to one side, rather than central, as shown.

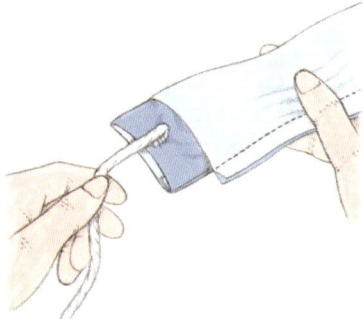

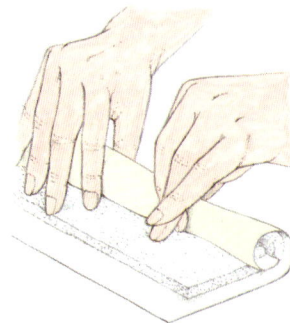

2▲ Make the padded roll Line up one long edge of wadding with one long edge of lining, so there is the same amount of fabric showing at each end. Then roll the lining and the wadding together to make a tube.

5▲ Make the fabric tube With the right sides together, fold the fabric in half lengthways and machine stitch the long edges together with cut edges matching. Pull the cord through the tube, so that you turn the tube through to the right side. Unpick the stitches and release the cord.

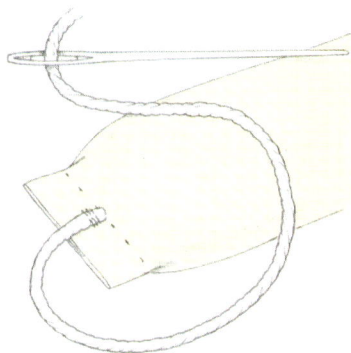

6 ▲ Attach the cord to the padded roll Secure the cord to one end of the padded roll by working a few stitches, then thread the loose end of the cord through a large-eyed blunt needle or bodkin.

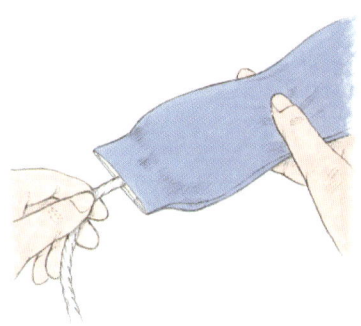

7 ▲ Complete the tube Insert the blunt needle into the fabric tube and pull the padded roll through. Once the padded roll is fully inserted into the fabric tube, cut the cord close to the stitching line. Repeat Steps 2 to 7 to make two more padded strips.

8 ▲ Make the plait Slightly overlapping the ends of each tube so they do not lie directly on top of one another, machine stitch through all three layers to secure them together. Then make the plait by winding the tubes around each other, check it for size around your curtains, and stitch the other end to match the first.

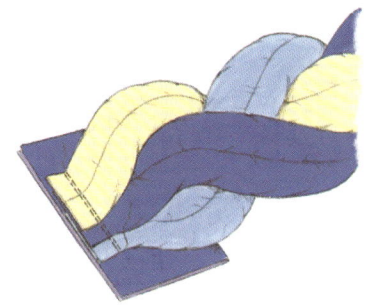

9 ▲ Bind the end Cut a 10cm (4in) square from one of the fabrics used to make the tubes, and with wrong sides together, fold it in half. Place the plait centrally along the cut edges of the folded fabric square and machine stitch through all the thicknesses.

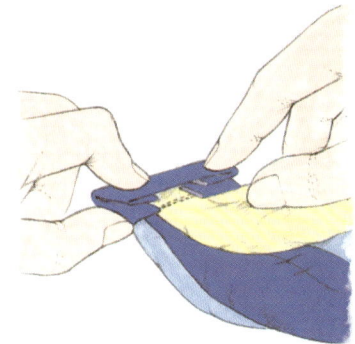

10 ▲ Finish the binding Turn the folded square over the end of the plait and fold in the side edges, then slip-stitch both sides and the final edge in place.

◄ Tartan tones on a dark curtain create a smart, formal effect suitable for dining room or hall curtains

use raffia

For a quick and easy natural-look tie-back with a touch of wit, use raffia and decorate with shells and other seaside accessories.

1 Take three braids of natural raffia (available from craft shops) and loosely plait them together.

2 Choose a variety of interesting seaside motifs, such as shells and starfish. Tie them on to the plait with a single length of raffia.

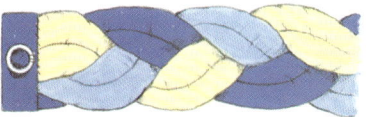

11 ▲ Complete the tie-backs On the wrong side of each completed tie-back, blanket stitch the curtain rings to the centre of the short edges (one ring on each edge), 2cm (¾in) from the end.

tied and trusted

*Plain wooden chairs take on a bright, contemporary look when
they are dressed up in new fabric. Transform your dining area
with these tie-on squab cushions and chair-back covers*

◀ *Choose a fabric colour to match your decor to integrate your chairs with the rest of your room*

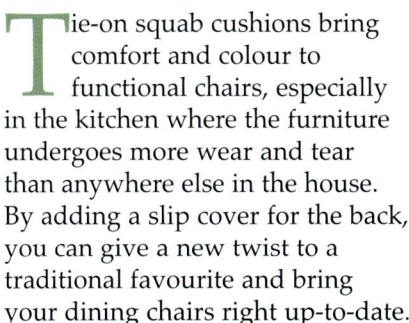

▼ *A plain hard-backed chair loses its harsh outlines with a tie-on cushion. The extra-long lashed ties complete the country feel*

Tie-on squab cushions bring comfort and colour to functional chairs, especially in the kitchen where the furniture undergoes more wear and tear than anywhere else in the house. By adding a slip cover for the back, you can give a new twist to a traditional favourite and bring your dining chairs right up-to-date.

Fabrics and fillings

Choose linens and cottons which match or contrast with your other soft furnishings. Try making cushions from the same fabric to bring together a collection of assorted chairs, or make a formal set look more individual by sewing each cover in a different shade. A piped edging or a pleated frill adds a personal touch.

A squab is made to fit the seat exactly, so its shape will vary according to the design of your chair. If it's square and the back of the seat is straight, you can use a ready-made pad inside the cover. Feather cushions will squash up to fit and come in many different sizes. The filling will settle with use, so it needs to be plumped up from time to time.

If the back struts project into the seat so that the corners of the cushions have to be cut out, or if it is rounded at the front edge, you may prefer to make a more tailored pad from upholstery foam. This is not difficult – the foam can be easily cut with large scissors. Purchase sheets of foam from good furnishing suppliers or quite often an upholstery workshop will supply foam to the public.

Easy to clean

Cushion covers will need to be cleaned, so it's important that they are easy to remove. When making up the cushion, leave a gap in the back seam for the pad. Close the seam by hand with a neat slip-stitch (bring the needle through the folded edge at one side of the seam, across the gap and along the opposite folded edge). Simply unpick the seam when the cover needs to be cleaned.

Cutting a template

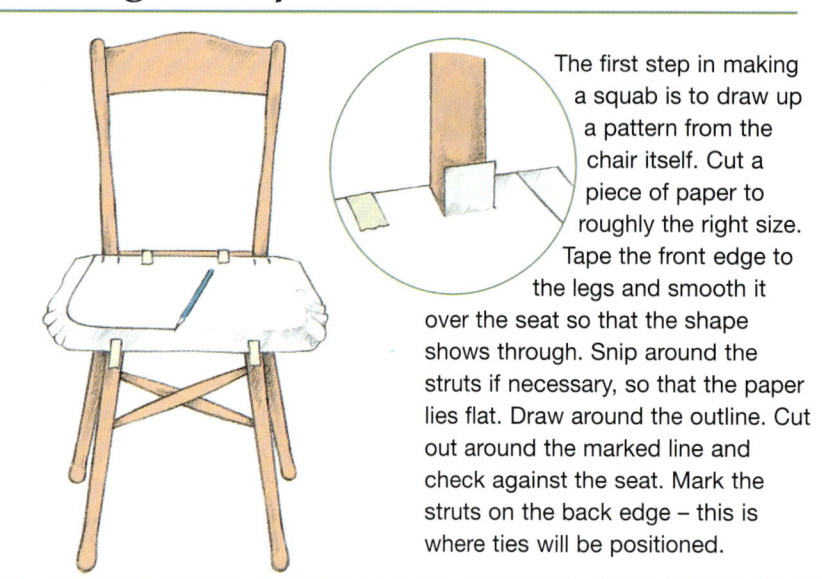

The first step in making a squab is to draw up a pattern from the chair itself. Cut a piece of paper to roughly the right size. Tape the front edge to the legs and smooth it over the seat so that the shape shows through. Snip around the struts if necessary, so that the paper lies flat. Draw around the outline. Cut out around the marked line and check against the seat. Mark the struts on the back edge – this is where ties will be positioned.

Measuring and cutting guide

- **For the front and back**
  Cut two identical pieces from the template, adding 2.5cm (1in) all around. For a thick pad, allow an extra 2cm (¾in).
- **For the ties** *(Cut four)*
  For a tie that is 12mm (½in) finished width, cut a 5cm (2in) wide strip. Tie a tape measure in a loose bow around the chair leg to find the required length, halve this figure for one tie, then add an extra 2cm (¾in) for the seams.

Essentials
- Fabric
- Matching sewing thread
- Cushion pad to fit seat or foam sheet cut to size from template
- Paper and pencil
- Masking tape
- Safety pin
- Pins

Ring the changes – tie your cushions on to the back of the chairs instead

Making the cushion

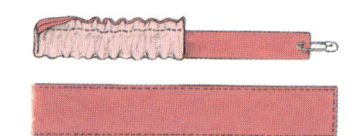

1 ▲ Make up the ties Fold the tie strip in half lengthwise with right sides facing. Pin and stitch along the long edge, taking a 12mm (½in) seam allowance. Trim the seam to 6mm (¼in). Fasten a safety pin to one end and push this back through the tube to turn it right side out. Turn in 5mm (¼in) on one cut end and press the tie so the seam lies along the top. Top-stitch around all three sides, 3mm (⅛in) from the edge. Make three more ties.

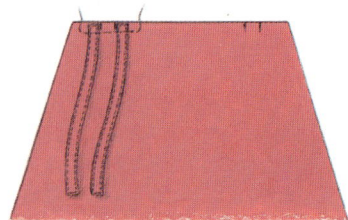

2 ▲ Position the ties Lay the template on the right side of one cushion piece. Use it as a guide to pin and tack the ties in place so that the cut edges line up – one each side of a cut-out corner or one on either side of a strut.

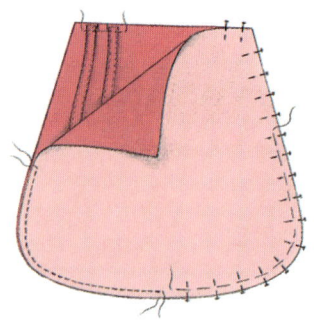

3 ▲ Join the back and front pieces Pin and tack the back and front together with right sides facing, taking care not to catch the loose ends of the ties. Machine stitch 1.5cm (½in) from the edge, leaving an opening for the cushion pad along the back, between the two inside ties. Sew an extra line of reinforcing stitching over the area where all the ties are attached.

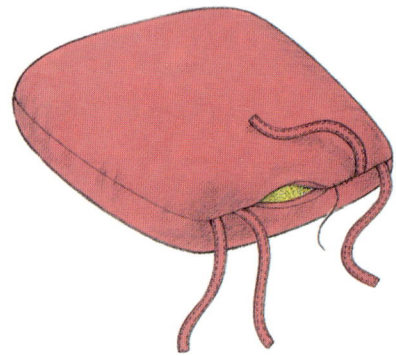

4 ▲ Finish off Make a cut into each corner (being careful not to snip the stitching) and cut tiny 'V's out of the seam allowance on the curves so that the cushion seam is smooth when turned right side out (see Step 3 opposite). Turn right side out. Fold in the seam allowance on the back edge, insert the cushion pad and slip-stitch the opening to close. Tie the cushion on to the chair.

add a bow

For a quick alternative, simply buy a ready-covered cushion and add a lavish fabric bow tie.

1 For each tie, cut two pieces of a matching fabric to the required length and width. Remember, the longer the tie, the wider it should be. Cut a diagonal line across the ends. Place the two pieces together with right sides facing and seam around all edges, leaving a small opening in one seam.

2 Clip the corners and turn the ties through to the right side. Slip-stitch the opening and then sew the centres of the ties on to the back corners of the cushion. Tie the cushion on to the chair, making large floppy bows.

▲ *Nothing could be simpler than slipping this chair-back cover over a straight-backed chair. Once you learn how to cut a template, the same steps can be used for any shape of chair-back*

Making the chair-back cover

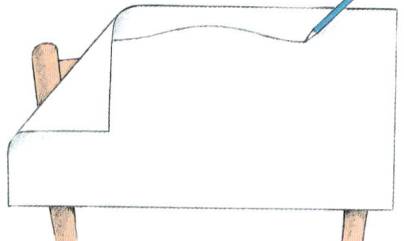

1 ▲ **Make a template** Lay a piece of paper over the top of the chair and trace the shape. Decide how deep you want the cover to be and mark the template to this length. Add on 1.5cm (½in) all around, plus an extra 2–5 cm (¾–2in) depending on the thickness of the chair-back. Make sure that the cover will fit easily over the chair. Cut two pieces from fabric.

2 ▲ **Join the pieces** With right sides facing, pin and tack the front and back pieces together around the side and top edges. Slip the cover over the chair itself to check the fit, and adjust the seams. Machine stitch together, taking a 1.5cm (⅝in) seam allowance. Cut the 'V's into the curves as described for the cushion.

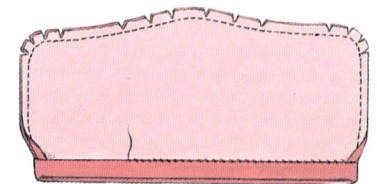

3 ▲ **Neaten the edge** Turn under and press a 12mm (½in) double hem around the open edge (turn under 12mm (½in), then 12mm (½in) again). Slip-stitch the hem in place. Turn the cover right side out and press the hem crisply, then press the curved seam lightly, easing the fabric into shape.

◄ **Tight finish**
For a snug fit, you need to glue the fabric in place. First, lay the pot on its side on the wrong side of the fabric. Mark the beginning point at the top of the pot, and trace the shape with a pencil while rolling the pot round and back to the beginning. Cut out the shape, allowing extra fabric along the top and bottom edges for folding under the base and into the inside at the top. Glue the fabric on to the pot, tucking the excess out of sight. Make a matching fabric bow (see 'In the frame', p158), then glue it to the front of the pot

ready-wrapped

Wrap a fabric remnant around a flowerpot or vase and tie it up to transform an ordinary container into a stunning style statement

A fabric covering works wonders for a humble container. Rummage in your remnants to reveal what you have at hand, then you can either wrap the fabric loosely round the pot, or glue it snugly in place.

Fabric wraps are ideal for jazzing up a boring plastic container, covering a damaged pot, disguising a vase, or simply creating a colourful gift. Set a potted plant, or bunch of flowers, inside your decorated pot, or use it as a storage jar for kitchen utensils, pencils or paintbrushes.

Bright felt glued to large pots and decorated with cut-outs makes great storage jars for kids' rooms.

Fancy fabrics

Choose the fabric to suit your room, highlight the colours of a bouquet or for a special celebration. Metallized organza, tied with silver or gold ribbon, is the perfect wrap for an anniversary; or white brocade tied with silk ribbons for a wedding. Study your leftover fabrics and ribbons, seek inspiration here – and you'll be raring to get wrapping!

Make it!

Dress your pots for special occasions with sheer fabrics, such as plain-dyed muslin and nets, and contrasting bows. Choose a contrasting ribbon, either in a pretty chiffon to continue the sheer theme, or double-sided satin for a touch of luxury. Our instructions on the right describe how to make the wrapped pots pictured below.

1▲ Net-wrapped pot To create this frothy effect, simply measure your chosen vase or pot and cut two squares of net, in contrasting colours, large enough to completely cover it. Set one square on top of the other, at an angle, and secure them with a bright chiffon ribbon, tied in a bow.

2▲ Muslin-wrapped pot For an attractive ruffle around the top of your pot, cut two circles of coloured muslin, one 5cm (2in) larger in diameter than the other. Pink the edges and place the smaller circle on top of the larger one. Stand the pot in the centre, then tie the fabrics around the neck of the pot with a satin ribbon.

Choose a bright printed fabric that colour co-ordinates with your flowers and wrap the pot for an impressive display. Turning in the cut edges, if necessary, loosely fold a wide strip of fabric until it fits the height of the pot. Hiding the join at the back, tape the fabric in place. Tie a generous strip of the fabric around the centre in a single knot; don't worry about the cut edges showing, they add to the charm

► It's a wrap
Disguise the shape and colour of a vase that detracts attention from a flower arrangement by wrapping it with a length of fabric. Turning the cut edges to the inside, fold the fabric into layers until it roughly fits the height of the pot. Tape one end of the fabric to the pot, then wrap the strip loosely around and tie it up with raffia

dyeing for a change

Bored with soft furnishings in the same old colours? Effect an instant transformation with easy-to-use fabric dye

Gone are the days of patchy, blotchy home-dyeing. Today's marvellous synthetic dyes come in bright, up-to-the-minute colours and give highly professional results.

You can dye soft furnishing fabrics as well as decorative trimmings, such as flowers and feathers, in a bowl, saucepan or washing machine – depending on the size and fragility of the item and what it is made of. The only thing you need to know is the type of fibre and the weight of the material you're using. This will help you choose the correct dye and the amount you need to obtain a good strong colour.

Methods of dyeing

Dyes are basically divided into those solutions which need to be heated and cold-water dyes. Hot-water dyeing can be done on top of the stove or, for larger items, in a washing machine. Follow our guide to achieve the best results.

Cold-water dyeing
This method gives a strong permanent colour to cotton and linen, such as bed and table linen, but lighter shades on wool and silk fabrics. Fix with salt combined with a special dye fix.

Hot-water dyeing
Use for small decorative items, such as feathers, buttons, dried flowers and grasses. Fix with salt. Also available is a dye that dissolves in hot tap-water, making it suitable for hand-dyeing. This type also gives a deep permanent colour to linen and cotton, but has a lighter tone on wool and silk fabrics.

Washing machine dyeing
Good for dyeing household linens. This type of dye produces a vibrant permanent colour on cotton, linen and viscose – all fibres found around the house. It is excellent for larger items such as towels and bedspreads. However the effect is much lighter on poly-cottons. Fix with salt.

Basic equipment

Gather together all the equipment you will need before you begin dyeing. You will find the majority of the items around the house.

Mixing and measuring

Pick a spacious container for the dye bath, such as a large flat-bottomed plastic bowl or a bucket. When using a hot-water dye, you will need a large saucepan or metal container that can be put on the stove so the dye can simmer. If you are going to be dyeing fabric regularly, look out for old pans in second-hand shops.

- Use an old plastic or metal jug for measuring and mixing up the dyes.
- Always wear rubber gloves when dyeing fabric at home.
- Choose a plastic or wooden spoon for stirring the dye mixture.

Fabrics

You can dye almost any type of fabric. However the majority of synthetic dyes work best on natural fabrics such as cotton, linen, silk and wool. You can also dye viscose, nylon and polycottons, but avoid acrylic fabrics and fabric impregnated with a special finish such as permanently pleated and flame-proof fabrics.
- Some fabrics react only partially to the dye and the result might be a paler colour than you expect, so read the instructions on the tin or pack carefully before you begin. The final result also depends on the original colour of the fabric. Traditional colour combining

principles apply when dyeing fabrics, eg adding a blue dye to a yellow material produces a green one, while fixing red dye on yellow fabric produces orange.
- Before you begin, wash and dry the fabric to remove any fabric dressing. Remove any stains as a dye can't disguise them – they will still show as a mark in the newly dyed fabric.
- To help return a fabric to a near-natural colour so you can obtain a cleaner dye colour, use a pre-dye solution to remove as much colour from the fabric as possible. You can dye patterned fabrics, but the dye tints the pattern as well.

Cold-water dyeing

1 Prepare the fabric Before you begin, wash the fabric and leave it damp. Fill a large plastic bowl or bucket with enough cold water to cover the fabric completely.

2 Mix the dye Put on rubber gloves. In a plastic measuring jug, dissolve the dye in 500ml (1pt) of very hot tap water and stir well. Add this dye mixture to the bowl.

3 Add salt and dye Mix together 125g (4oz) of salt and one sachet of special cold dye fix in very hot tap water. Stir into the bowl.

4 Place the fabric in the dye Immerse the damp, unfolded fabric in the bowl of dye and leave for one hour. Begin by agitating the fabric in the bowl for approximately 10 minutes. Keep the fabric submerged and agitate occasionally throughout the dyeing

time, lifting it out of the bowl and squeezing the solution through the material to prevent the fabric from forming into folds.

5 Rinse the fabric After one hour, remove the fabric from the dye solution and rinse it thoroughly until the water runs clear. Wash the fabric in the usual way, then dry it naturally, away from direct heat or sunlight.

Hot-water dyeing

1▲ Prepare the fabric Wash the fabric and leave it damp. Fill a saucepan with sufficient hot water to cover the fabric.

▲ *An ethnic mix of cushions in bright rainbow colours is easy to achieve with DIY dyes*

2▲ Dissolve the dye Put on rubber gloves. In a measuring jug, dissolve the dye in 500ml (1pt) of boiling water and stir well.

3▲ Combine the dye and salt to fix Add the dye solution to the saucepan with 30g (1oz) of salt, stirring well until the salt has dissolved.

4▲ Heat the fabric in the dye Put the unfolded, damp fabric into the dye solution in the saucepan and turn down the heat to simmer. Simmer, stirring constantly, for 20 minutes.

5▲ Finishing off Remove the fabric and rinse thoroughly. Wash the fabric in the usual way with fabric detergent, then dry it naturally, away from direct heat or sunlight.

Washine-machine dyeing

1 Prepare the fabric Wash the fabric first and leave it damp. Put on rubber gloves, empty the dye into a dry drum; tap the powder through the holes. Add the salt, then put the damp, unfolded fabric into the machine.

2 Use the machine Run a 60°C colourfast cotton cycle. When the programme is finished, add wash powder and run through the hottest programme for the fabric. Remove the fabric. Before using the machine for washing clothes, run it on a very hot programme to wash away any traces of dye.

checklist
Successful dyeing

● **How much dye?** Always follow the manufacturer's instructions and use the amount of dye and salt specified. Weigh the dry fabric to check how much dye you need. Using too little dye will result in a pale shade and if you add too much it will saturate the fabric, making it difficult to rinse later.

● **Colour test** When you are dyeing fabric for soft furnishing projects, test dye a spare piece of material first.

● **Correct temperature** If you are dyeing ready-made bed linen or curtains, check the label to determine the fabric content and any special washing instructions that need to be followed. Dye the fabric at the specified washing temperature.

● **Pre-washing** Wash all fabric and linen to remove stains and prepare the fabric. Do not use a fabric conditioner in this wash. Check that the fabric is wet through before dyeing it.

● **Big is best** Use a container that's large enough to immerse the fabric. Make sure it can move freely around during dyeing to obtain an even colour.

● **How long?** Keep the fabric in the dye for the required time or until the fabric has reached the desired shade.

● **After care** Always rinse thoroughly after dyeing, then wash the fabric in the usual way. Be careful when washing dyed fabric for the first few times as some colour may still come out.

the main draw

Draw-string bags offer storage with style and will add a burst of colour to any bedroom or bathroom

Fabric draw-string bags have a dual role. Firstly, they offer the perfect solution when storage space is limited or when you want to keep a set of items all together in one place. And secondly, they look good too.

All together now

Large draw-string bags make tidy holdalls for bulky items, such as laundry, toys and shoes, while smaller bags can be used to store your sewing kit or to keep make-up items together. Hang the bag from a hook on the wall, from a door handle or over the back of a chair and add a splash of colour to brighten the dullest of corners.

It's easy to match fabric prints to the use of any bag you're making. The toy bag featured here is a cartoon bird print in bright colours to appeal to a young child and encourage tidy habits. Alternatively, you could choose your fabric to co-ordinate with the curtains hanging in a room, or pick out the colours of a duvet cover or other bedding instead.

Rapid results

You won't need a great deal of time, patience or expertise to create this project since draw-string bags are no more than two rectangles of fabric stitched together and threaded through with a draw-string cord. So get started now – you'll be amazed how much these bags can contribute to keeping a room tidy while adding their own individual touch of style.

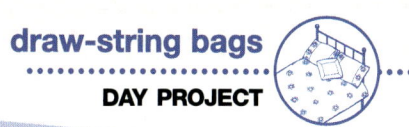

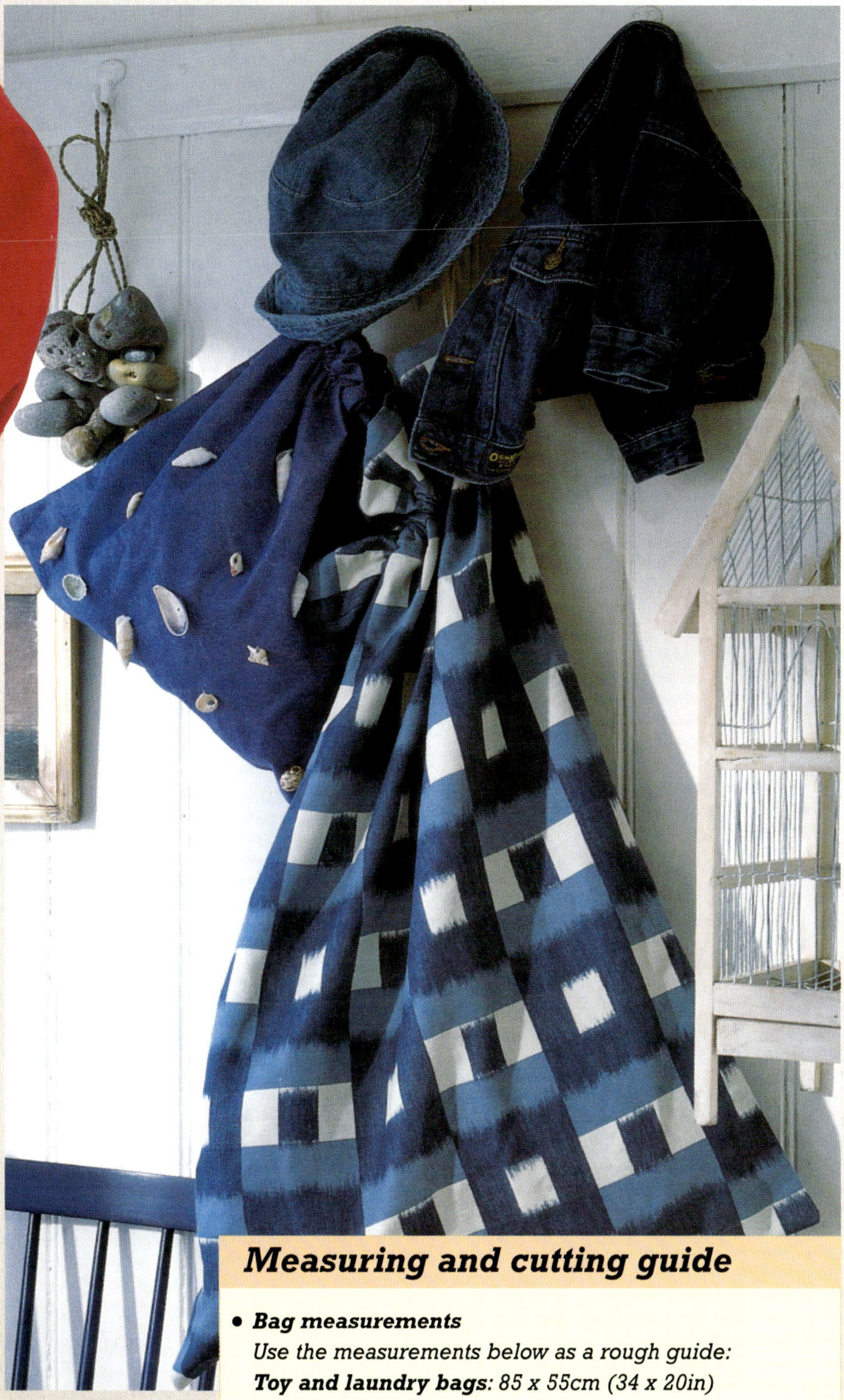

▲ ***Decorate draw-string bags with sea shells against a background of deep blue, or use cool checks to create the ultimate in bathroom accessories***

Measuring and cutting guide

- ***Bag measurements***
  Use the measurements below as a rough guide:
  Toy and laundry bags: *85 x 55cm (34 x 20in)*
  Shoe bags: *45 x 30cm (18 x 12in)*
  Wash bags: *35 x 25cm (14 x 10in)*
  Pot-pourri bags: *12 x 9cm (4¾ x 3½in)*
- ***Cutting out***
  Decide on the size of bag you are going to make and the depth of its frill (the fabric above the casing for the draw-string cord). The frill is usually 7.5-10cm (3-4in) deep, depending on the size of the bag. Cut out two rectangles of fabric to your chosen size, adding twice the frill depth, plus 6.5cm (2½in) to allow for the casing and hems, to the depth of the bag. Add a 3cm (1¼in) seam allowance to the bag width.

Essentials

- Fabric
- Scissors
- Matching sewing thread
- Pinking shears
- Tape measure
- Pencil or tailor's chalk
- Cord, cut into two equal lengths
- Adhesive tape
- Safety pin

Making the bag

1 ▲ Mark the casing openings Place the fabric rectangles with right sides and cut edges together, then pin and tack the side and base edges. Measure the depth of the frill down from the top edge of the bag along each side edge and mark with a pin on each side. Mark 2cm (¾in) below in the same way: this will be the position for the casing openings.

2 ▲ Stitch the side and base seams Machine stitch around the sides and bottom edge, taking a 1.5cm (⅝in) seam allowance. Stop and start stitching again on either side of the pins you have used to mark the casing. Work a few stitches in reverse on either side of the openings to secure the stitching.

3 ◄ Form the bag base
Neaten the cut edges with pinking shears and press the seams open. To form the base, stand the bag upright and open it up with your hands. Press the fabric at the corners of the bag flat to form a small triangle. (You can check that the triangle is even on both sides by making sure that the side seam of the bag runs through its centre – see above). Measure approximately 7cm (2¾in) from the corner points – or more if you would like a wider base – and insert a pin on either side of the triangle to mark the stitch line.

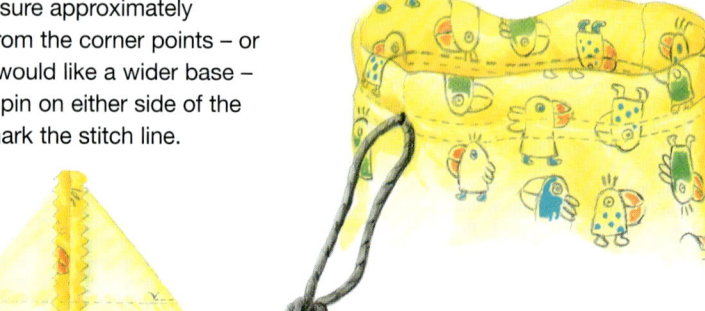

4 ▲ Stitch the base Stitch straight across the triangle where you have marked, then trim the excess fabric from the corners, about 1.5cm (⅝in) from the stitching. Neaten the cut edges with pinking shears.

5 ▲ Make the top frill Press 1cm (⅜in) to the wrong side around the top edges, then turn under the frill depth so that the bottom fold just covers the slits for the side openings; pin. Stitch around the bag top, close to the lower fold. Stitch a second row, 2cm (¾in) above the first row to form the casing and frill.

6 ▲ Thread the first draw-string
Turn the bag right side out. Wrap the adhesive tape around the cut ends of the cord to prevent it from unravelling. Fasten a safety pin into one end and thread the cord through the casing, bringing the pin out of the same opening. Stitch or knot the cord ends together.

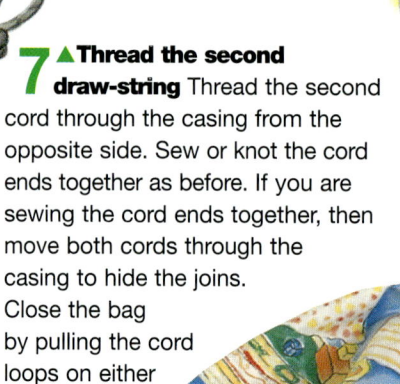

7 ▲ Thread the second draw-string Thread the second cord through the casing from the opposite side. Sew or knot the cord ends together as before. If you are sewing the cord ends together, then move both cords through the casing to hide the joins. Close the bag by pulling the cord loops on either side of the bag.

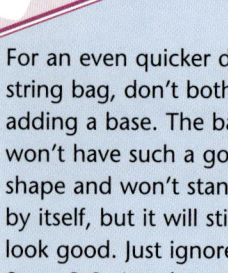

MAKE IT SIMPLE

quick fixes

For an even quicker draw-string bag, don't bother adding a base. The bag won't have such a good shape and won't stand up by itself, but it will still look good. Just ignore Steps 3 & 4 and use the base seam as the bottom of the bag.

For a different look, make a bag without a frill. Instead of sewing two seams for the casing as in Steps 1, 2 & 5, press 1cm (⅜in) to the wrong side around the top edge of the bag. Turn under 2.5cm (1in) and stitch a single row 2cm (¾in) down to form a casing directly at the top of the bag. Thread cords through as before.

TAKE ANOTHER LOOK

bag an elephant

STAMP IT

◄ *Choose motif fabrics in bright colours to give all your bags an individual look*

Here we have used an elephant stamp (available in most art and craft shops, limited DIY stores, or by mail order) to make a child's draw-string shoe bag. Before making up the bag, stamp a parade of elephants (each one in a different colour) along each main section, near the lower edge.

If you need a reminder of the simple techniques involved in stamping, refer to 'Stamp of approval', p20. Be imaginative – you can stamp any fabric item, using whatever arrangement of motifs you find attractive. You could use one repeat motif over an item, or you could buy a selection of stamps and create a variety of images randomly positioned for an eye-catching result.

child's play

From birds and elephants, to stars and fruit, these patterned fabrics are perfect for making draw-string bags with loads of child appeal

Children love to store all their accumulated bits and pieces in draw-string bags. Give the bags added appeal by selecting a fabric with a printed pattern – there are so many to choose from that it's easy to get carried away. For a baby or toddler, go for a favourite nursery motif, such as animals or a story book character. Or if the bag is being used by an older child, look for a print that's more appropriate, such as stylized animals or cartoon characters.

1 Experience jungle fever with some vivid multi-coloured parrots. These bold birds would look just as good as fabric furnishings in a child's room

2 Starry nights look brighter with this golden celestial motif. It's great for small items such as our draw-string bags

3 These animated chickens will cheer up the children on a dull day. Make them a bag for carrying their shoes to school. Then, when the bag is on the peg-rail, they'll recognise it instantly

4 Use small sea creatures and shells for an aquatic bathroom theme. Line a draw-string bag in this fish print with plastic for a practical wash-bag

5 A lemon print draw-string bag looks luscious in a sunny kitchen setting. For an extended citrus fruit theme, alternate with bags of tasty oranges, limes and tangerines

6 Elephants never forget when these regal animals grace draw-string bags. This fabric is also a good choice for curtains and bed linen

7 This lively floral design would look elegant in an older girl's room. For a co-ordinated look, use it for cushion covers as well as a bag to brighten a dark corner

8 Look out for familiar characters, such as this Peter Rabbit, which will have great appeal in a nursery. Slightly older children may prefer something more zany, such as a cartoon character

● See 'The main draw', p152, for details of how to make draw-string bags.

⑧

checklist
Motif-printed fabrics

● **Wash and wear** Go for printed cotton for draw-string bags as it's generally strong material that can be washed frequently. Buy a good quality cotton and you'll find that the colours won't fade.

● **Neat seams** As printed cotton fabrics are a woven construction, the seams will fray if they aren't neatened. For the inside of draw-string bags you can simply trim the finished seam allowances with pinking shears, or work over the edges using the zigzag attachment on your sewing machine.

● **Complementary styles** Choose a printed pattern that fits into the room where its being used; for example fish motifs in the bathroom or fruit and vegetables in the kitchen. Think about using your chosen fabric for co-ordinating soft furnishings, such as matching cushions and curtains, in the same room.

● **Variety of colours** You'll probably find that most popular prints come in a number of different colourways, so you should find one that fits in with your colour scheme. You could even be so bowled over by a design, that you decide to use it as the starting point in planning a new look for your room.

▲ *Matching motifs and complementary fabrics add magic to a nursery setting. Note the useful, over-sized draw-string bag hanging from the end of the cot*

in the frame

Picture frames can be transformed in no time at all by covering them with fabric. Go for sleek, straight lines or add bows for a truly individual look

What do you do? You've got a favourite photograph or picture that deserves to be displayed in pride of place, but you can't find a frame to do it justice. The answer is to take one of your existing frames, or to buy one ready-made, and to cover it with fabric.

Simple technique

Covering frames with fabric is an easy, no-sew technique. Use PVA adhesive, which you can buy from any DIY or department store, to fix the fabric in place.

You can make the frame as plain or ornate as you want. If you go for the plain option, all you have to do

is follow the steps starting right for a simple, but effective, result. But if you want to make a frame that really stands out, then you can make a bow as well.

Fabric-covered frames are very versatile and can be used to provide a visual link with other elements in a room scheme. Alternatively, frames can be covered in contrasting fabrics and arranged boldly on a wall.

The best fabrics to use are fine cottons and silks, small prints, bright, plain colours or lightly textured fabrics such as moiré. And if you grow tired of the design, you can simply peel off the old fabric and start again with something new.

Essentials
- Wooden frame   • Fabric
- PVA adhesive and a mixing bowl
- Scissors   • Small paint brush
- Soft pencil (B or 2B)

Covering the frame

1 ▲ Mark out the frame Press the fabric and lay it out flat, wrong side up. Place the frame centrally on the fabric. Using the pencil, mark around the inner and outer edges. Remove the frame and then mark the cutting lines 5cm (2in) inside the marked inner line and 10cm (4in) from the outer marked line. Cut out the frame shape.

2 ▶ Seal the frame Pour some more PVA adhesive into a bowl and dilute with a little water to the consistency of single cream. Paint PVA adhesive over the frame to seal it and leave on one side to dry.

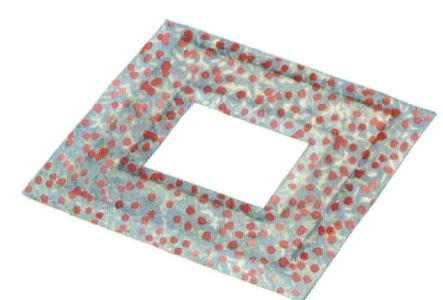

3 ▲ Mould the fabric to the front of the frame Brush diluted PVA over the wrong side of the fabric. Place the fabric centrally over the frame, and match up the marked inner line on the fabric with the inner edge of the frame. Press the fabric in place, moulding it over the front of the frame.

4 ▲ **Neaten the inner edge** Turn and stick the fabric around the inner edge to the back of the frame. On square frames, cut into the inner corners, taking care not to cut too far, and fold the fabric flat against the back of the frame. On oval frames, snip slightly into the fabric all around the inner edge and mould it to the back of the frame.

5 ▲ **Neaten the outer edge** Turn the outer edge of the fabric to the back of the frame, making neat corner folds on square or rectangular frames (see above). On oval frames, mould the fabric over the outside edge in a series of tiny pleats.

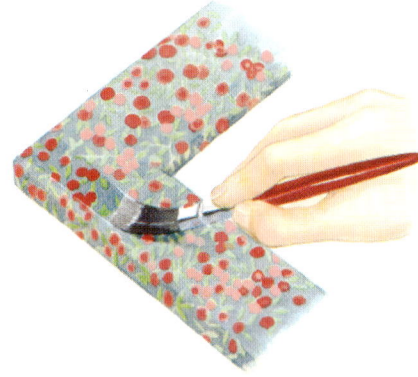

6 ▲ **Complete the frame** Brush another layer of diluted PVA over the entire frame to finish and leave to dry.

Making the stiffened bows

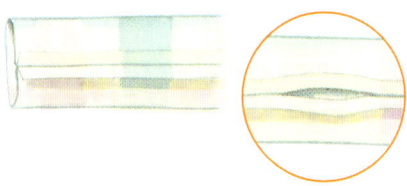

1 ▲ **Prepare the bow strip** Fold the fabric strip in half lengthways, right sides facing, then pin and stitch down the length leaving a small central opening for turning through. Press the seam open so that it lies in the centre of the bow strip.

Essentials
- *Fabric*
- *Pins*
- *Matching sewing thread and a needle*
- *PVA adhesive and a mixing bowl*
- *Small paint brush*
- *Kitchen foil*

Measuring and cutting guide

● *The width of the bow should complement the frame width. The bow strip on the frame pictured below measure 4cm (1½in) wide by 50cm (20in) long.*
If you are unsure about what size to cut your bow strip, simply cut a strip of paper and bend it into a bow shape. Place the bow at the top of the frame to check that it's in proportion. Then cut one strip of fabric to twice the intended bow width by the chosen length, adding a 1cm (⅜in) seam allowance all the way around.

▼ *Choose sugar almond colours for fabric to frame a sweet baby photograph. Top it with decorative bow which is shaped with the aid of scrunched-up kitchen foil*

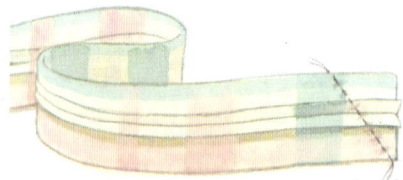

2 ▲ Form diagonal ends Pin and stitch diagonally across each end. Trim the excess fabric and turn the strip right side out. Stitch the opening and press flat.

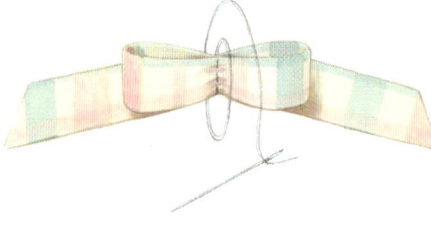

3 ▲ Make the bow loops Fold the strip in half. Measure twice the intended length of your bow loop from the fold and pin. Machine stitch across the strip at the pin mark. Press flat with the centre fold over the stitching to form the bows and tails.

4 ▲ Gather the centre Using double thread in the needle, work a few running stitches through the bow centre and pull up to gather the fabric. Wind the thread around the centre several times and fasten off with a few stitches, one on top of the other.

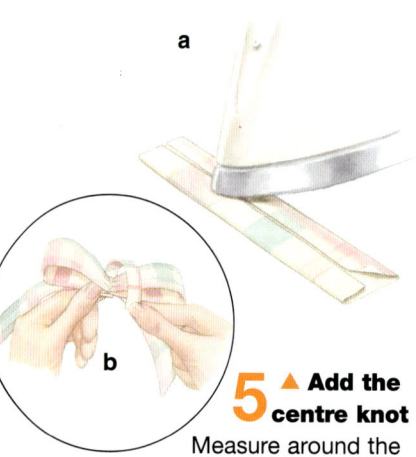

a

b

5 ▲ Add the centre knot Measure around the centre of the bow and cut a strip of fabric to this length plus 1cm (⅜in) by twice the chosen width. Turn in and press both long edges of the strip to meet in the centre (a). Holding one end at the back of the bow, wrap the strip around the centre (b). Hand sew to the back of the bow to secure in place.

◀ Co-ordinating fabric made up as a country style wall hanging perfectly complements this fabric-covered frame and gives it extra presence

▲ Silk ribbons make an attractive substitute for stiffened bows and can be fixed on to a frame in an instant

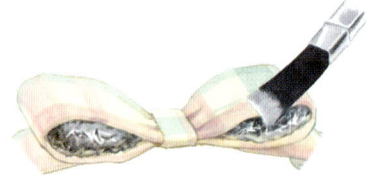

6 ▲ Stiffen the bow Dilute some PVA with water to the consistency of single cream. Brush over the bow and arrange the loops into your chosen shape, then leave to dry. Use small pieces of scrunched-up kitchen foil to help keep the bows in shape.

7 ▲ Stick the bow to the frame When the bow is completely dry, remove the foil. Stick the bow to the frame with undiluted PVA.

▶ Sunny style

Sunshine colours give an instant lift to a room. The soft creamy yellow on the walls provides the starting point in this dining room. Fabrics at the windows and on the table add accents of brighter yellow, combined with soft browns and mossy greens

▼ Bright white

Zingy lime, red and orange bed linen and curtains help to stop a room with white walls feeling too cold. Pick up the bright accents with accessories

Malabar

Vantona

clever colours

Using colour effectively is easier than you think, especially if you follow a few ground rules

Colour can completely change the mood of a room, even give the illusion of changing its shape. Paint, wallpaper and fabrics are available in all the colours of the rainbow, so understanding colour helps you combine tones and shades successfully.

Whether you are decorating one room, or a whole house, first think about the kinds of colours you like around you. Do you like bright primary colours, warm autumnal shades, cool blues, or a neutral palette of soft greys and creams?

Whatever the current colour fashion, it is important to choose colours you won't tire of quickly.

The science of colour

Colour is simply the way our eyes interpret light waves. There are three primary colours – blue, red and yellow. They combine to make secondary colours – green, violet and orange – which then combine with their adjacent primaries on the colour wheel to give tertiary colours. All colours are a combination of these in differing proportions.

Sanderson

▲ Cool blues
Above, soft
creams are high-
lighted with wintry
blue accessories
in this Nordic
room. The bright
tones of the
leaves and berries
on the wreath
add warmth

▶ Red hot
On the right, a
basically neutral
room is brought
to life with rich red
voile curtains. The
lime cloth on the
table adds a colour
contrast and stops
the room looking
too heavy

Anna French

Primary and secondary colours opposite each other on the colour wheel (there is a simple colour wheel in 'Getting the right mix', p39) are thought to make a pleasing combination: red and green, blue and orange. Every colour has a range of shades and tones, for example yellow can range from bright sunshine to pale primrose or buttermilk; blue can range from the darkest navy to palest duck egg.

Colours are often called advancing or receding. This is basically an optical illusion. Dark, warm colours based on the red/orange/yellow end of the spectrum can appear closer to us, effectively reducing the size of a room and making it seem cosier. These advancing colours work well in

colder north-facing rooms. Light, cool colours from the blue/grey/violet end have the opposite effect, making a room seem bigger and lighter. These receding colours work best in sunny south-facing rooms. Neutral colours – creams, off-whites, light greys, beiges – balance the other colours and work well in most rooms.

Working with colour

Try out colours first before you commit yourself. Use sample pots to paint a large piece of paper, then pin it up in the room. See what the effect is like in daylight and at night, on a gloomy and a sunny day. Colours often look darker on the wall than on the paint chart, so it is worth buying a sample pot one

shade lighter too. Add as large a sample of any wallpaper or border as you can. Buy a metre of your chosen fabric and pin it up to check that the whole effect works well.

It is tempting to match exactly a background fabric colour for paint, but this can end up looking a bit monotonous, try instead to pick out a detail colour, or go for a shade lighter or darker.

Colour tricks

To heighten a low ceiling, use a reducing colour, or white, on the ceiling. Extend the wall colour on to the cornice and skirting boards to make the room seem taller. Narrow vertical stripes can also add to the illusion. To lower a high ceiling, use an advancing colour on

Crown Paints

Dulux Colourways

**▲ Compare
and contrast ▶**
*Two schemes
shows just what
a difference
colour can make
to a kitchen. One
is bright and
modern with
opposite walls
painted in deep
green and blue.
In the other
scheme, the
corner is given a
traditional cosier
treatment with
terracotta tones*

Crown Paints

▲ Link up
*Soft pastel
colours give a
gentle air. The
clotted cream of
these breakfast
room walls works
well with the soft
pink glimpsed in
the room beyond.
Touches of
pink in the
accessories help
to link the two
rooms visually*

**▼ Create a
feature**
*In Mediterranean
countries it is
traditional to
paint bands of
bright colour
around windows.
Here a green
band frames a
small deep
window, and
complements
the soft yellow of
the wall*

the ceiling, continuing it down to
the cornice or picture rail. Match
the flooring and skirting board
colour to the ceiling.

Rooms with sloping roofs often
look bigger if the same colour is
used on walls and ceiling. Similarly
a one-colour scheme can give a feeling
of spaciousness in a small flat.

Either paint small rooms with
cool receding colours, with the
skirting board the same colour as
the floor covering to make the area
seem larger; or give them a
dramatic warm colour scheme
which enhances the cosiness of the
room. Make large rooms warmer
with dark colours or leave them
bright and airy with a cool or
neutral palette.

Colour can also be used to link
rooms. The easiest way is to keep

to one colour for all the woodwork
in a home, usually white, cream or
a similar neutral colour. When you
plan a room, think about what the
scheme will look like when seen
from an adjacent room. While an
occasional dramatic clash can be
fun, harmony is easier to live with
in the long term.

And finally, bring colour into a
neutral room with accessories –
lampshades, tablecloths, wall-hangings,
cushions, curtains, blinds, even
vases, ornaments and flowers.

• Browse through the 'Fabric
files' in this book for
inspiration on patterned,
plain and textured fabric to
liven up the colour
schemes in your home.

Dulux Colourways

pole to pole

For the ultimate in no-sew chic, and when curtains don't need to be drawn, wrap long lengths of fabric around a wooden curtain pole and just let it hang

◄ Single sided

For a narrow hall or landing window, make loose, informal drapes and then hang the excess fabric just to one side to maximise the light

Draping a curtain pole with a long length of fabric is a novel way of dressing a window. It can be a permanent solution or it can just allow you to live with a fabric for a while and experiment with different effects before committing yourself to one style of curtain or drape.

Adjust the length of the loops around the pole to match the height of the window. Stand back to get the full effect and then, when you are happy with the result, fix the fabric in place with a few carefully placed drawing pins in the back of the pole.

► Bathroom splendour

The rich red, black and gold fabric of these drapes creates the perfect finishing touch for a period bathroom complete with a claw-footed bath

cover story

Freshen up a tired stool, or breathe new life into a junk shop bargain, for no sew style in living areas

A low padded stool makes a wonderful focal point for a sitting room. It elicits the aura of old world luxury and comfort, but blends in effortlessly with contemporary settings. Fitted with castors, a stool can be moved easily around the room and be used as a coffee table, or extra seating.

Revive your stool with a new cover – it's simplicity itself and requires no sewing skills. Just choose a fabric for the new cover, then add a loosely woven fabric to cover the underside, and wadding for a perfect finish.

Colour matters

Make sure you select a durable and closely woven upholstery fabric for a new cover since a stool gets a lot of wear. Take your time in choosing

the right colour, as this is the key element in co-ordinating the stool with the rest of the room.

Try matching the fabric colour to a contrasting colour used in other details in the room such as curtains, cushions or sofa covers. Or link the stool's fabric to the main colour theme, but in a contrasting print.

Ready, steady, go

An old stool that is still in fairly good condition with a cover that's faded or just doesn't match a new decor is an ideal candidate for basic revival. Just add a new layer of wadding and a new cover. A tattered and lumpy specimen might need attention from a professional upholsterer before re-covering.

If you choose an upholstery fabric that's pricey, test your measurement calculations before purchasing the fabric. Cut some spare cheap fabric, such as calico, to the correct size and wrap it over and around your stool. Make sure there is enough extra all around to overlap the bottom and to allow you to easily manoeuvre the edges while you are mounting the cover.

Re-covering the stool

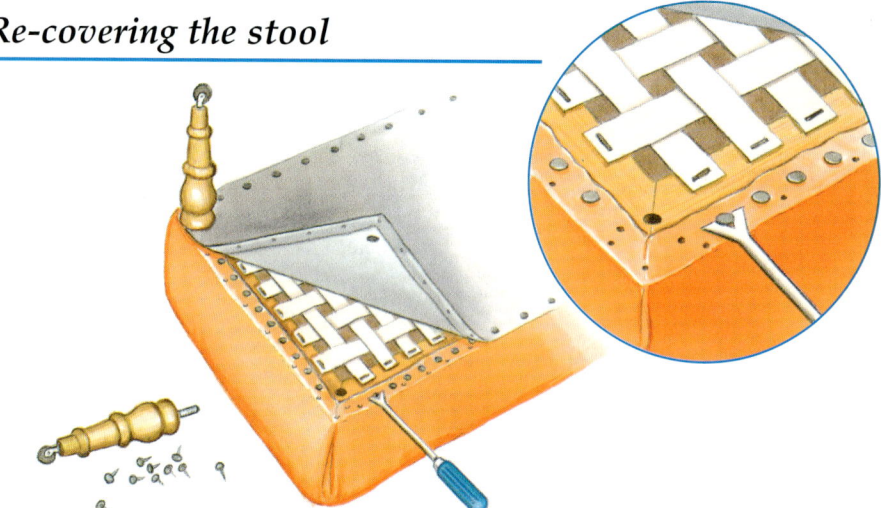

1 ▲ **Remove the old cover** Turn the stool upside down and unscrew the legs. Remove the bottom cover, and then the top cover, by pulling out all the tacks with a tack lifter or a claw hammer. Turn the stool the right way up and then remove the first layer of old wadding as well.

◄ *Here's a clever co-ordination of colour and tapestry-patterned fabric. Cushions and a rug match the stool*

2 ▲ **Smooth the wadding into place** Place the upholstery fabric right side down and smooth it out; then place the wadding on top of it. Turn the stool upside down and place it centrally on top of the two layers. Pull the wadding up over the sides of the stool, pinch it together at the corners and cut off the double triangles of excess fabric to eliminate the bulk. Then, trim the edge of the wadding so that it will overlap the bottom of the frame by about 12mm (½in).

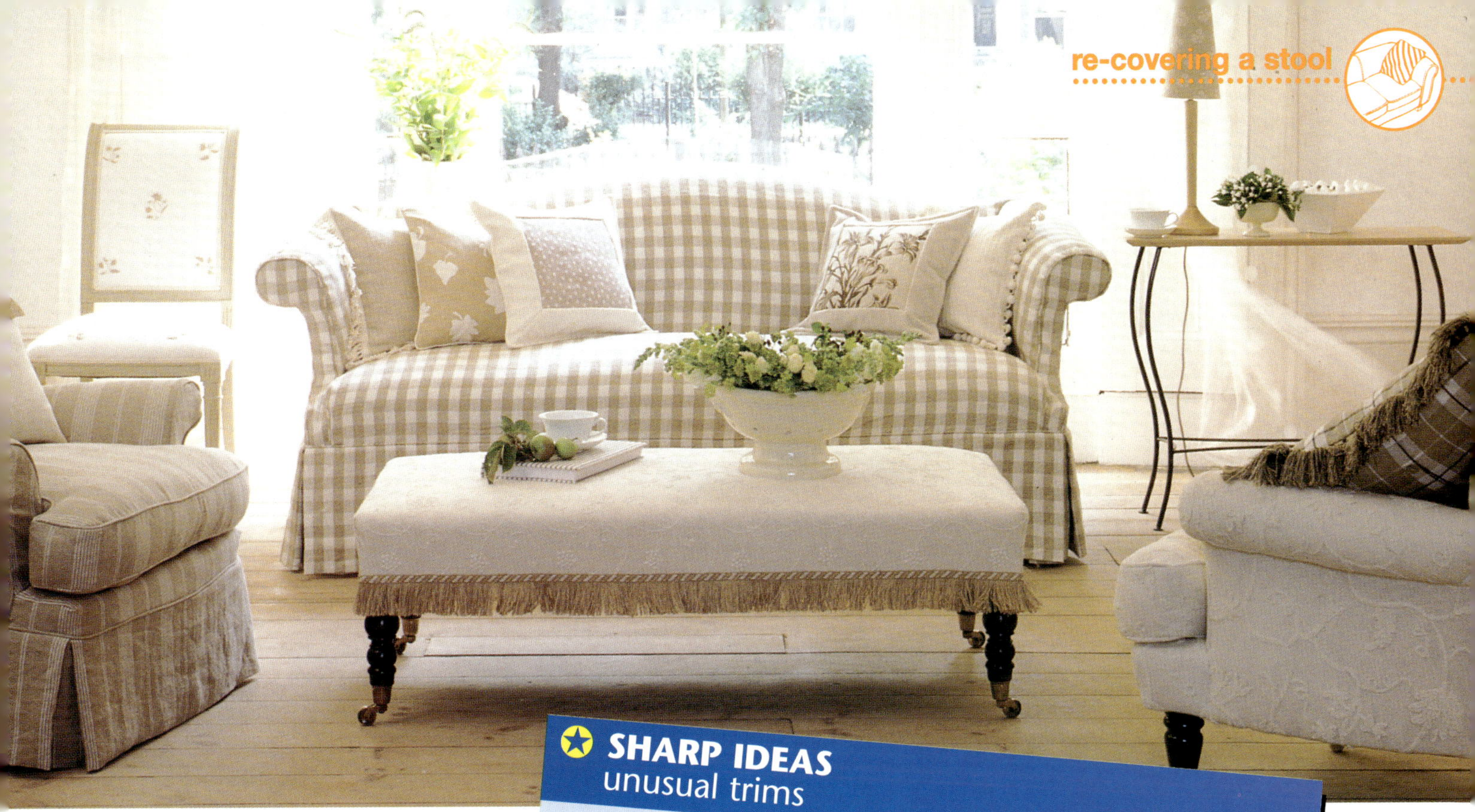

▲ *The cool charm of the embroidered cover and the discreet beige fringing make this long stool a handsome centrepiece for a neutral-coloured room*

SHARP IDEAS
unusual trims

- Add one of the traditional decorative fringes or braids which are widely available in haberdashers and furnishing fabric shops. Tack or glue it in place around the lower edge of the stool.
- To give a stool a really eye-catching finish, use a more unusual trim, like bead fringing, bobbles, antique crochet lace or a zigzag scalloped fabric valance.
- For a trimming to complement traditional fabrics, scour second hand shops and even local jumble sales for cushions and chair seats with braids that can be re-used and attach them with decorative antique-look tacks.

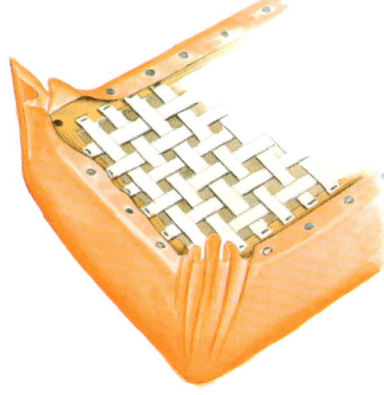

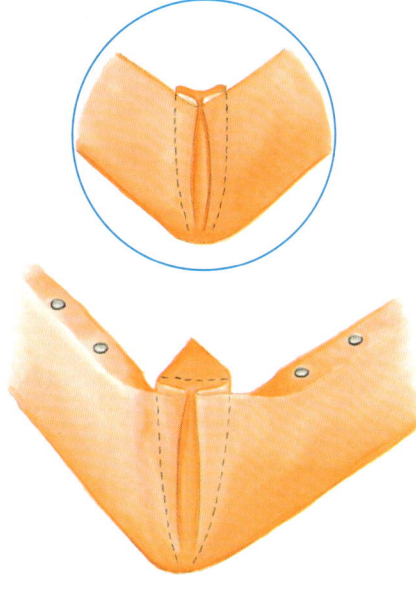

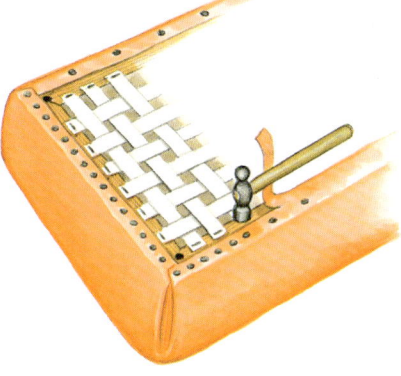

3 ▲ Temporarily tack the sides Keeping the wadding in place over the sides, pull the upholstery fabric up and secure it to the bottom of the frame at the centre of each side with a temporary tack (drive the tack in just far enough to hold the fabric in place). Working out from each centre tack, secure the cover to the bottom of the frame with more half-inserted tacks placed about 5cm (2in) apart and ending about 13cm (5¼in) from each of the corners.

4 ▲ Fold the corners on the cover To form neat corners, with a slightly rounded effect, fold a double pleat at each edge as above. Trim away the point at the top of the pleat.

5 ▲ Tack the cover in place Smoothing the cover out as you proceed and repositioning the temporary half-inserted tacks if necessary, tack the cover to the frame. Working from the centre of each side outwards, position the tacks 12mm (½in) apart and the same distance from the edge of the frame. Trim the fabric close to the tacks with scissors or a craft knife, ensuring that the leg screw holes are not covered.

6 ▲ Tack on the underside cover Press 2cm (¾in) to the wrong side all round the edge of the underside fabric, folding the corners neatly. Tack the cover to the bottom of the stool, working from the centre of the sides towards the corners and placing the tacks close to the edge of the cover and about 2.5cm (1in) apart. Again, avoid hammering the tacks into the screw holes for the legs.

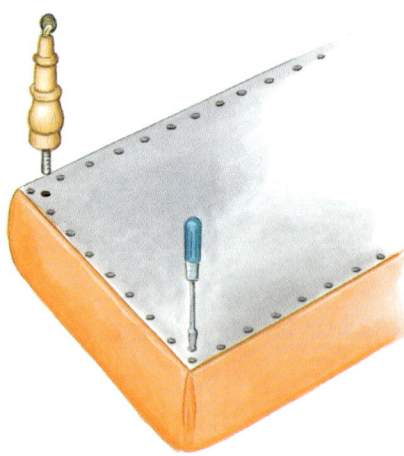

7 ▲ Screw on the legs Using a screwdriver or a knitting needle, poke a hole through the underside fabric at the position of each leg screw hole. Then, screw in the legs.

✓ SO EASY tack tips

● You must remember to remove all the old tacks to make way for the new ones. Don't be tempted to re-use old tacks as they'll probably be bent and rusty. Avoid accidents by never kneeling on the floor without first checking for stray tacks.

Covering a stool with fixed legs

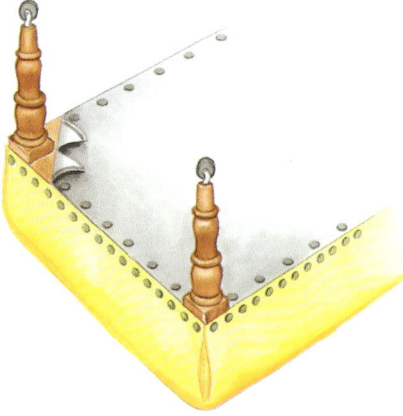

1 ▲ Renew the cover Follow Steps 1 – 4 as before, smoothing on the wadding, but trimming it to 12mm (½in) from the lower edges. Tack the main fabric in place around the side of the frame, rather than the bottom, trimming and turning under the edge. Then, tack on the new bottom covering, clipping into the corners at the legs as shown.

2 ▲ Cover the tacks Disguise the tacks which will show on the sides by gluing on a decorative braid. Alternatively, use brass headed pins when you finally secure the fabric.

▼ *A boldly striped stool makes a statement in a country setting. Team it with checks for clever mix'n'matching*

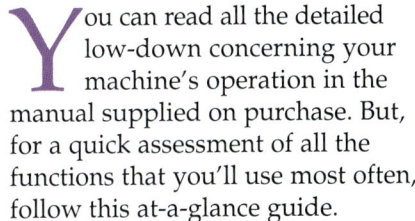

You can read all the detailed low-down concerning your machine's operation in the manual supplied on purchase. But, for a quick assessment of all the functions that you'll use most often, follow this at-a-glance guide.

Stitch length and width

The finer the fabric, the more stitches you'll need. Generally, allow 6-7 stitches per cm ($^3/_8$in) for fine fabrics; 5-6 per cm for light or mediumweight fabrics; and 3-4 per cm for heavyweight fabrics. The regulator is marked in range from 0 to 4/5. For most soft furnishing projects, set the dial between 2 and 3.

For the width, leave the dial at 0 for straight stitching. For zigzag stitching, vary the length and width (see p30).

Pressure

Lower the pressure foot to hold the fabric layers together as they feed through the machine. Too much pressure and the fabric won't move smoothly under the needle, causing it to pucker. Too little pressure, and the fabric slides, causing uneven stitches.

machine magic

Tension

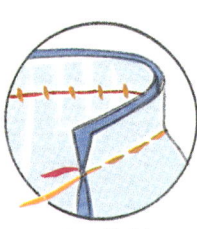
too tight

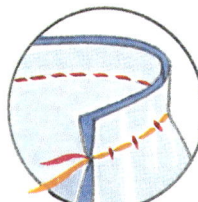
too loose

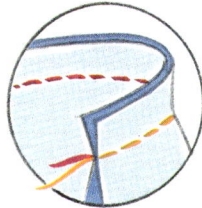
perfect

The tension between the upper (spool) and lower (bobbin) threads must be evenly balanced to produce the perfect stitch. A stitch forms when the upper and the lower threads link together between the fabric layers. Once the tension is properly set, you only need to change the tension when stitching extra heavy or very fine fabrics.

A dial sets the tension of the upper thread. When the top tension is too tight, the fabric puckers as the lower stitches are pulled up to the surface. When the top tension is too loose, the upper stitches are pulled to the bottom causing weak, loose stitches.

You can alter the tension of the lower thread by adjusting a screw on the bobbin case, but you shouldn't need to tinker with this as you should always be able to produce a good stitch by altering the top tension alone. It's wise to have the tension balanced by a service engineer every year.

Make friends with your sewing machine to whizz up professional projects in an instant

Checklist – before you start

- **Test the machine stitch** on a double piece of your chosen fabric.
- **Stitch at an even speed**, not in spurts. If you are a beginner, see if your sewing machine can be set at a slower stitching speed, making it easier for you to gain confidence.
- **Guide the fabric** through the machine. Don't push it from the front, or pull it from behind the needle.
- **Be careful with pins** – place them at right angles to the seams, with their heads on the right-hand side, so you can stitch over them, and remove them as you stitch. Don't leave pins in the underside of the fabric where they can damage the feed teeth.
- **Clean the machine** regularly and, when not in use, cover it to keep out the dust.
- **Fit the correct needle** for the chosen fabric and make sure that it's sharp. Check that you've got the right thread – refer to your sewing machine manual or pattern details.
- **Change your needle** regularly, not just when it breaks.

Basic machine stitches

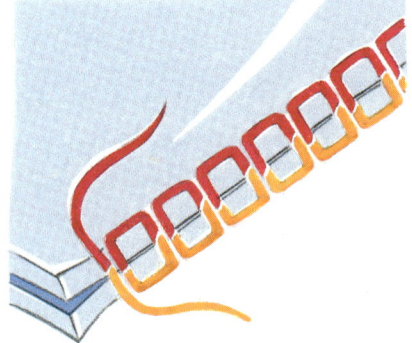

Machine stitches form when the needle goes through the fabric above the bobbin. As the needle is withdrawn from the fabric, the top thread loops round the bobbin case and locks around the lower thread.

Tacking Set the stitch length to the longest length 4/5. Loosen the upper tension. Stitch the fabric layers together in the usual way, removing any pins as you stitch. Work just outside the seamline, so that the main stitching can be worked alongside the tacking stitches. You can thread the machine with a contrasting colour to make the stitches easy to see and therefore quick to remove.

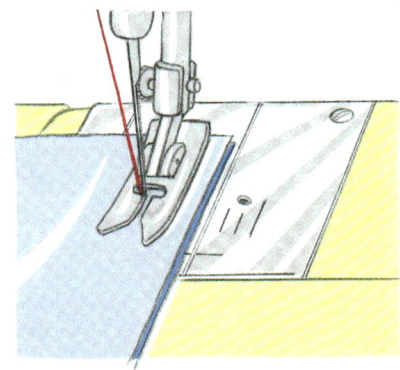

Straight stitching Novice stitchers should work slowly and always have a stitching guideline to follow – either a line of tacking stitches or a marked line. It's also helpful to follow the marked distance lines etched on the needle plate or use the machine foot as a guide – position the outside or inside edge of the foot against a previously stitched line, against the fabric edges or a fold of fabric.

Staystitching Stabilize an edge that's likely to stretch out of shape, such as a curve or loosely woven fabric, by working a line of machining on each piece of fabric just inside the seamline before you stitch the seam. On inward corners, which need to be clipped, increase the number of stitches per cm and work along the seamline before you start work to strengthen the fabric.

Topstitching Add a decorative touch, with a hint of durability, to a plain seam by topstitching it. Press the finished seam allowances to one side on the wrong side of the work. Then, on the right side, hold them in place with a line of straight stitching worked along the seam allowance. Lengthen the stitch slightly and loosen the tension to create a more prominent stitch.

Gathering

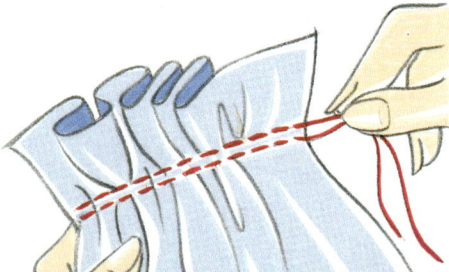

Loosen the upper tension slightly before stitching. Work two rows of machine stitches 6mm (¼in) apart, one row above the seamline and the second row just beside the seamline. After stitching, pull up both rows of gathering by drawing up the bobbin threads only; tie them together to secure.

Neatening seams

Although the idea of extra stitching on long seams for bed linen or curtains may not be appealing, some seams will have to be neatened – just take the quickest option to the best result.

Why neaten? To avoid fraying which can mean that the seam eventually comes apart, and to strengthen the seam line, which is a weak area.

Quick options The quickest way to neaten a seam on a firm fabric is to trim the seam allowance with pinking shears. In fact, you can cut out with pinking shears when cutting simple shapes. A better way to use pinking shears is to run a line of stitching down the seam allowance and then trim the remainder of the fabric away

with the pinking shears. The most frequently used method of neatening is by zigzagging down the seam allowance and this gives a fairly good, fray-proof finish. However, light fabrics will roll and crease under the zigzag foot, which creates a lumpy result. These fabrics are better neatened with a very narrow hem.

Neatening difficult fabrics If you have to neaten a fabric that is going to fray badly then you will have to make a french seam. Stitch the seam with wrong sides together first taking a very narrow seam allowance. Trim close to the stitching, turn the fabric right sides together, press carefully, then stitch again on the seam line. Your raw edges will be encased in the seam.

Beginning and ending

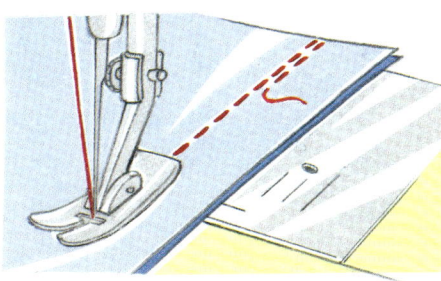

The easiest way to begin and end a seam is with a few stitches worked in reverse at each end. Position the fabric so the needle is approximately 1.5cm (⅝in) from the end of the stitching line. Set the machine in reverse and stitch almost to the fabric edge. Change to forward stitching and stitch the seam almost to the opposite edge. Set the machine in reverse and backstitch for 1.5cm (⅝in). Alternatively, leave long thread ends so that you can knot the spool and bobbin threads together so the knot is against the seam ends. Trim the ends close to the knot.

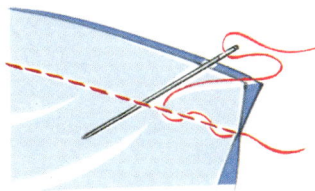

On very fine fabrics, thread each end in turn through a needle and weave them in and out of the stitches for a short way down the seam.

Best foot forward

Straight stitch foot This is the best foot for straight seams. It's a slim foot with one side slightly shorter than the other and the straight vertical slot makes it easy to keep track of the stitching line.

Multipurpose/standard foot The wide slot in the centre of this foot makes it easy to work zigzag stitch. The vertical slot in the front of the foot lines up with the needle to provide a good stitching guide.

Zip foot This is a narrow foot with an indentation on each side for the needle that's ideal for stitching in zip fastenings. The needle can be positioned to the right- or left-hand side. It's also a good foot for stitching against piping and bulky trimmings.

Machine fault checklist

● **When a fault occurs**, study your manual for help. There are a number of faults that are quite common, so study the list below so that you'll be prepared and should be able to correct the problem yourself quickly and easily.

● **If the thread breaks**, the machine is incorrectly threaded; the needle is too fine for the fabric; the needle is bent or not positioned properly; the tension is too tight; the thread is caught round the spool.

● **If the needle breaks**, the wrong needle has been fitted in the machine; the needle is bent; you have stitched over a pin; the bobbin has not been set into the machine properly.

● **If there are irregular or missed stitches**, you are sewing erratically or in spurts; the needle is the wrong size for the fabric and thread; the pressure is too light for the fabric; you are pulling the fabric from behind the needle as you stitch.

▲ *Perfectly stitched, neat hems are an essential part of home furnishings – especially where they are clearly seen, as on the edges of these unlined curtains*

stylish storage

Solve your storage problems with a versatile hanging shelving unit. Made from heavy calico, it's both durable and economical

Take your wardrobe up a style notch, with a set of hanging storage units – and get organized into the bargain. Hanging neatly from the clothes rail, a shelving unit makes use of the space in your wardrobe that would otherwise go to waste.

Everyone has different requirements, so plan what you need to store and vary the size of your units and shelves accordingly. The size of the unit we feature is ideal for larger items of clothing such as sweaters and shirts; or could be used to store towels.

Heavy duty

Use a heavyweight calico, to make an economical storage system that can be tailored to your needs; narrow units and compartments for shoes and socks, wider units for sweaters and T-shirts. Keep the weight in the shelves evenly distributed and avoid very heavy weights which may cause the pockets to sag.

Go for display

The storage unit we have made is in a neutral colour, but you can choose colours to match your room style. Then make a series of the units in different sizes and colours (see the sharp ideas box, right) and hang them on a clothes rail. You'll have made your storage great to look at as well as practical.

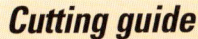

Cutting guide

Amount of fabric to buy	5.2m (5½yds) x 96cm (38in)
Case section (cut 2)	96 x 136cm (38 x 53½in)
Top section	34 x 76cm (13½ x 30in)
Shelves (cut 6)	34 x 62cm (13½ x 24½in)
Other materials Hardboard (7 pieces)	30 x 30cm (12 x 12in)
Wooden batten	26 x 5 x 2cm (10¼ x 2 x ¾in)

Essentials
- Heavyweight calico fabric
- Matching button thread
- 3 screw-in hooks from wooden coat hangers
- Tape measure
- Pins
- Hammer
- Bradawl
- Wooden batten
- Panel pins
- Scissors
- Hardboard

Making the shelf unit

back

front

1 ▲ Make the shelves Cut six shelves and fold the fabric in half widthways with right sides and cut edges together. Stitch along the two side edges, taking a 6mm (¼in) seam. This leaves the edge opposite the fold open for the back. Turn the shelf right side out; press. Topstitch along both side edges, 1cm (⅜in) from the edge. Insert a piece of hardboard into the shelf, then tack the opening closed, stitching close to the hardboard. Make all the shelves in this way.

▲ *Tidy up open-fronted wardrobes in the sloping ceiling of an attic with a variety of hanging storage made in fabrics to match the bedroom's decor*

★ SHARP IDEAS
different looks, different sizes

- Add a touch of colour to the inside of your hanging storage by using two different fabrics. Cut one case section from a contrasting-coloured or patterned fabric and use this on the inside.
- To alter the size of your unit, decide on the shelf size and number first. The width of the case is the sum of the three sides of the shelf; the length is the number of shelves multiplied by the shelf depth.

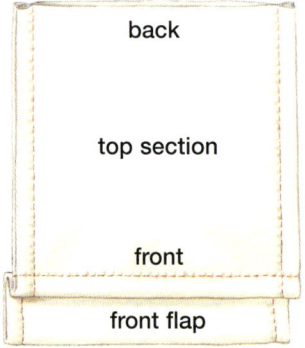

2 **Make the top section** Cut the top section and fold the fabric as in Step 1. Pin, stitch and topstitch the piece as given for the shelves. Now form the front flap that neatens the top of the hanging storage. Turn the front edge under by 6cm (2½in), then pin and tack in position. Topstitch along 1cm (⅜in) from this folded edge. The 5cm (2in) between this stitching line and the front folded edge forms the hanging unit's front flap.

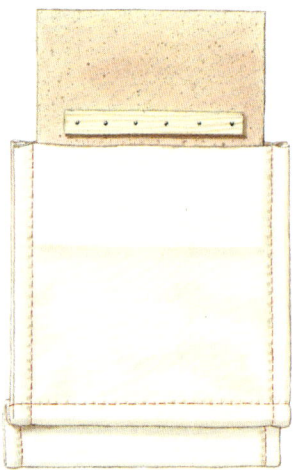

3 **Mark positions for the hooks** Position the wooden batten centrally on the remaining hardboard and secure with panel pins (tap the pins through the hardboard and into the batten). Insert the hardboard into the top section with the batten uppermost. Tack the back as in Step 1. Using the bradawl, make three holes for the hooks through the fabric and into the batten, the first hole at the centre and the other two 10cm (4in) each side.

▶ *A tough, cream and beige striped denim fabric looks good and is a practical choice for a range of hanging storage. Here, narrower units are perfect for shoes*

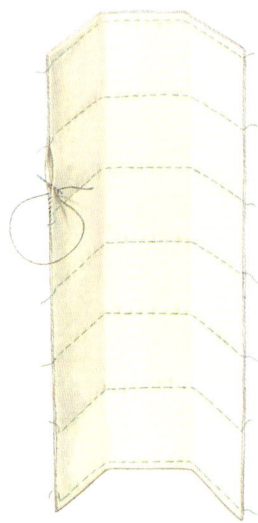

4 **Make the case and mark positions for shelves** Place the two case sections together with right sides and cut edges matching. Stitch all around the outer edge, taking a 6mm (¼in) seam allowance and leaving a 10cm (4in) opening in one edge for turning through. Trim the corners and turn right side out. Slip-stitch the opening and press. Work tacking stitches to denote the shelf positions across the width of the fabric, the first and last 1cm (⅜in) from the top and lower edges, and the others at 22cm (8½in) intervals (seven lines in all). Fold the case along each tacked line and press the fold.

SO EASY
touch fastening

- Instead of using screw-in hooks to hang up your shelves, use touch-and-close fastening in a wide width. Attach it to the top piece of the top section before inserting the hardboard (omit the batten). Cut a 28 x 20cm (11¼ x 8in) piece of calico. Stitch a double hem, 1cm (⅜in) wide, along each side. Attach the hooked side of the touch-and-close fastening along one long edge and the other strip along the opposite edge on the right side. Sew the calico fastener to the top of the casing with a double line of stitching so the fastener will wrap round the rail.

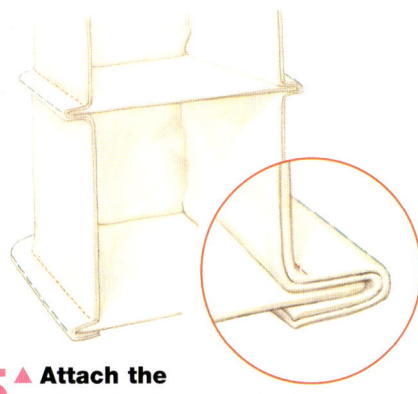

5 ▲ Attach the shelves Beginning at the lower edge, place the pressed fold on the case around the outer edge of one shelf, with its fold at the front, and pin. Position each shelf in this way, slotting it into the pressed fold on the case each time. Leave the last folded position free for the top section. Using the zipper foot on your machine, stitch round the three sides of each shelf to secure them, taking a 1cm (⅜in) seam.

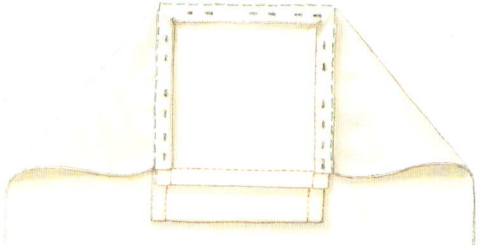

6 ▲ Attach the top section Place the final pressed fold line of the case around the outer edge of the top section and pin in position, having

the flap at the front. Using the zipper foot on your machine, stitch round the three sides, taking a 1cm (⅜in) seam, to secure the top. Slip-stitch the sides of the flap to the case. Remove all the tacking stitches.

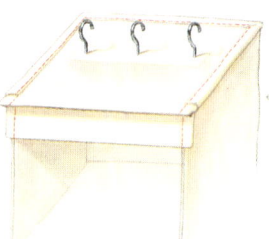

7 ▲ Attach the hooks Screw a hook into each of the positions marked on the top section, ensuring they are held firmly in the wooden batten.

cover-up storage

By cutting the case section wider and creating extensions to the sides of the hanging storage you can cover up your belongings completely. This storage case has no shelves but uses the same method of making the base and the top section as shown in the steps, left. A zip added down the centre front means that whatever you have put inside can be completely hidden from sight.

This type of unit is particularly suitable for bulky items. By adding a row of hooks to the underside of the wooden batten, you can create a hanging space inside the cover-up too.

pulling strings

Make an attractive Roman blind and not only will your windows look brighter – you'll save money as well

Their name may be ancient history, but their neat looks are stylish and definitely modern. Roman blinds, with their deep-pleated folds, require less fabric than any other type of window dressing, apart from roller blinds. The size of the finished blind is the same as the window being covered, so it is bound to be good for your budget.

Roman blinds suit just about any room in the house. They're ideal for recessed windows or windows where space is restricted, such as above a sink or worktop, a bath or a desk. Altering the fabric and the depth of the pleat folds produces dramatically different effects.

In window treatments where the curtains are kept tied back yet more privacy is required, Roman blinds are a good solution. When pulled up the blind lets in all the available light, making it a smart choice for a small, dark room as well. And, of course, they are not very expensive to make. You could even piece the blind together from remnants of fabric by stitching them at the channel seams.

Stained glass effects

Most mediumweight curtain cottons are suitable for Roman blinds. If you choose another fabric make sure it's one that falls nicely into pleats and is light enough to pull up easily. Make the lining in a matching cotton sateen.

Light handiwork

There are two things to remember when buying your fabric; first, it must be wide enough to cover the width of the window, plus extra for side turnings. Secondly, and more importantly, the blind needs to look right with the light shining through as it totally alters the effect of the colours and patterns. To make sure of your choice, pin up a large swatch of fabric and lining at the window. Then, check out the effect at various times of the day, as well as in the evening.

The mechanics of the Roman blind are fairly simple – just pull up into pleats with strings threaded through rings at the back. It couldn't be quicker, easier or cheaper, so don't delay – give your windows an instant uplift today!

Measuring guide

- **Width of blind** First work out the length of batten your blind will hang from. It needs to be 4cm (1½in) wider than the width of the window, measuring out from the outer edge of the frame.
  Both the main fabric and the lining need to be this width plus an extra 3cm (1¼in) on each side.
- **Length of blind** Prepare the batten and screw it to the wall (see Step 1 overleaf). Then, measure from the top of the batten to just below the window sill. This is the finished length of the blind and the main fabric needs to be this figure, plus an extra 3cm (1¼in) for both top and bottom.

Batten 2.5 x 5cm (1 x 2in)

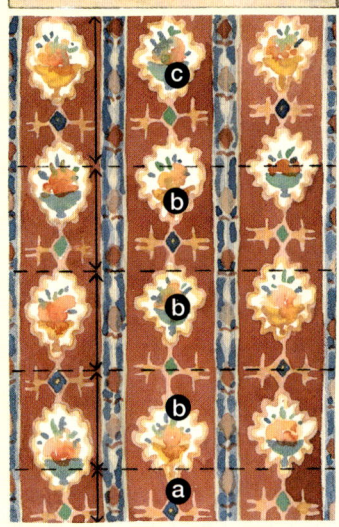

- **Pieces of dowelling** Divide the finished length of the blind by 30cm (12in) which is the pleat length (each folded pleat is half this). The first dowelling position is half a pleat length from the lower edge (a), the rest a pleat length apart (b), with any excess above the last dowelling position (c). Work out how many pieces of 12mm (½in) dowelling you need. Each piece should be 1.5cm (⅝in) shorter than the finished width of the blind.
- **Length of lining** Take the cut length of the main fabric as described left and add 5cm (2in) extra for each dowelling channel.

Essentials

- Blind fabric
- Lining fabric
- Matching sewing thread
- Wooden batten
- Staple gun
- Three 4cm (1½in) long screw eyes
- Screws for attaching batten to wall
- Touch-and-close fastening
- 12mm (½in) wooden doweling for each pleat
- 6mm (¼in) × 3cm (1¼in) wooden lath
- Small plastic curtain rings
- Nylon curtain cord, 4 times the length of the blind

Making the blind

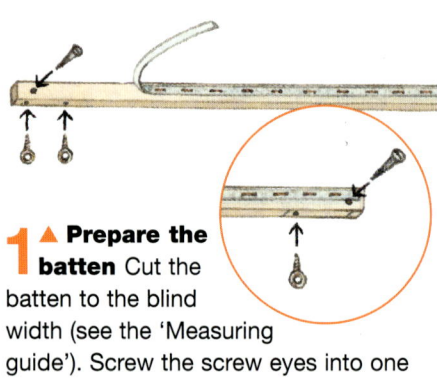

1 ▲ Prepare the batten Cut the batten to the blind width (see the 'Measuring guide'). Screw the screw eyes into one of the 2.5cm (1in) wide sides of the batten (the lower edge), positioning one 13cm (5¼in) from each end and the third 2.5cm (1in) from one end for the cord. Staple the hook side of the touch-and-close fastening to the top, front edge of the batten, then screw it to the window, in the position shown.

▲ *When the scene on the blind is as fantastic as the one outside, you'll long for a sunny day to see the full effect. Cut the fabric to show a different aspect on each blind and you will never tire of them*

◀ *Shades of pale – classic toning cream fabrics and furnishings make this bedroom a haven of relaxation*

2 ▲ Neaten the cut edges If necessary, trim the blind fabric to the size explained in the 'Measuring guide'. Mitring the corners (see 'One layer's enough', p94), fold and press the cut edges to the wrong side, 3cm (1¼in) from the edge, and set aside. Then, trim the lining to the correct size, allowing the extra for the doweling channels as explained in the 'Measuring guide'. Press the cut edges to the wrong side as given for the blind fabric, but folding back 2mm (⅛in) more all the way around the edge.

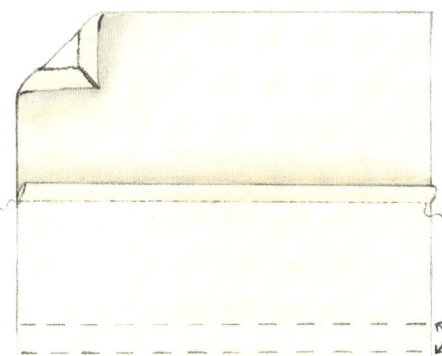

at each channel seam. Then stitch through the lining and the blind fabric along each channel, close to the seam.

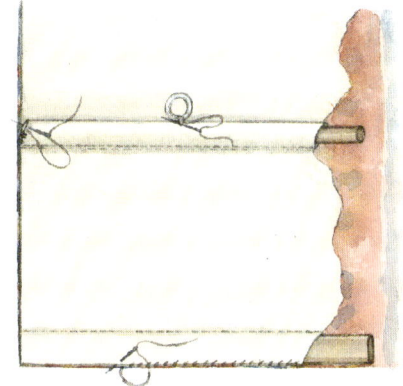

3 ▲ Stitch the channels on the lining Mark 5cm (2in)-wide doweling channel positions on the right side of the lining. Keeping the side edges turned under, form a pleat at each channel position by pinching the marked lines together. Pin and machine stitch the channels, leaving the ends open.

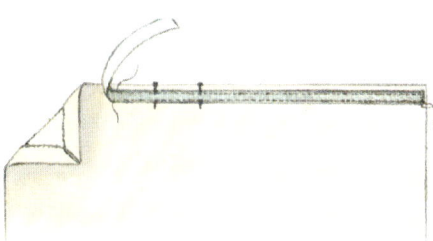

4 ▲ Attach the touch-and-close fastening to the lining Pin and stitch the loop side of the touch-and-close fastening to the top of the right side of the lining, close to the edge. Press the channel seams.

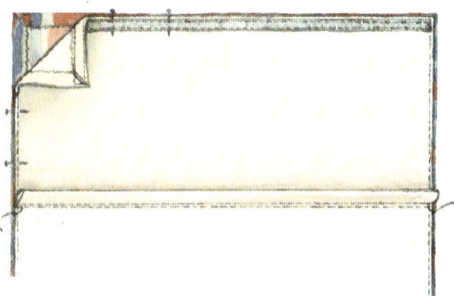

5 ▲ Stitch the lining to the blind With the wrong sides together, pin the lining to the blind fabric around the outside edge and then along each channel seam. Leaving the lower edge of the blind open, join the lining to the blind along the three remaining sides, stitching close to the edge and keeping the ends of the channels open by stopping and restarting the stitches

6 ▲ Insert the doweling and lath, and stitch on the rings Insert the lath into the bottom of the blind between the lining and the blind fabric, and hand stitch the opening closed. Slip the doweling into the channels in the lining and hand stitch the ends closed. Then, sew two plastic rings to each doweling channel, 13cm (5¼in) from each side edge of the blind to correspond with the two screw eyes on the batten.

> ⭐ **SHARP IDEA** omit the lining
>
> ● To simplify making a Roman blind, the lining can be omitted and the doweling channels stitched directly into the blind fabric. Simply follow the instructions as given for the lining, but making a double hem around the outside edge before stitching the channels.

7 ▲ Mount and string the blind Attach the blind to the batten with the touch-and-close fastening. Cut a piece of cord to twice the length of the blind. Tie one end to the lowest ring on the same side as the two screw eyes and string the cord up through the rings. Tie the remaining cord to the other lowest ring and string it in the same way. String the cords through the screw eyes as shown. With the blind still down, pull the cords taut and knot them together near the screw eye to create the pull cord.

▶ *Crisp green and white is the perfect colour combination for a kitchen. Gingham is an ideal choice for the blind as it's so easy to launder*

take a bow

Big and bold, decorative or functional – it's easy to spice up your fabrics and furnishings with ribbons and bows

Large, confident bows look resplendent in any room setting. Reminiscent of sumptuous gift wrappings, they add a festive, jaunty flare. Try using big, bold bows to tie back lush curtains and to fasten plump pillows and cushions. Or, introduce bows as a fabulous feature on chairs, table settings or picture frames.

Made in either complementary or sharp contrasting colours, bows of all sizes will add a touch of pizazz, and sit comfortably throughout the house. Depending on the desired effect, you can introduce these quirky

▲ A class act
Black and white curtains look dramatic in a sitting room. The striped bow tie-back adds a whimsical note with its ruffled tails

◄ Witty cushions
These plump, plain cushions, festooned with candy-coloured bows, look a real treat all lined up in a row

▶ Dreamy drapes
A blue-and-white gingham ribbon bow functions here as a quirky tie-back for a sheer bed drape. The cut-out blue-bird motif on the wall focuses attention on this eye-catching design detail

details sparingly as subtle accessories, or lavishly as focal points.

Pleasingly plump

Make large, thick and plump bows for the best decorative effect. For a luxurious look, cut a strip that's twice the required width from a firm, crisp fabric. Fold it in half, with right sides together, and stick two sides with fabric glue, leaving one short edge open. Turn the strip right side out, fold in the short edges and glue them to close the strip. Bind the centre with another strip of fabric to make a generous, double-layered bow.

For even speedier results – no glueing necessary – simply cut a long strip of fabric that's triple the desired bow width. Then, fold the fabric into a three-layered strip and bind it at the centre. Leave the fabric edges raw, or simply fringe or pink them. Extra-wide satin, or paper, ribbons also make good chunky bows.

◄Pretty pouches
Make a collection of jewellery pouches in luxurious, soft velvet. Tie them with plump satin bows and emphasize the points with glittering gold tassels

▶ Wrapped with roses
A wicker chair wrapped with a gigantic floral fabric bow makes a feature for a bedroom

▶ All dressed up
On special occasions, dress up chair-backs with stunning, glittering double bows, tied in place with matching golden thread. Be extravagant! If the celebration warrants it, tie matching bows all around the room – on door knobs, lampstands and vases

cream tea

Impress your guests with beautiful linen table mats featuring the subtle highlights of drawn thread work. Simple embroidery skills make it all so easy

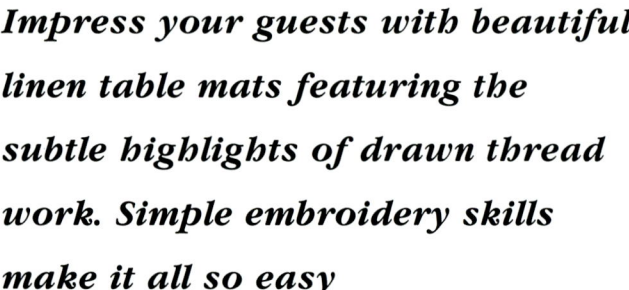

Fast, everyday life often means that there's little time to spare for gracious living. Yet, for those special occasions, when you really want to make an impression, what could create more of an impact than beautiful table linen – especially when the handiwork is all your own, even the embroidery.

Don't be put off by the stitching. We're not talking intricate designs which will take hours on end to complete; just a neat technique that involves removing threads from the fabric, then decorating the edges.

Looks for linen
You can create lots of interesting effects with drawn thread work and the results are particularly eye-catching on table linen. Openwork areas in the fabric are created by withdrawing threads in one direction, and working simple embroidery stitches to gather the remaining strands into a design of regular-patterned spaces in the fabric. Often the design is very simple, such as a drawn thread border highlighting a hem, although more decorative effects can look spectacular. An even-weave, mediumweight fabric is essential – linen is perfect, especially for its cool, good looks – so that you can count the threads

Essentials
- 28-count cream linen
- One skein of single strand embroidery cotton
- Small piece of cotton fabric for lining napkin
- Tapestry needle
- Matching sewing cotton
- Tacking thread
- Sharp scissors

Making the table mat

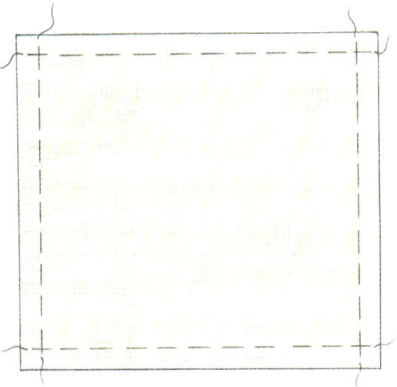

1 ▲ Mark the hemlines Using a contrast-coloured thread, tack horizontal and vertical lines 2.5cm (1in) from the cut edges for the hemlines.

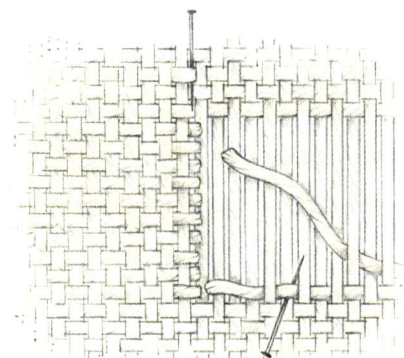

2 ▲ Withdraw the threads for stitching Insert a pin to mark the centre of one side. Measure down 5cm (2in) from the tacking and, with another pin, gently ease up and snip a thread *parallel* to the hemline. Working from the centre outwards to each side, use the pin to ease out the thread to within 3cm (1¼in) of each vertical hemline. Withdraw nine more horizontal threads. Repeat along the opposite side.

and withdraw them cleanly.

Subtle effects, where the embroidery thread tones with the fabric, look extremely classy. But you can also change the appearance of the design with a thread in a colour that contrasts with the fabric. Using a mixture of threads in different textures adds another dimension, but don't overdo the colours or the effect will be more confused than co-ordinated.

Fabric cutting guide

Amount to buy for one mat and napkin ring

Linen	50 x 50cm (19½ x 19½in)
Lining	21 x 8cm (8 x 3¼in)

Cut linen fabric into two pieces as follows:

Table mat	45 x 40cm (18 x 16in)
Napkin ring	21 x 8cm (8 x 3¼in)

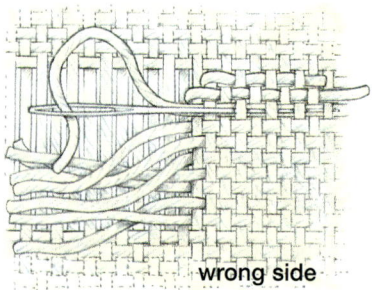

wrong side

3 ▲ Darn in the loose threads
Thread each loose withdrawn thread in turn through the tapestry needle and weave it into the wrong side of the main fabric at the edge of the border. Cut off any excess thread.

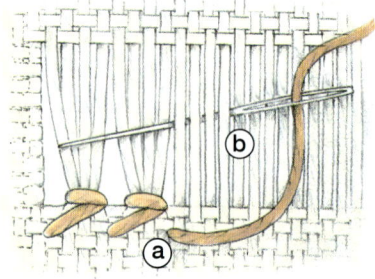

4 ▲ Commence the hem stitch
Thread the tapestry needle with embroidery thread. Begin to work along one side of the withdrawn threads. On the wrong side, lay a short length of thread along the border to be covered by the stitching, then work from left to right. Bring out the needle to the right side of the work, two threads down from the withdrawn edge (a). Insert the needle behind four loose threads (b).

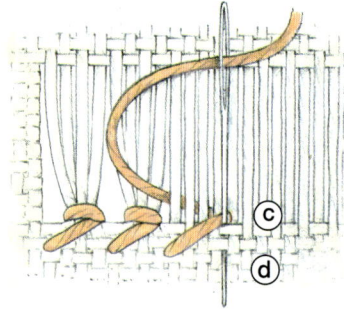

5 ▲ Continue with the border
Now insert the needle vertically behind the edge at the right of the group of stitches (c) and bring it to the front again two threads down into the linen (d). Pull the thread firmly to draw the four loose threads together, so binding them into a loose group.

Continue in this way along one side of the withdrawn threads; finally, anchor the end of thread in the back of the stitches on the wrong side.

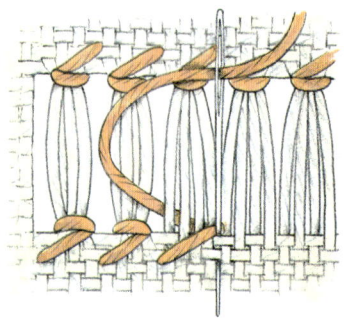

6 ▲ Complete the border with ladder stitch Turn the fabric around to the unworked side of the border. Work another row of hem stitch along this side of withdrawn threads, again working from left to right. Work around the same groups of four stitches as previously, so making a 'ladder'.

7 ▲ Hem the mat Press the finished embroidery on the wrong side. Fold over the hems along the tacking lines, mitre the corners (see 'One layer's enough', p94) and fold under the cut edges. Pin, tack and hem stitch with matching sewing cotton. Press the hems on the wrong side.

Making the napkin ring

1 ▲ Work the drawn thread decoration Find the centre of the linen for the napkin ring and count out five horizontal threads lengthways to either side (10 in all). Cut these threads and withdraw them to 2cm (⅝in) of the edge of the fabric. Work a row of hem stitch along one side of the withdrawn threads, grouping four loose threads together each time (as given for Steps 4–6 of the table mat).

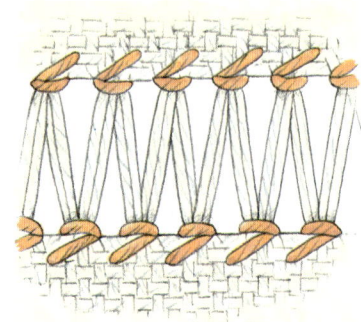

2 ▲ Finish embroidering the napkin ring Turn the work around and make another row of basic hem stitch, but this time divide the group of four vertical threads as shown above to make a zigzag effect.

3 ▲ Make up the napkin ring Fold the fabric in half widthways and stitch the short sides together, taking a 1cm (⅜in) seam. Turn right side out and press 1cm (⅜in) to the wrong side on each long edge. Make up the lining in the same way (but don't turn out); slip it inside the ring. Slip-stitch the lining and linen together around the top and bottom edges.

Laced alternative

1 Make a hem stitch border
Work a border of basic hem stitch around the withdrawn threads as given for Steps 4–6 of 'Making the table mat', making sure that you have an equal number of bound groups of stitches.

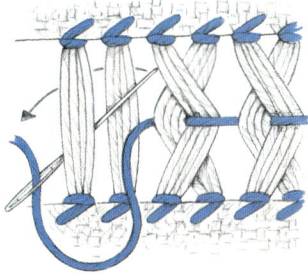

2 ▲ Lace the threads
Cut a length of embroidery thread, long enough to go from one end of the border to the other, and secure it at the right-hand side of the withdrawn stitches. Working from right to left, work over four threads, turn the needle back and pick up two of them, then position it over the remaining two. Turn the needle point to the left, so twisting the two sets of threads. Pull the thread gently, but firmly, through the twist. Continue in this way to the end.

▲ *Linen needn't be natural – instead, colour co-ordinate it with your room scheme. A double drawn thread border, interlaced with herringbone stitch, makes an attractive option*

◄ *Oatmeal-coloured linen with blue stitching contrasts with the striped china for a tasty breakfast setting*

Brighter outlook ▶

Detract from a dismal outlook with a dramatically different window treatment that draws the eye away into the interior. Here blinds obscure the view but not the light, while a swagged fabric heading adds visual interest

tricks of the trade

Use fabric tricks to create all sorts of clever effects in every room of the house

Blind faith ▶

For windows that need extra privacy without blocking out natural light, nets are not the only solution. A sheer roller blind serves the purpose beautifully and filters sunlight at the same time

▲ Keep it clean

Pale background colours and the clean lines of contemporary furniture create an impression of space in a small sitting room. Meanwhile, attractive curtains hanging from an extended pole improve the proportions of a modern window

Awkward spaces, small windows, long corridors or ugly architecture need not ruin your interior schemes. Even the quirkiest design feature can be cleverly disguised with a visual trick or two. Get to know how to use the colour, drape and texture of fabric to achieve near-perfect proportions and a spaciousness that you never knew you owned.

Colour continuity

Solid, deep colours appear to pull in walls and lower ceilings, and the same is true of strident patterns on carpets, curtains and upholstery. So if you are short on space, try to use the same basic colour of fabric on large items, such as furniture, curtains and carpeting, and make more dramatic changes in the smaller furnishing items, for example cushions and lampshades.

Patterned upholstery or curtains can work well, however – although you should make sure that if the colours are bright or the pattern is bold, you use it in moderation to avoid a cluttered effect. Also remember that while traditional heavy, dark furniture can work well in high-ceilinged rooms, it will make a smaller, modern interior appear crowded.

Making space

It's worth knowing too that reds, oranges and yellows appear to bring surfaces closer, while paler, cooler shades such as blue, lilac and green have the opposite effect. Bear this in mind when you choose fabrics for soft furnishings to coordinate with your decor, particularly in small rooms.

Choosing just one colour for a room can in fact be just as effective as opting for a combination of two or three shades. With a single colour choice, you can make imaginative use of different textures and fabric weaves for varied effects.

Using texture

Compare different grades of cotton, for example, and you'll be amazed at the variety available. Mix some of these cottons with other fibres, such as linen, muslin, hessian and silk, and the effects you'll achieve will be as diverse as if you had used a range of different colours.

A simple change of lighting will have a dramatic effect on the atmosphere of a room. Apart from achieving this in the obvious way – using a number of lights situated at different levels in the room – you can also

◄ **Classic touch**

Introduce a hint of tradition in a modern setting with classical fabric designs and wallpaper borders to substitute for architectural features, such as picture and dado rails

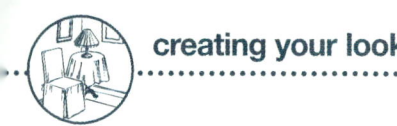

Elegantly dressed ▶
*Elaborate swags
and drapes are best
suited to tall windows
and French doors.
Used with smaller
dimensions, they can
appear over-bearing*

can be improved just as well by disguising
any unsightly areas, such as an old, damaged floor or a cracked wall.

If painting, wallpapering or carpeting
over the eyesore is too costly or time-
consuming a prospect, then there are other
options. You can use fabric wall-hangings
to disguise uneven walls for example, or
drape fabric over an ugly mantlepiece.

Window wizardry

Windows can also present a problem in
certain rooms – they can be too small,
awkwardly shaped, or even ugly – but
there are various ways in which you can

▲ Cool interior
*Everything apart from
the patterned bed
linen in this charming
cottage bedroom has
been kept plain to
make the room
seem bigger*

seemingly 'alter' their appearance . For
example, short windows will look taller
with a pelmet suspended well above the
frame, so that the bottom of it just covers
the top of the window recess.

A wider view

In a similar way, narrow windows appear
wider if you extend the track or pole well
beyond the outer edges and add gathered
curtains. Dormer windows, on the other
hand, have no room for curtains, so the best
option is to choose simple blinds instead.

Arched windows need a special treatment
that does not detract from their character,
such as a sheer curtain that will reveal the
silhouette of the window behind. For bay
windows, create more space by hanging
curtains inside, rather than across the front,
using a shaped track.

No home is perfect and each will have
its own foibles. But by using some of these
tricks, you can quickly transform unsightly
features into attractive ones.

create special lighting effects using fabrics.

A room that lacks natural daylight is
brightened instantly by swapping heavy,
long curtains for a light fabric blind.
Alternatively, you can use sheer fabrics to
filter light without blocking it, or layers of
fabric to vary the intensity of the natural light.

Creative camouflage

One of the main reasons for revamping a
room is to highlight its attractive
architectural features. However, a room
that lacks unusual or impressive features

▶ Hidden agenda
*A clever disguise
for the uneven wall
underneath, this
simple wall hanging
makes an atttractive
feature in its
own right*

flower borders

Large or small, striped or checked, floral prints lend a gentle touch to a plain blind

Bring the garden in through the window all year round with this selection of printed floral cotton fabrics that would make great Roman blinds (see 'Pulling strings', p176). These window dressings are more graphic than pretty, so don't overdo the flowers – instead look out for striped, or checked, combinations that harmonize with the surroundings.

A range of scales

There's such a choice of checks and stripes with floral motifs that the mixture can be very heady. If the window also has curtains, then choose the fabric for the blind carefully – if the curtains are bold and brightly patterned, then your fabric could be more restrained with a small, regular print. A bold print would be stunning with plainer curtains.

1 *Big, blowsy roses, of the traditional variety, get an instant update when placed against broad stripes in pastel pink and green*

2 *Go rustic with these stylized flower arrangements on a distressed-effect background. Warm shades of gold and terracotta give an earthy appeal*

3 *Modern florals are cheerfully opulent – just look at these wonderful sprays of hydrangea boldly displayed on a bed of broken stripes*

4 *Relax in the cool striped charm of this sweet mixture where individual bunches of lily of the valley are combined happily with cornflowers*

5 *Give your furnishings a touch of Jane Austen with Regency roses. They look really fresh displayed against buttery cream and white stripes*

6 *Change the scale – if your curtains have a bold print, then a blind with these rosebud-dotted checks would complement them perfectly*

INDEX

PICTURE CREDITS

Abode: 53 (tl), 174; **Laura Ashley**: 83 (tr), 136 (tr), 188 (cr); **Jan Baldwin /Options**: 88/89; **Charles Barker PR**: 92, 135 (tr), 163 (tl, c) 186 (top); **S Bartholomew**: 22, 24, 25 (tl), 28 (c), 143, 152; **D Blackmore/Homes and Ideas**: 188 (cl); **Bloomfield Associates**: 186 (b); **Michael Brockway**: 178 (tr), 179; **Camera Press Ltd**: 19 (tl), 38, 44 (tl), 49, 58 (cr, tl), 63 (cr), 70 (br), 77 (br), 87 (br), 94 (main, bl), 95, 98, 113, 125 (tr), 173; **Camron PR**: 92, 102, 175 (tc), 176, 187 (bc); **Marie Claire Idees**: 71, 121, 150/151, 172, 181 (br); **Condor PR**: 136 (bc), 137 (tc); **Crown Paints**: 135 (tr), 163 (tl, cl); **Crowson Fabrics**: 187 (t); **Steve Dalton/ Woman & Home** 167; **David & Charles**: 134; **Christopher Drake/Country Homes and Interiors**: 168, 170; **Delbanco Meyer**: 85 (cl); **Dulux**: 135 (bl), 163 (cr, br); **Michael Dunne/ Homes & Gardens**: 178 (bl); **Anna French**: 111 (tr), 157, 162 (tr); **Forbo/Lancaster**: 110; **Lara Grylls PR**: 57 (cr), 75 (bc), 83 (bl), 84 (tl, tr), 109 (2), 161 (top); **Robert Harding**: 9 (tl), 10, 11 (br), 12, 13 (2), 17, 19 (tr, bc), 20 (br), 21, 26, 29, 31 (tc, cl), 36, 37 (br), 44 (bl), 45, 46, 53 (bl), 54, 63 (tl), 68, 69, 75, 76, 76/77, 78, 80, 81 (tl, tr,), 85 (ct), 92 (br), 93 (cr, br), 97, 103 (tl, cr), 104/105, 105 (2), 108, 112 (2), 113 (tr, bc), 114 (tr), 115 (bl, main), 116, 117, 118 (tl), 124, 125 (cl, tr), 126, 128, 129, 131, 141 (tr), 142, 143 (bl); 144 (bl); 145 (tl, br), 153, 154/155 (2, centre), 160 (main, tr), 165 (c, tr); **Harlequin Fabrics**: 32, 33 (bl); **Ikea**: 136 (bl), 137 (tl); **Homes and Gardens**: 180 (bl); **Interior Archive**: 15, 17 (lr), 81 (bl); **Di Lewis/ Ideal Home**: 181 (bl), 188 (tc); **Malabar**: 57 (cr), 161 (tr); **Neil Mersh**: 1, 39, 40 (bl), 61, 62, 64, 66/67, 102, 122/123, 146, 155 (tr, b), 182, 183 (tl), 184, 185, 189; **Munro & Forster PR**: 149 (2); **Natural Fabric Company**: 87, 88; **Next**: 84 (br); **Nimbus**: 111 (bl); **Osbourne & Little**: 31 (tr), 58/59, 59 (c); **Lyndon Parker**: 42, 47 (6), 51 (3), 79, 140; **Period Living**: 27; **N Pope/ Ideal Homes**: 91; **PWA International**: 20 (top), 56 (cr), 65, 82 (2), 141 (bl), 148 (2), 181 (cr); **Jonathan Reed**: 35, 37 (tl), 70, 72, 73, 90, 99, 119, 120, 127, 132, 133; **VV Rouleaux**: 180 (tr); **Sanderson**: 33 (tr), 110, 162 (tl); **John Suett/ Homes and Ideas**: 181 (tr); **Steve Tanner**: 9 (r), 11 (top, bc), 14, 16, 25 (tr), 28 (tr, cr), 48, 50, 158 (tl), 159 (br); **Tilbury/ Sandford/Brysson**: 33 (c), 161 (bl); **Pia Tryde/IPC Syndication**: 175 (cr); **Vantona**: 161 (bl); **Welbeck PR**: 135 (bl), 163 (tr, bl) ; **Elizabeth Whiting & Ass**: 18 (2), 30, 34 (2), 40/41, 57 (tl), 57 (tl), 59 (tr, bl), 60 (2), 86 (2), 123 (r), 137 (cr, bl), 146 (tl), 164 (2); **John Wilman Fabrics**: 177; **Polly Wreford/ Homes & Gardens**: 167.

ARTWORK CREDITS

Peter Bull: 15, 16, 21, 35, 36, 37, 38, 62, 63, 89, 90, 126, 127, 153, 154, 158, 159, 160, 166, 167; **Terry Evans**: 18, 30, 41, 74, 75, 82, 91, 114, 120, 121, 138, 147, 150, 151, 169, 170, 171; **John Hutchinson**: 50, 51, 67, 68, 69, 107, 108, 116, 117, 118, 140, 141, 144, 145, 183, 184, 185; **Julia Illingworth**: 10, 11, 55, 56, 78, 79, 95, 96, 97, 129, 130, 131, 177, 178, 179; **Kevin Jones Associates**: 27, 28, 82; **Tig Sutton**: 23, 24, 25, 43, 44, 45, 71, 72, 73, 90, 101, 102, 104, 133, 134, 155, 174, 175.

<u>KEN FIN</u>

First Published in Australia by Ken Fin Books in 2000
6-10 Keele Street Collingwood Victoria 3066
Telephone: (03) 9417 6699
Fax: (03) 9417 5574
www.scb.com.au

ISBN 1 86458 085 2

Packaged by De Agostini Rights/brady-hercun

Editorial & Design by Craft Plus Publishing Ltd

Reprographics by Modern Age Repro House Ltd

Printed in the Czech Republic